From Darkness Into Light:

The Biography of a Holocaust Survivor Family

Marco Manfre

Ronald Isaacson

From Darkness Into Light

Also by Marco Manfre

The Outcast Prophet of Bensonhurst

Returning to the Lion's Den: Life in an Organized Crime Family

Blue Blue Sea

A Place To Call Their Own
(a short story)

www.marcomanfre.com

Please post reviews of this book on amazon.com

I've given my life to the principle and the ideal of memory and remembrance.

Elie Wiesel

This book is dedicated to

The memory of Walter and Margot Isaacson, who survived the dark years of the Holocaust and were later able to bask in the sunlight and enjoy the blessings of life in the United States of America; Oskar and Jenny Landau and Sally Isaacson, who lost their lives in the death camps of the Third Reich; Emma Isaacson, who died longing for her sons, both of whom had been driven away by the Nazi rise to power; the millions of others who were innocent victims of the savage hatred and communal insanity of Europe during the years 1933 – 1945; and the courageous sisters of Couvent de la Miséricorde in Heverlee, Belgium and other convents throughout Europe who risked their lives to shelter children who were not of their faith.

A special thank you is owed to Lucy Isaacson for her helpful comments regarding significant events in Ron's life and for her careful reviewing of the draft manuscript of this book.

From Darkness Into Light

Preface

This is the story of Ronald Isaacson and his family. They endured years of persecution and anguish during the grim era of the Third Reich. This book is, at the same time, an attempt to remember and honor the larger but ever diminishing group of people who suffered and were forever marked by their suffering during that period of time. The fact that people were persecuted, in this case because of their religion and heritage, is not an uncommon occurrence in the history of the world. Thousands of books have been written about the astoundingly vicious ways in which governments, social organizations, followers of religions, and others have treated their fellow human beings. Many of those volumes, whether they are historical accounts, memoirs, or novels, deal with the period of time from 1933 to 1945 in Europe, the bleak time referred to as the Holocaust.

By telling the moving story of one German-Jewish family, this book attempts to shed some light on a specific aspect of the Holocaust: the personal agonies experienced by those who lived through the long, cold night of that calamitous era.

The information about Ronald Isaacson, his sister Eva, his parents, his grandparents, other family members, and friends of his family has come from interviews with Ron and from notes that he has provided. Much additional information was derived from a slim book called *Story of My Life* that Ron's mother, Margot Isaacson, wrote and self-published in October 1986. Her spare, unadorned writing is clear and literate, which is a testament to her innate abilities and intelligence, since she was not fluent in English until, in mid-life, she and her loved ones emigrated to America.

The story of this family, while it is replete with instances of harrowing distress and enormous danger, also bears witness to and demonstrates the great possibilities that life has to offer.

From Darkness Into Light

The Epoch of Darkness

When people, historians and laymen alike, talk about the *Shoah* (or *HaShoah*), more commonly referred to as the Holocaust, they generally make mention of the Nuremburg Laws, yellow Stars of David, ghettoes, rail cars jammed with people being transported to death camps, and genocide. Those are academically correct images and appropriate historical aspects of the horrifying story of what happened to the Jews of Europe from 1933 to 1945. Other people feelingly remark, "Oh, what a shameful period of time!" or they whisper about the six million who were murdered or they sadly state that the Holocaust is a prime example of man's inhumanity to man. Some ask, "What was the world doing while those atrocities were happening?" Others, in utter disbelief, pose the question, "What was God doing while the Nazis were committing mass murder?" Those are all valid sentiments and reasonable questions to ask in reference to the moral issues raised by the Holocaust.

However, what most people do not understand, cannot begin to grasp—for which those of us who did not experience *HaShoah* should be eternally grateful—is that those historically correct and coldly clinical depictions and representations of what occurred, those heartfelt declarations of revulsion, and those pointed questions do not come close to describing what the victims experienced, which is, after all, the most important consideration.

Many, perhaps most of those who survived the monstrous evil of that time clearly remember, actually still sense, and reside in (at least on occasion) the reality of the terrifying scenes that they witnessed as they peered from behind drawn drapes, what they heard as others were being dragged away, crying and begging for mercy, and what they saw and felt and smelled as they hid, ghost-like, for weeks, months, or years in their dark places and, later, as they attempted to endure yet another day in the harsh nightmare of the death camps.

For the victims of the Nazis, it was a time of icy-cold clammy hands and unmitigated fearful trembling as they held their breath in dim rooms and damp cellars and drafty attics. It was a seemingly endless period of gut-wrenching terror for those souls as they planned and prayed and held out hope that they would be able to secure their own safety and that of the ones they loved, until finally, with silent, gloomy resignation, they accepted the fact that it was only a matter of time until men with rough hands would come through the door to take them to cold, shadowy places from which they were unlikely to return.

What we call the Holocaust was an interminable night of terrifying, hellish proportions from which the vast majority of victims were not able to escape. The grievous misery that it caused occurred on two levels. On the one hand, it was a time during which the ones being persecuted—those whom the Nazis had designated sub-human vermin whose very existence was considered a menace and an affront to members of the "Master Race"—wanted nothing more than safe, routine lives for themselves and for their families. They longed to return to the ordinary humdrum tasks, headaches, and disappointments of everyday existence. When those doomed souls finally, despondently, came to understand that nothing would ever be ordinary again, they attempted to find refuge in places of warmth, light, and relative safety, but found, more often than not, only cold, murky corners and dark, empty despair. When they sought the assistance of or, at the very minimum, compassion from those who they believed were friends, all too often they were met with, at best, frightened stares and, at worst, bestial hatred.

The second level of the long, dark nightmare of *HaShoah* entailed the annihilation of more than a millennium of Jewish life in Europe. How many synagogues, museums, cultural and educational institutions, *shtetlach* (the plural of *shtetl*, which refers to a Jewish town or settlement in Eastern Europe), works of art, and other tangible features of

European Jewish culture were destroyed during those 12 hideous years? Certainly, thousands were obliterated. And, what of the best and brightest among the Jews who perished? How many physicians, scientists, artists, and inventors who, if they had not been murdered as part of the Final Solution, might have achieved distinction and been able to enhance the lives of tens of millions of others? How many of the other, more ordinary victims of the Holocaust, if they had been allowed to live out their years, might have added to the richness of life in routine but still beneficial ways? And, lest we forget, after the Allied liberation of Europe, when Jewish survivors wearily returned to their towns and villages, all too often they found that their homes had been confiscated by their gentile neighbors. While, in some instances, survivors were warmly greeted, more often they were met with hostility and, not infrequently, violence. Many came to the bitter conclusion that although the "Thousand-Year Reich" had been vanquished, Jewish life in Europe was no longer tenable.

The goal of this book is to give life to the story of those who suffered the very personal torment of those ugly years, to remember and honor the millions who perished, and to recognize those righteous souls who risked all to shelter victims of the Third Reich, in particular, the most vulnerable ones, children.

To achieve that goal, this book tells the story of a particular man and his family, one out of a countless number of families that endured the indignities and the losses that were the appalling consequences of the Holocaust. It also recounts the tale of how, with enormous effort and courage, despite great peril, much suffering, and numerous daunting obstacles, the members of that family were able to create a new, better life in a land of safety, limitless opportunity, warmth, and light.

From Darkness Into Light

Part I

Darkness

From Darkness Into Light

ONE

Years of Innocence and Delight

Heverlee, Belgium, 1985, Couvent de la Miséricorde.

Above, the golden-yellow disk of the sun shone brightly at the midpoint of a flawless sapphire sky. The man looked up. Behind him were the flaking stucco walls and darkened windows—empty now, no small faces peering out—of the ancient convent and its adjoining school. Before him and on both sides, beyond the dusty courtyard in which he stood, his eyes took in a dreamlike scene: a stunning array of luminous yellow and orange and red blossoms dancing and quivering in the warm, silky breeze. Smiling wistfully, he sniffed the pungent scent of pine. The only sound was the soothing chatter of songbirds hidden in the surrounding trees.

He thought back to when he had lived here, a small child in hiding, protected by women in floor-length black habits. He had a fragmentary memory, a sense recollection of being frightened and feeling abandoned. He and his sister had been brought here 43 years before. He had been two and a half years old; Eva had been four and a half. They had lived in this place for fourteen months. That had been during a bleak time when the outside world had been hellishly permeated with enormous dangers, vicious brutality, institutionalized prejudice and loathing, and what to many seemed to be unendingly cold darkness. He had been too young to understand, but he wanted his mother. Years later, she told him about his time at the convent because he did not completely remember it. Nonetheless, standing there now all of those years later, he shivered as he felt—was *almost* able to recall—something. It was a deeply concealed, indistinct recollection, a vague, uneasy sense, a fragment of a forlorn, dusty image of dim places, loneliness, and a trace of old smells, such as the odor of a coal fire and fresh-baked bread and warm milk in a mug.

It was there, but it was not.

He looked at the elderly nun who stood next to him; she was staring into the surrounding foliage, as if she was searching, as if she was also trying to remember. He turned to the other side, to his wife. He looked at her through tear-filled eyes. He wanted to smile, but found that he was not able to do so. He did not want to weep, so he forced himself to focus on the verdant woods before him and remember that he had much to be grateful for and that there were more reasons to rejoice than to cry, but it was a struggle; despite the good years that he had lived, he knew there were also reasons to shed a river of bitter tears, if not for the frightened little boy who had missed his mother, then for all of the pain and anguish and brutality of that dark era and for those who did not survive.

He remembered what he had been told about his family's history, particularly, the story of his mother and father and how they had suffered and how much they had risked to protect him and his sister during the years of the calamity known as the *Shoah*.

Ron Isaacson, born René Rudolf Isaacson in 1940, closed his eyes and remembered what his mother and father had said: that as far back in the shadowy, remote past, for as many generations as his family could count, they had been German, and exceedingly proud of that heritage. They were also Jews, and proud of that too. He had read that the history of the Jews in Germany dated from at least the 5th century CE. None of his ancestors had ever imagined that one of those ancient ancestries would be cause to cancel out the other.

Ron's maternal grandmother, Jenny, was born in Hemelingen, a little village near Bremen, on July 11, 1884. She had an older sister, Rosa, and a brother, Adolf, who died in service to the Fatherland during what people had called the Great War. Ron had been told that Great Uncle Adolf's name had been engraved, along with those of other local war heroes, on a monument at the entrance to the cemetery in Duisburg. As Ron stood there, in the courtyard of the convent in Heverlee, he wondered,

Is his name, that of my Uncle Adolf, still there? Is the cemetery still there? Although throughout his life he had been told bits and pieces of the family saga, Ron realized that now, at the age of 45, there was so much he did not know. He desperately wanted to fill in the blank spaces.

Ron had been told that his maternal great-grandmother, Elise, had lived with his mother and his mother's parents until she died of breast cancer in 1923 at the age of 78 or 79.

Ron's maternal grandfather, Oskar Landau, had been born on November 20, 1881. According to family lore, that joyful event had taken place on a ship called the Sofia, although no one had ever recorded where the ship had been or where it had been headed on the day of his birth. Oskar's father, Ron's maternal great-grandfather, Salomon, had, for years, traveled back and forth between Germany and the United States, teaching languages, generally leaving his wife, Johanna, and their children in the care of relatives in Mikolschutz, a small town in Upper Silesia.[1] Johanna died at a young age in an institution of some sort; that part of the story is lost in the mists of time. The relatives who had been left with the responsibility of raising Oskar and his siblings were hard, disciplined people. When, as a child, Oskar misbehaved, he had to kneel on dried peas for what seemed to the boy to be never-ending periods of sheer agony. Resolute and determined, with solid Teutonic self-control, he never shed a tear or uttered a complaint. Aside from the harsh discipline, he was well taken care of and received an outstanding liberal education, developing fine penmanship and a superb command of spoken and written German. Years later, he would puff out his chest and proudly tell his children that he had to walk to and from school in all kinds of weather and that the trip had taken a full hour each way.

Oskar was drafted into the Austrian army shortly after he and Jenny were married at City Hall in Duisburg, and was immediately sent to

---

[1]Mikolschutz was annexed by Poland in 1919 under the terms of the Treaty of Versailles.

the killing fields of World War I. He survived the war healthy in body, but suffering from debilitating chronic wounds to his soul.

Jenny Landau gave birth to her first child—who would, in time, become Ron's mother—with the help of a midwife, Frau Kaufmann, on the ancient kitchen table in her apartment in Duisburg on January 21, 1916, nine months after she and Oskar had married. She named the child Else Margot. Six weeks later, April 4, 1916, Oskar returned home on leave, at which time he and Jenny solemnized their marriage in the synagogue in Duisburg.

When Frau Kaufman had attempted to register the birth of the child, using the name chosen by Jenny, the clerk at the Civil Registry refused to fill out the papers because he said that the name "Margot" sounded French and was, in the midst of the brutal, drawn-out war against those people, unpatriotic and offensive. Thinking quickly, the midwife changed the name to Else Margarette; "Else" was in honor of the child's grandmother, Elise. From the beginning, despite her official name, the family referred to the little girl as Margot.

During Margot Landau's first 13 years, she and her family lived in a sunny three-story apartment house on Sonnenwall, a thoroughfare with a busy streetcar route. A cleaning establishment occupied the ground floor of the building; the second and third floors were reserved for tenants. Margot's mother used the large front room of their apartment as a men's clothing store which she called Etagengeschäft Herz; the name was emblazoned in bold letters on the windows so that it could be seen from the street. Margot's father, Oskar, worked as a dry goods salesman.

The family lived on the third floor of the building in an apartment consisting of a small kitchen with a balcony, two bedrooms, and a spacious dining room. The bathroom was located half a staircase below the apartment. It was not until Margot was about ten years old that her parents had a bathtub installed in the apartment; it was placed in their bedroom because there was no other space for it, and it was curtained off to provide privacy. The water was heated by a coal burner that was positioned next to the tub. Even though Margot preferred the local bathhouse, she dreaded walking home wet on cold days, so she made use of the family bathtub during inclement weather. Other families in the apartment building continued to use only the bathhouse, which offered, besides regular baths, *schwitzbader*, or sweat baths.

Since, during the time that Margot's father was at war, her mother and grandmother completely devoted themselves to caring for her, with no one else to occupy any portion of their attention, the child was used to being indulged. She was breastfed until she was more than a year old; when she cried and demanded to be taken from her crib, her two caregivers placed her between them on the bed that they shared and gently massaged her back and legs and feet until she slipped off to sleep.

A good deal of that undivided attention abruptly vanished when Oskar Landau returned home from war at the end of November 1918. Shortly after he walked into the apartment, he unhesitatingly informed his wife that, beginning immediately, Margot would no longer sleep in their marital bed. *Oma* (Margot's grandmother) had moved into the second bedroom a few days earlier, when she learned that her son-in-law was coming home. Oskar ignored his wife's protestations and her explanations about how the baby needed time to adjust to the change. Later that night and for many nights after that, he closed his ears to Margot's screams, saying that the child would have to get used to sleeping in her crib.

When Margot was four years old, her parents enrolled her in a Froebel Kindergarten in order to give her the opportunity to socialize with other children and develop more fully as a unique individual. Her father rode her to school and back each day on his bicycle. Froebel schools are based on the philosophy of Friedrich Froebel, a nineteenth century thinker who influenced many educators, most notably, Maria Montessori. His approach can best be summarized by his own words: "The play of children is not recreation; it means earnest work. Play is the purest intellectual production of the human being, in this stage … the whole man is visible in them, in his finest capacities, in his innermost being."[2]

Later that year, 1920, Margot's mother gave birth to a second child. Even though they named her Johanna Ruth, from the very beginning everyone in the family referred to her as Ruth. Margot thoroughly enjoyed playing with her little sister and taking on the role of second mother to her.

After a year at the Froebel Kindergarten, right after Easter—which is when the academic year began in Germany in those days—Margot was enrolled in the first grade in the Buchenbaum School, which was a fifteen-minute walk from her home. Her teacher, Dr. Lategan, who was also the rector (the principal) of the school, was a kind, wise, and patient educator who encouraged all of the students to stretch their minds. Using a slate and chalk, Margot and the others learned the alphabet and how to read and write simple words. According to Margot, her most challenging subject in later years was, of all things, knitting. She found working on her first project, a potholder, so difficult that she was often reduced to tears. Despite that, she loved school and, along with five other girls—three gentiles and two other Jews—Margot was allowed to skip fourth grade and enter the "Studienanstalt," or "lyceum," which was an intermediate-level school. Before she left the Buchenbaum School, a class photograph was taken, but with all of the moving in which her family was engaged in later years, it was lost. For decades, she would become misty eyed when she talked about that photograph. Then, in 1985, when Margot was living in the United States, she was astonished to find in the mail a copy of that treasured picture. Even more incredible was the fact that it had been sent to her by one of her good friends from childhood, Ruth Neumark, who had emigrated to Israel a number of years earlier. Ruth Neumark's father had been the highly respected—and sole—rabbi in Duisburg for as long as anyone could remember.

The principal of the new school that Margot attended, Dr. Feigel,

---

[2] http://www.froebelweb.org

a man who she often referred to as "a teacher in the truest sense of the word," always set aside time to tutor her and the other girls who had been allowed to skip fourth grade. Among the subjects that the students were required to learn was French. Decades later, as she leafed through her old notebooks, Margot smiled in wonder as she recalled the huge number of vocabulary words that she had to memorize, along with the conjugations of many dozens of verbs. Despite all of the studying involved, Margot enjoyed learning French and took pride in her ability to speak it fluently, which, ironically, was to be vital in terms of her survival and that of the rest of her family in years to come. In addition to French, she took classes in Latin and in English.

Margot considered herself very fortunate that her parents' retail clothing business was successful because it enabled them to make regular tuition payments and provide a comfortable, middle-class lifestyle for their children. Each summer, Margot, Ruth, and their mother were able to spend short periods of time at various local resorts; her father, too busy with work, was never able to travel with them. One of the places they visited was Berchtesgarten, an astonishingly lovely alpine destination that they thoroughly enjoyed. Years later, the National Socialist German Workers' Party[3] would establish its headquarters there and use it as a retreat for senior leaders.

For her tenth birthday, Margot's parents bought a stunning black-lacquered piano and arranged for a gifted, demanding teacher named Gustav Stern to provide lessons for her and her sister. Despite the fact that Margot did not always want to practice, she did as she was told, eventually becoming a very fine, if not accomplished pianist. Decades later, she took advantage of an opportunity to visit Gustav Stern in Seattle, Washington, where he served as the conductor of the Seattle Symphony Orchestra. During their brief visit they talked about the "old days," when Germany

---

[3] *Nationalsozialistische Deutsche Arbeiterpartei* or *NSDAP*, generally referred to in English as the Nazi Party.

was home and life was beautiful.

Margot would smile wistfully and say that she credited her father for inspiring and encouraging her to love music. The exquisite theater in Duisburg—built in 1912, damaged during World War II, refurbished in 1950, and still standing today—was a major source of culture and entertainment for Margot and her family. Her parents had drawers full of librettos from scores of operas; her father knew the main arias to most of the well-known productions. After seeing her first opera, Richard Wagner's "Der fliegende Holländer," Margot was captivated by the main tenor and the leading soprano, often standing outside of their homes, hoping she would have a chance to talk to them.

Family friends, such as Sam and Ottie Schneider—who Margot and her sister referred to as "Onkel and Tante"—along with their children, Martin and Reni (The latter became one of Margot's best friends), were always allowed to luxuriate in the Landau family bathtub. However, since heating the water and filling the tub took over an hour, bath times were arranged according to a strict schedule; each person in Margot's family and each of the Schneiders made sure to be available for his or her bath at the precisely correct time.

When Margot was 13 and Martin Schneider was 17, she decided that she was in love with him. Why wouldn't she? He was kind and engaging, with blonde wavy hair; he was also an inspired poet and an excellent mathematician. A born teacher, Martin patiently taught Margot how to play chess. He also had a pleasant singing voice; his dream was to become an opera singer.

Margot's family and the Schneiders spent most Sundays together, generally visiting nearby parks and wooded areas. While the adults walked and chatted, the children excitedly pretended to be engaged in dangerous treks through the wilderness. During games of Hide and Go Seek, Margot and Martin sometimes secluded themselves in the undergrowth, holding hands and exchanging sweet, innocent kisses. They were unsophisticated adolescents who enjoyed life and saw only sunshine and bright vistas; they had no idea that the sublime, stable world that they took for granted was on the verge of a cataclysmic disruption that would lead to the violent deaths of millions.

Years later, Margot would wonder out loud whether her affectionate relationship with Martin would have developed into the kind of love that lasts a lifetime, if political turmoil and monstrous brutality had not intruded and torn their world apart.

In 1929, Margot, Ruth, and their mother, along with Tante Ottie, Reni, and Martin, vacationed in Switzerland. Shortly after they returned home, Margot's parents, who had decided to expand their business, rented a large ground floor store with expansive living quarters above it on Kasino Strasse 16 in Duisburg. After a short period of heady success, during which Margot's parents hired a salesman and a secretary, they suddenly began to lose business. They soon learned the cause: a branch of a chain store that also sold men's clothing had opened nearby. Margot's parents had to face the fact that they were not bringing in enough money to pay the rent for the store and the comfortable apartment above.

When, in the midst of the worldwide depression, the business completely collapsed, Margot's mother and father sadly and reluctantly moved the store back to the previous, smaller location on Sonnenwall; the family relocated to a less expensive apartment. During the next few years, they moved again and again, each time to a smaller apartment at which the rent was less.

During the stressful years that followed, the number of Nazi Party members elected to the Reichstag increased almost ten-fold. At the beginning of 1933, when the Nazis came to power and Adolf Hitler was appointed chancellor, the Schneider family, understanding just how precarious life for Jews would soon become, fled Germany, ultimately settling in Seattle, Washington. Reni married a Jewish boy she met there, Julius Lesser, who was also from Duisburg. They eventually moved to

Chile, where Reni gave birth to three daughters. Margot always hoped she might be able to see Martin Schneider again. Years later, in America, when she found his name in a telephone directory, she called, only to learn from a woman who said she was his widow that he had died of a heart attack in 1971.

Over the decades, after so much joy and so much pain and a heartbreaking amount of loss, Margot would, from time to time, gently take from a bureau drawer a sheet of creased, yellowed paper and unfold it. She would look at the words written on it. Sometimes she would hold the paper up to the light because the pencil marks had begun to fade with the passing years—not that she really needed to do that: the words were etched in her memory. She would read aloud the short poem that Martin had written for her when they were young and happy and untested during that bright, buoyant time of innocence and delight. She would smile and then her eyes would become wet as the words floated across her field of vision and through her brain.

The following is a translation of what was on the sheet of paper:

Whatever is for us in store,
Love, pain or grief,
Once we aren't here anymore,
It was worthwhile to live.

TWO

Sunset

Toward the end of 1931, Margot's parents told her that they could no longer afford her tuition; they explained that they had to use the money to allow her sister Ruth, who was four years younger, to remain in school for a while longer. To soften the blow, they said that they would pay for Margot to attend a private business school for a few months to learn practical skills such as shorthand, typing, and business math, after which she would have to find a job.

Six months later, after she had completed the business course, Margot began what was to be a three-year apprenticeship in the yard goods section at Cohen & Epstein, a well-regarded department store in Duisburg. The female employees of the store had to adhere to a strict dress code: a navy blue dress with a white collar or a navy blue skirt and a white blouse, all perfectly ironed, and they were required to make as many sales as possible. Whenever a potential customer left the store without having purchased at least a small item, each of the young women who had waited on that person was reprimanded.

Margot was told that in order to be allowed to move up to the position of full-time salesperson, besides being successful as an apprentice, she had to attend twice-weekly classes at a vocational school. She worked diligently at her studies and pushed herself—despite her withdrawn, reserved personality—to be effective at her job. Little by little, Margot learned how to assert herself and interest customers in the items on display, eventually becoming adept at sales. Because of that and her relatively high level of education compared to those of the other women who worked in the store, within her first year, Margot, who was still considered an apprentice, was allowed to become assistant to the buyer, a highly prestigious position which she thoroughly enjoyed. Her new responsibilities included pricing merchandise and completing general office work, such as typing, filing, and using the telephone. Her salary, while higher than that of the other apprentices, was still meager. Nevertheless, when Margot turned over the bulk of her weekly earnings to her unceasingly anxious parents, they looked relieved and she felt proud.

On January 30, 1933, a disheartening day for Jews the world over, Adolf Hitler was appointed chancellor of Germany. Despite their fear and loathing of the man, most German Jews believed that Hitler's political ascension would be a short-term circumstance which would have no lasting effect on their lives. *After all*, they thought, *this is Germany, our home. Surely, our fellow citizens will vote Hitler and his party out of office once they understand how awful they are.*

During the beginning of that fateful year, most Jews and Christians maintained their normal good relations, and even though a few of Margot's Jewish friends fled Germany, the vast majority of them remained watchful and wary but optimistic about their future.

Now that Margot was contributing most of her modest salary to the household, her parents felt that they could afford a short stay at a boarding house in a small resort town on the Rhine near Koenigsberg. The owners, who were Christian, were warm and gracious to their Jewish guests. Their daughter, Marianne, who was 19 years old, became friends with Margot, who was 16. At one point during that week, Marianne asked Margot to attend a carnival with her and her boyfriend, a young man named John. Margot, who had not had many opportunities to attend fairs or other similar types of entertainment, enjoyed the vivid colors, the glittering lights, and the exhilarating rides. Most of all, she was thrilled by the lively music.

She also met a young man with whom she danced over and over again. Marianne and John, seeing that Margot had a companion, tactfully left the couple alone and went off to find a secluded spot.

At the end of the evening, when Margot was unable to find Marianne, she assumed she would have to return to the boarding house via bus. Then she realized with dismay that she had missed the last bus. The young man with whom she had danced offered to ride her back on his motorcycle. With a combination of excitement at this new adventure and more than a bit of apprehension, Margot climbed on the motorcycle behind her companion and braced herself by gripping the bottom edge of her seat. However, once the young man kick-started the deafeningly loud motor and shot forward at what seemed to be rocket-like speed, Margot instinctively wrapped her arms around his waist. As they bounced along a narrow, dimly lit road that followed the faint outline of the river, the man, steering with one hand, reached around to grope his now-terrified, helpless passenger, who, still holding onto him, moved back on her seat, almost losing her balance. A short while later, he slowed down and drove to a roadside clearing, where he parked the motorcycle, jumped off, and helped the exceedingly frightened girl down; then he escorted her to a bench, wrapped his arms around her, and repeatedly—against her will—kissed her. Alarmed for a new reason now, Margot vigorously fought off the man's attempts to fondle her. When she started to cry, rather than backing off, the young man squeezed her more tightly and then he hotly whispered into her ear, "I recently joined the SS," perhaps hoping that bit of information would impress the girl and make him seem more desirable as a lover. Struggling to overcome her terror at the advances of the man, Margot croaked that she was Jewish and—between violent, choking sobs—she added that she was a virgin and that she intended to remain that way until she married.

Decades later, each time Margot told this story, she said she always wondered whether it had been her obvious fear and her anguished words that moved the man or whether it had been due to some unseen protective force, but at that point, to her great relief, her grasping companion unwrapped his arms and sat back on the bench. Then, glaring at Margot and speaking in an authoritative voice, he lectured her, saying that she should have known better than to go off with a stranger. After that, he drove her back to the inn.

Margot's best friend from when they were in first grade was Lieschen Gaetner, an outstanding student and gifted artist; she was also a gentile. In April of 1933, after years of what Margot had thought of as an intimate, durable friendship, Lieschen informed her that they could no longer spend any time together. This unexpected announcement came as a great shock that wounded Margot to her very core. Lieschen politely, coldly explained that they could no longer be friends because Margot was Jewish and their relationship was not compatible with the morals of the New Germany. To compound matters, Lieschen added, her boyfriend, a dedicated and enthusiastic member of the Hitler Youth, had strenuously objected to her relationship with Margot.

Margot's heavy pain and sense of profound dislocation were not in the least alleviated when her parents told her that breakups of all kinds were occurring throughout Germany: friendships called to a halt; love affairs torn asunder; business partnerships terminated; Jewish men and women dismissed from their jobs; and Jewish students told that they were no longer welcome in their schools and encouraged to enroll in institutions for people of their faith.

Margot had never felt significantly different from her Christian classmates and neighbors. As with most German Jews, she had always assumed the fact that she attended a synagogue for services and for religious instruction while her gentile friends went to churches was a minor difference of no real significance. Her parents, who held a similar view, fervently believed that despite the fact that they were Jewish, their German citizenship and proud observance of ancient national traditions and customs made them indistinguishable from their fellow citizens who were Christian. They were only moderately observant. They did not strictly follow the rules of kashrut (kosher), but neither had they ever eaten pork or shellfish. Although they did not refrain from work and other activities on the Sabbath, as more pious Jews did, they did observe some Jewish holidays, such as Passover and Hanukkah. In addition, they attended High Holy Day services and they reflected and fasted on Yom Kippur. Margot's mother often said that she enjoyed attending services at the synagogue to which the family belonged—at which the organ player was Christian. Although it was a Conservative synagogue, the congregation adhered to some of the Orthodox traditions, such as women being seated in an upstairs gallery while the men prayed downstairs and allowing only men to read from the Torah. While Margot's father fluently read and prayed in Hebrew, her mother, who took lessons as an adult, read from a *siddur* (a prayer book) written in German.

Along with most German Jews, Margot and her family believed that they were, quite simply, Germans who happened to be Jewish, just as others in their neighborhood were Germans who happened to be Christian. They did not remember ever having heard of incidents of outright anti-Semitism in Duisburg and had, over the years, read about only a handful of instances in other cities in Germany. They did not know it—in fact, most Jewish Germans could not conceive of it—but the years ahead would become progressively darker and gloomier for them and would culminate in catastrophe. Even those who were grimly realistic about the radical, anti-Semitic beliefs and pronouncements of the political group in power, the National Socialist German Workers' Party, and the wildly inflammatory rhetoric of its charismatic leader, Reich Chancellor Adolf Hitler, could not begin to imagine the horror that would consume them, their fellow Jews, and their country, along with most of Europe and other parts of the world in the years to come.

The situation for Margot's family and for the rest of the Jewish population of Germany remained unpleasant but unchanged during the next year and a half. Then, on September 15, 1935, they experienced a devastating shock when they read about the ratification of the so-called

Nuremberg Laws, more formally known as *The Law for the Protection of German Blood and German Honour* and *The Reich Citizenship Law*. Those two statutes were based, in part, on Friedrich Nietzsche's theory of the *Übermensch*, literally the "over," "above," or "across" man, generally translated as the *Superman*. While Nietzsche's Superman is depicted as a strong, moral individual who, without the help of God, creates positive values for society, Hitler's Nazi Party used the concept to describe a race of mighty Germans and other northern Europeans—known as "Aryans"—who were blessedly untainted by the blood of *Üntermenschen* (the plural form of *Üntermensch*), "undermen" or "sub-humans." The laws deprived Jews and other *Üntermenschen* of the rights of citizens and required them to remain apart from "true Germans" in business and in personal relationships, leaving them bewildered and traumatized.

At that early stage of the Third Reich, despite the Nuremburg Laws, large numbers of German Jews still believed that, in time, Hitler and the Nazi Party would become more moderate because the German people would never allow the persecution and demonization of Jews to continue. They were also convinced that, should Hitler and the Nazis attempt to pass more severe legislation to legally deprive Jews of their remaining rights, those people would eventually be voted out of power.

In the wake of the Nuremburg Laws, Margot's parents, shaking their heads, wondered how a society which had produced Beethoven, Brahms, Heigel, Kant, Heiner, and Gropius, to cite just a few of the great ones, could sit back and allow its Jewish citizens to be treated as if they were vermin. "No," they asserted, "We are citizens just like the Catholics and Protestants with whom we have worked and sat next to in the theater and with whom we have shed blood for the Fatherland. This set of obnoxious laws will not stand. Our fellow Germans will not allow it."

However, little by little, throughout Germany, signs were posted that coldly stated, *Verboten für Juden* (Forbidden for Jews). At the same time, thousands of German children joined the Hitler Youth and virtually all contact between Jews and gentiles disintegrated. Although it was painful for them, some Jews—many of whose families had lived in Germany for hundreds of years, in some cases, for more than a millennia—chose to flee the country which no longer recognized them as citizens and, instead, considered them sub-human parasites. They traveled to countries in Europe, hoping to find refuge; many of them were refused entry. Small numbers of Jews, to their great good fortune, were able to migrate to South Africa or North or South America or a few other parts of the world where they would be safe from persecution.

The vast majority, who stayed, believing that the political situation would, with time, improve, eventually regretted their false optimism. Most of the 500,000 Jews whose families had long called Germany home, along with millions in other countries that would be occupied by the Nazis, would become victims of the Final Solution.

Margot's parents, because of their unyielding faith in the goodness and wisdom of the German people and due to the fact that they were still struggling financially and could not afford to move, closed their eyes to the darkly ominous political climate and made a point of attending to their daily tasks.

Although Margot read news reports and listened to radio broadcasts and fully understood what the new laws meant for her, her family, and all of the Jews of Germany, she still trusted that everything would work out well in the end. She decided to ignore, as much as possible, the gathering storm clouds of intolerance and hatred that were darkening the skies over her homeland. Instead, she focused on the good and the luminous and the cheery aspects of her life, refusing to believe that the looming twilight would last, let alone that it would usher in a long, dark night of despair and bitter anguish.

THREE

When Walter Met Margot

Because they maintained their steadfast faith in the goodness of the German people, Margot and her family ignored the bitter political atmosphere and stubbornly believed that they would be able to continue to live in their homeland. *Besides*, they asked, *where would we go?*

They worked hard and continued to engage in their normal activities. Although social doings that involved being in contact with Christians were officially forbidden, they still went to the movies and the theater on occasion, believing it was unlikely that anyone would know or make an issue of the fact that they were Jewish.

Despite the fact that Margot had never expressed any interest in sports, because she had been dropped by her Christian friends she began attending soccer games played by an amateur Duisburg team that was part of a local Jewish sports league. One afternoon in 1934, on the special bus that transported players and fans to and from games in nearby towns, she met an avid soccer enthusiast named Walter Isaacson. Amidst the general revelry and cheerful noise of the dozens of animated people aboard the bus, the two young people, shy at first, eventually struck up a conversation. They talked all the way to the soccer stadium. At the game they sat next to each other and continued to talk. Afterwards, they sat side by side on the bus ride home. Walter, who was 26—eight years older than Margot—worked as a salesman in the carpet and curtain department of Cohen & Epstein, the same large store at which she was employed. They laughed and said it was amusing that they had never seen each other at work. He lived with his parents and his brother Heinz in Ruhort, a brisk 45-minute walk from Margot's house. They began meeting after work so that Walter could walk her home.

A few weeks after they had met, when Walter made it clear that he was very interested in her, Margot invited him to visit her at home so that he would be able to meet her parents. Oskar and Jenny Landau, despite their deep misgivings about Walter because he was so much older than their daughter, were gracious to him and did their best to make the young man feel comfortable. After a bit of small talk, Walter mentioned that he was an accomplished chess player, a revelation that led to a highly contested game between him and Oskar. Over the next few weeks, their chess games led to a friendship and eventually a warm bond between the two men.

Walter's father, Sally,[4] who owned a butcher shop in neighboring Ruhort, had served in the German army in both the Boxer Rebellion in China in 1900 and during World War I. Walter's mother's family was able to trace their ancestry to Westphalia, a region of western Germany, to as far back as 1786. Sally and Emma Isaacson were pleased that their son had found a "nice Jewish girl." That sentiment has been shared by generations of Jewish parents who fear that their children might marry gentiles and, little by little, ignore their religious practices and eventually discard their heritage. It is, therefore, gloomily ironic to contemplate the fact that German Jews of Margot's and Walter's generation—young people who had grown up believing that they were indistinguishable from other Germans and who considered their religious background to be a minor part of their identities—would be the last ones for many years to even give a passing thought to intermarriage. For at least the next decade, the very fact that they were Jewish would represent their full identity; for millions of them, that religious classification would be like the mark of Cain.

In 1933, the company at which Walter Isaacson had worked for as a salesman in the curtain and carpet department, Gebrüder Alsberg, in a town called Bochum, had become *arisiert*.[5] Although it came as a shock to

---

[4] Although uncommon, this was, at one time, used as a male Jewish name.
[5] Aryanized, that is, taken from its Jewish owners and given to Christians.

Walter and to other Jewish workers, that outrage had been occurring throughout Germany. Shortly after that, Walter was able to obtain a job at Cohen & Epstein, in Duisburg, where Margot was employed. Two years later, Cohen & Epstein became *arisiert*. Walter was, once more, dismissed from his job, but Margot was not. After a desperate search, he considered himself fortunate to obtain a low-wage position with a branch of Gebrüder Alsberg, located in Neuss, which was still in the hands of its Jewish owners. Since the store was about 90 minutes by public transportation from Ruhort, where his parents lived, and Duisburg, where Margot lived with her family, Walter rented a one-room apartment in Neuss. He returned to his parents' home each Saturday night after work and was able to spend time with Margot on those evenings and on Sundays.

During those weekends, Margot and Walter often traveled to nearby cities along the Rhine, such as Düsseldorf, which was much larger and more culturally rich than either Duisburg or Ruhort. On those occasions, they walked along the tree-lined banks of the river or, if they felt daring, they would defy the laws, which were now being more vigorously enforced, and, smiling so as to appear unconcerned, purchase tickets for a movie. One Sunday afternoon, Walter invited Margot to see his austere bachelor's quarters in Neuss. While they were there, the landlady, Fräulein Vasen, who was also Jewish, stopped by to say hello. She was so taken with Walter's lovely young friend that she invited them to stay for dinner. A few days later, Walter wrote a letter to Margot in which he said he was pleased that she had seen his room, and added that Fräulein Vasen had enjoyed meeting her and hoped to see her again. Margot, without thinking, left the open letter on the dining room buffet, where her mother took the liberty of reading it. When Margot arrived home from work that day, her parents angrily confronted her, saying that they were shocked and distressed that she had visited the apartment of a young man without a chaperone. Then they admonished her for the additional offense of not informing them about this scandalous rendezvous after the fact. Margot, knowing that her parents' criticism was appropriate, looked down and remained silent.

The following Saturday, Walter appeared at the apartment in Duisburg. After pleading for forgiveness for his lapse of judgment, he asked Margot's parents for permission to marry their daughter. They looked at each other for a few seconds, and then they gave their consent.

On June 12, 1936, a Friday, two years after they met on a bus on their way to a soccer game, Else Margot Landau and Walter Isaacson were married in a civil ceremony in City Hall in Duisburg. Two days later, Sunday, June 14, 1936, Rabbi Neumark, who had married Margot's parents 21 years earlier, united the couple according to Jewish law in the same synagogue. Margot was 20; Walter was 28.

Six years later, when the world was embroiled in World War II, Dr. Neumark, who had held the post of rabbi in Duisburg since 1905, was arrested by the Gestapo and transported to Theresienstadt, where he died—whether from disease, malnutrition, or at the hands of his captors is unknown. While Theresienstadt served as a holding station, and not a death camp,[6] many thousands of Jews and other prisoners died there. Throughout the war, the Germans transferred well over 100,000 inmates from Theresienstadt to Treblinka, Auschwitz, and other death camps, where they were systematically murdered. Forty-one years after the war, the town of Duisburg, perhaps in an effort to heal or else out of a sense of guilt, honored Rabbi Neumark by dedicating a street in his name.

After Walter and Margot's wedding ceremony, the Isaacson and Landau families hosted a festive dinner, after which the newly married couple left for Bad Honnef, a resort town along the Rhine between Cologne and Bonn. During the dreadful years that came after that, Walter

---

[6] In fact, in 1944, the Nazis made cosmetic improvements to the camp and used it as a "showpiece." They allowed Red Cross inspectors to tour it in an attempt to dispel the notion that Jewish inmates were being subjected to harsh treatment there or in any other camp. They also produced a motion picture called "Theresienstadt" which they used for propaganda purposes.

and Margot often scolded themselves for having spent money on their brief honeymoon, as if the situation in Germany had been normal and their future bright and secure. In the years to come, on more than one occasion, they asked themselves why they had not heeded the recommendation of friends who had repeatedly advised them to use their savings to legally emigrate from Germany and begin their married life in a country where being Jewish represented an interesting but not hazardous cultural distinction. But, Margot and Walter asked, where could they have gone? Many European countries had begun to limit the number of Jews they would allow to cross their borders. Additionally, the process of legally emigrating from Germany was, for the average individual or family, prohibitively expensive and extraordinarily complicated. Layers of bureaucratic red tape had to be overcome and substantial bribes had to be paid to officials to move the process along. Of course, many German Jews chose to simply cross the border to neighboring countries and live in the shadows as strangers, hoping not to be caught by immigration officers.

Since the young couple did not earn enough to pay for rent in a decent apartment, they had to live with the Landaus in the room that Margot used to share with her sister; Ruth, now 16, was told that she would have to move into a small alcove behind the kitchen. As she relocated, she complained, but it was mostly for show. Walter, who had given up his apartment in Neuss, now had to travel each day for nearly two hours by public transportation both to and from his job in that city.

During that early period of the Third Reich, it was becoming clear that Germany had grand territorial ambitions which would surely lead to war. That understanding led the young couple to consider the fact that if they ever felt compelled to escape to Belgium or the Netherlands or France, those countries might eventually be invaded and occupied by German troops. If that were to occur, they would find themselves subject to the same anti-Semitic laws as in their homeland. They thought about America. After asking friends, they learned that in order to emigrate to the

United States they would have to procure an affidavit from relatives or friends living in that country which indicated that they would provide for the young couple.

In addition to that obstacle, the very thought of traveling so far from their parents—across the Atlantic Ocean—distressed and horrified Margot and Walter. They could have fled to Shanghai, a city chosen by many German Jews at the time; however, not only was that exotic location just as far from Germany as America, but they thought of it as a place with a totally alien culture in which they might never feel at home.

Walter and Margot and their families clung to the hope that the political and domestic situation, as appalling as it was, would improve after a while. After all, this was Germany, a bastion of high culture and civility that was the centuries-old home of a half million Jews, huge numbers of whom had, over the centuries, risen to positions of importance in business, the arts, science, medicine, law, education, government, and the military. In addition to that sentiment, they were both working and had the support of each other and their families. They believed that despite the menacing whirlwind surrounding them, the political climate in Germany would eventually return to normal and their future would be luminous.

A few months after their marriage, Margot finally completed her apprenticeship at Cohen & Epstein. When she was told that there were no full-time positions at that time, she applied for a job as a salesperson in a small Jewish-owned store in Duisburg. Since the shop, like most other Jewish businesses in Germany, was just barely surviving (because most gentiles no longer patronized stores which displayed the required Star of David), the owner, Joseph Boehm, told Margot that part of her job would involve tutoring his children and occasionally helping his wife with housework. Because she did not have any other options, Margot agreed to this arrangement. Then, after having endured the exhausting, expensive daily commute between Duisburg and Neuss for several months, Walter reluctantly told Margot that they would have to relocate to that city. In addition to the fact that this meant Margot would have to find a new job, the idea of moving away from her parents and seeing them only on weekends was difficult for her to accept. However, she agreed because the long commute was not good for her husband.

In Neuss, they found a small but tidy furnished room. Margot found employment as a governess to a four-year-old boy whose parents, also Jewish, owned a millinery store. This position, at which she earned only a few *Reichspennig* (small change), evaporated a few months later when her employers abruptly emigrated to Johannesburg, South Africa. After a frantic search, Margot found a position as a salesperson in a local clothing store. Besides serving the occasional customer, she had to help Frau Mansbach, the wife of the owner, to clean her apartment, which was located in the rear of the store.

A few months after she began this job, a bit less than a year after she and Walter had been married, when Margot missed two menstrual cycles, she became alarmed and thought she had a serious illness. She had no knowledge or understanding of reproduction because no one—neither her mother, other female relatives, friends, nor any of her female teachers—had ever explained that subject to her. In fact, years before, when, one day after school, Margot had begun to menstruate for the first time, her mother, too embarrassed to discuss that topic, told her daughter that she must have hurt herself in gym class. Now, concerned about the absent menses, Margot rushed to Duisburg. Her mother, only slightly concerned because she suspected the cause of the missed cycles, took Margot to the family physician, Dr. Julich. After examining Margot, he said, "There is nothing to worry about. In due time, a little Isaacson will come out." Upon leaving the doctor's office, Margot innocently asked her mother, "Where will the baby come out?" Her mother hesitated, and then uncomfortably replied, "Where it went in, it will come out."

Margot continued to work in the store until she was unable to climb the ladder to retrieve and replace sales goods or lift heavy boxes.

On February 22, 1938, Margot gave birth to a girl in a hospital in Neuss. She named her Eva. Since no other Jewish women had given birth that day, in accordance with the Nuremburg Laws which prohibited contact between Jews and gentiles, Margot was in a room all by herself. In the midst of ever harsher conditions in Germany, this baby brought great joy and a glimmer of hope to the new parents and to their families.

Little by little, as the situation for German Jews became increasingly dire, families began to fragment; children, who generally felt more willing than parents to uproot themselves, attempted to flee the country. Margot's sister Ruth, who had been unable to find a job in Duisburg, secured employment as a domestic for a family living in München-Gladbach. Even though she dreaded the thought of working as a servant, Ruth was grateful that whatever money she was able to give to her parents helped them to make ends meet. She spent little, saving as much as possible because she had been considering "making" *aliyah* (Hebrew for "going up") to Palestine, a plan that alternately excited and frightened her. Although she wanted to live in *Eretz Yisrael*, the Land of Israel, where she would be safe, she knew that if she emigrated to that untamed wilderness she might not see her family for years, if ever again. She also understood that if the situation for German Jews were to become worse and something were to happen to her parents and sister, she would not have any idea in terms of where they were.

After a great deal of thought and several discussions with her parents, who encouraged her, Ruth decided that she would, after all, emigrate to Palestine. However, before she could implement her plan, she was picked up by the Gestapo. For the next two days, her parents, sick to their stomachs because they did not know where she was, sat in their darkened apartment, jumping at each sound in the hallway, hoping, praying that their daughter would come home. Each time they went to the police station to ask about her they were rudely turned away. Finally, one official admitted that she was being held; he told the Landaus to go home and to await official word regarding her fate.

Days later, Ruth returned with a Gestapo officer, and said that she had to pack. She explained that she had been stopped on the street, brought to Gestapo headquarters, and questioned. Then she had been placed in a cold, dirty cell. That morning, a Gestapo officer had abruptly told her that she was being deported to Poland. This was happening throughout Germany to Jews who were considered foreign nationals or "stateless Jews." Ruth was classified a Polish national because, as stated earlier, her father had been born in Mikolschutz, a town in Upper Silesia which, 12 years after his birth, had been granted to Poland as one of the terms of the Treaty of Versailles. According to the Nuremburg Laws, Oskar and his children (and other Jews who had been born in parts of Poland that used to belong to Germany) were Polish citizens. This technicality did not apply to German Christians who had been born in those regions, and no previous German government had ever considered this technicality a matter of consequence. Now it mattered a great deal.

Oskar and Jenny wondered why Ruth had been picked up to be questioned by the Gestapo and why they had not. The apparent randomness in terms of who the Gestapo or the police stopped, questioned, and detained and who they allowed to move down the street unmolested imposed another dark layer of fear and uncertainty on top of the heavy burden that had become the lives of German Jews.

As Oskar and Jenny cried in frustration and alarm because they were unable to protect Ruth, they assumed that, sooner or later, they and Margot would suffer the same fate as their younger daughter.

They were horror-stricken and inconsolable with grief and guilt as Ruth was escorted by the officer from their apartment to the train station. In the months that followed, during which they had no contact with their daughter, they frantically tried to find out where in Poland she was and what, if anything, they could do for her. Everyone they consulted told them to be patient and pray and hope for the best. They considered traveling to Poland to find Ruth, but they did not know where to look and they feared that they would not be allowed to return to Germany.

The following is a translation of a letter that Ruth wrote to Margot several years later:

The reason I was deported was that the Polish (and very Fascist) government issued an edict that all Poles living outside of Poland had to get a special stamp in their passports, only available in Poland itself, or lose their citizenship. The Germans got wind of this and did not wish to have thousands of stateless Jews in Germany. We were taken in special trains over the border at Benschen in the Polish corridor. Benschen was a very small farming village and completely unprepared as train after train rolled in with all these people. There were women, children, babies and people in their eighties with only some hand luggage and no food. Some of us were housed in horse stables with manure still on the ground; others just stayed at the station. Later on, open horse-drawn wagons arrived with loaves of bread, which were thrown into the crowd. If you were lucky, you caught one, and, if not, you hoped that someone would give you a piece.

Conditions were dreadful. More and more people arrived. Finally, the Polish authorities allowed those who had relatives inside Poland proper to leave Benschen, providing they had the train fare. I remembered that we had a cousin from our mother's side in Lodz, so I went to Lodz. I was allotted accommodations with a family of four who all lived in one room. The man earned his meager living stitching leather uppers for shoes—piece work— at home. Our cousin, who was involved with the Refugee Aid Committee and was expecting her own father from Benschen, found my name on the list. She found out where I was staying and insisted that I stay with her and her family. They had two children, an eight-year-old daughter and a six-year-old son.

They were sheltering already another cousin from Cologne. A week later, our cousin's father, who was nearly seventy, a strictly Orthodox Jew, came. The room had been partitioned to house a small wood-burning stove and a bench with buckets of water on it. The tap was on the landing. There were about ten rooms on each landing, each housing an entire family and often lodgers on night shift. The beds never got cold. One lavatory was for all these people at the end of each landing. Need I describe our living conditions further? We ate, slept, cooked, washed and everything else in this one room. Seven of us! It was horrible!

Thanks to you, Margot, and a girlfriend of yours who was already in England, I got out six weeks before the Germans marched into Poland. The tanks and other machinery were standing at the frontier as the train brought us back. Due to the outbreak of war, I was unable to keep in touch with the wonderful people who took me under their wings, even though they themselves lived under the most dreadful circumstances. I presume they all lost their lives in Auschwitz or Bergen-Belsen.

One night a few weeks after Ruth had been torn from her parents and sent to Poland, Gestapo officers pounded on the Landaus' apartment door. The men searched the apartment and then they escorted Oskar and Jenny to the local police precinct, where they were questioned for hours.

In the weeks before they were picked up, the Landaus had discussed how they would handle this dreadful situation if it occurred. Would they admit that they were, according to the new laws, Polish nationals? If they did that, would they manage to be reunited with Ruth? If they were actually deported to Poland, would they be able to find their daughter? Where would they look?

They had no passports to show to the Gestapo because, years before, they had allowed them to expire and had disposed of them. After a great deal of frantic discussion, Oskar and Jenny had finally decided that if they were picked up by the authorities they would remain silent about their alleged Polish citizenship.

After hours of questioning, because Oskar and Jenny insisted that they were German citizens who had never had passports and had lost their birth certificates, the police and Gestapo officers, who had many other people to interrogate, sent them home.

Later, the Landaus sat in the dark at their small kitchen table, drinking tea. Neither one spoke. The fact that they had not been imprisoned or deported to Poland served as no consolation to them. As they silently prayed that they would hear from Ruth and fervently hoped that Margot would not be picked up by the Gestapo, they reluctantly accepted what they had for so long rejected: this was the reality and only the beginning of what were sure to be years of hell for their family and for the rest of the Jews of Germany.

FOUR

Kristallnacht

At around 10:30 p.m. on November 9, 1938, a Wednesday, as people in cities and towns throughout Germany and Austria were preparing for bed, the silent calm of that late fall evening was interrupted by strident sounds emanating from outside. People who parted their drapes or opened their windows saw groups of shadowy, strutting figures. The thud of heavy boot steps rose alarmingly from the cobblestone streets and coarse, angry, hate-filled shouts and vile curses slashed through the still air, echoing from building to building and into the places where people lived. Those disturbing sounds were almost immediately followed by the jangling, sharp-edged icy-cold clatter of glass shattering ... over and over again; the mobs shouted obscenities as they methodically smashed house and shop windows—but only those belonging to Jews. Then the roving gangs chased down and savagely beat men and women who had been identified as Jewish. After a while, some of those in the streets, torches in hand, set buildings on fire. Soon, the thick, acrid odor of burning timbers filled the air, leaking into houses and apartments.

As that beastly, violent night turned into still-dark early morning, the chilly air was rent by the echoing thunder of falling bricks and wooden beams as buildings, many of them smoldering ruins, collapsed heavily onto their foundations and spilled onto sidewalks.

The dimensions of the outrages committed during that appalling night would not be clearly discernible until daylight: on the streets of cities throughout Germany and Austria lay shards of glass from the thousands of shattered windows of Jewish homes, businesses, hospitals, schools, and social organizations; the smoky ruins of burned-out, plundered synagogues;[7] scores of dazed, bloodied Jewish victims hiding in alleys or huddling in doorways; and the bodies of other Jews hanging from lampposts. In all, 91 Jewish men and women were murdered that night and in excess of 30,000 Jewish men were picked up by the police and sent to concentration camps.

The main perpetrators of that night's violent, carefully planned government-sanctioned *pogrom* were *gauleiters* (local leaders of the Nazi party); members of the SA, the *Sturmabteilung*, the Storm Detachment or Assault Division, also known as the Brownshirts; and the *Schutzstaffel* (*SS or ⚡⚡*), the Defense Corps, who served as the paramilitary wing of the National Socialist German Workers' Party. An unknown number of everyday German citizens also took part in the frenzied assaults, which finally ended during the early morning hours of November 10. Police throughout Germany and Austria had been officially instructed to make no efforts to curtail the violence; fire departments had been under orders to allow synagogues and other Jewish buildings to burn, taking action only to protect adjoining non-Jewish structures from the raging flames.

The pretext for the attacks was the November 7th assassination of Ernst vom Rath, a low-level German diplomat stationed in Paris, by Herschel Grynszpan, a 17-year-old German-born Polish Jew living in that city. Grynszpan—who made no attempt to flee from the German embassy after he fired five bullets from a newly purchased pistol into the first official he had seen—said that he had been tormented by the dire plight of his family, which had been deported from Germany to Poland, as Margot's sister Ruth had been. Grynszpan voluntarily confessed to the killing. In one of his pockets French police found a postcard that he had planned on sending to his family; on it Grynszpan had written, "With God's help. My dear parents, I could not do otherwise, may God forgive me, the heart bleeds when I hear of your tragedy and that of the 12,000 Jews. I must protest so that the whole world hears my protest,

---

[7] Estimates range from several hundred to as many as 1,000 in Germany and Austria, some of them hundreds of years old.

and that I will do. Forgive me."

Ironically and tragically, the victim, vom Rath, had made his deeply held anti-Nazi views widely known and was, at the time of his death, being investigated by the authorities.

The day after vom Rath was killed, the German government declared that Jewish students would be barred from attending state elementary schools;[8] it suspended all Jewish cultural activities throughout Germany and Austria; and it halted the publication of Jewish newspapers and magazines. Then the government encouraged members of the SA and other paramilitary organizations to go on the rampage throughout Germany and Austria. The widespread riot became known as *Kristallnacht*, meaning "The Night of Broken Glass."

Early on the morning of November 10, Margot was playing with eight-month-old Eva, and Walter was—despite the turmoil and bloodshed that had taken place in the streets of Neuss all night (which seemed to have finally subsided)—preparing to leave for work. Just then, the couple was startled by violent pounding on the door of their small apartment and the rasping of angry, official-sounding voices. As Walter cautiously opened the door, two uniformed Gestapo officers roughly pushed their way in, knocking him aside, and coldly surveyed the apartment. They focused for a few seconds on the baby and then on Margot. Without a word, they seized Walter and shoved him into the hall, down the stairway, and to a van that was parked on the street. They opened a door and heaved him into the vehicle.

With tears streaming down her terrified face and her heart beating violently in her chest, Margot, feeling weak and faint, observed the horrifying scene on the street below from a window in the apartment. As the van pulled away from the curb, Margot cried, first gently, and then with body-shaking sobs. When she sensed that Eva, who was in her

---

[8] This rule had been in effect from the time of the Nuremburg Laws, but had been only loosely enforced.

playpen, was becoming upset, Margot used her reserves of inner strength to calm herself. Then, forcing a smile, she picked up the baby, kissed her cheek, and held her close. Through her tears, Margot sang a soothing lullaby to Eva and tried to convince herself that her husband would be home soon. *After all*, she mused, *once the police question him, they will realize that he was not involved in the bedlam of last night*. At that point, since neither she nor Walter had gone out and since the government-controlled radio news reports were vague (and almost completely lacking in truth), she did not know exactly what had happened the night before, other than the fact that windows had been broken and buildings had burned and people had been fighting.

Hours later, when Margot had not heard from her husband, she picked up Eva and timidly ventured out of the apartment. She learned from other women in her neighborhood that just about all of the Jewish men in Neuss had been rounded up and taken directly to Dachau, a concentration camp. During that early stage of the Third Reich, concentration camps were large prisons that held mostly political detainees. They were not yet being utilized as slave labor facilities or as death camps—huge factories whose function was to murder their inmates.

A few days later, frightened and bewildered after she had been told that she was utterly powerless to bring about her husband's release—or even obtain permission to visit him—Margot packed a few belongings and, with Eva, traveled by bus to her parents in Duisburg. She was relieved to see that the upper floors of the building in which they lived (Their apartment was on the third floor.) seemed not to have been damaged during the government-organized riot that was now being called *Kristallnacht*. However, the clothing store on the first floor, which was owned by Jews, had been ransacked and left in ruins.

Margot and her parents, with Eva between them, held each other tightly and cried; then Margot's mother and father assured her that Walter would be allowed to return home at some point. But Margot could not sit still. Leaving Eva with her parents, she walked out of the apartment, telling herself that there had to be something she would be able to do to help her husband. She heard from neighbors of her parents that Jews with visas to other countries or valid proof that they intended to emigrate from Germany would be released from the concentration camps in which they were being held. After asking directions, she walked to the nearest foreign consulate, where she planned to ask how to obtain a visa for herself and her family. Of course, she was not the only Jewish person on that mission that day. An official instructed her to fill out a form and said that it would take months before she would receive a response. She spent the rest of that day frantically walking from consulate to consulate, desperately hoping that an official from one of the countries—any country—would grant visas for her and her family. At nightfall, she returned to her parents' apartment and collapsed onto a couch. After a few minutes of playing with Eva on her lap, she fell asleep. The next morning, after downing a cup of coffee and a buttered roll, she returned to the street ... and her desperate search for a visa. After a week of this agonizing, seemingly futile task, when she felt that she was drowning in a deep well of depression, Margot was able to convince a sympathetic official at the consulate of the Dominican Republic to write a letter stating that she and her family would be allowed to enter that country.

Margot rushed to her parents' apartment, where she happily held out the letter to them. With a combination of relief that Margot, Walter, and Eva would be safe—and regret because their loved ones would be moving to a distant country—Oskar and Jenny told their daughter to go straight to the authorities with the letter. Picking up Eva, Margot rushed to Gestapo headquarters in Duisburg, where she showed the letter to a receptionist. As she nervously waited on a wooden bench, watching people bustle from office to office, Margot prayed that the letter would free her husband from what she believed might be years or possibly a lifetime of internment in a prison camp.

After several tense hours, at the point when Margot knew she had to return to her parents' apartment to feed her restless, whimpering baby, a secretary informed her that the letter was sufficient proof of the Isaacsons' intention to emigrate from Germany and that Walter would be released, although she did not know when that would be. As Margot took the letter, she asked the woman to write her new address—that of her parents' apartment in Duisburg—on her husband's file so that he would know not to return to Neuss when he was released. The woman noted the information and told Margot to go home and wait.

A full, anxious month later, at the end of December 1938, Walter knocked on the door of the apartment. Margot stared in shock and dismay at the pale, emaciated, frail-looking man she loved. His clothes were shabby and dirty and his hands were red and raw with frostbite. In a voice barely above a whisper, Walter told her not to worry about his condition, explaining that other than the drastic loss of weight, he was in good health. He sat wearily on a chair at the little dining table in the apartment, and then he wolfed down six hard rolls with butter and drank four cups of steaming hot coffee. In between mouthfuls of food, he weakly, gratefully smiled at his wife, Eva, and his in-laws.

When Walter could eat no more, Margot brought a basin of tepid water to the table and gently bathed his hands. Then she carefully dried them and, ignoring his assertion that he did not need any additional care, she slipped a pair of woolen mittens over his red, raw hands. With tears dripping down the creases and furrows of his care-worn face, he looked at Margot and whispered that he was one of the lucky ones. He said that at Dachau a fellow prisoner, Fritz Kaiser, a teacher at a Hebrew school in Ruhort, had developed gangrene in one arm due to frostbite and had to undergo an amputation with only a mild anesthetic to mask the pain. Then Walter asked to hold Eva. When the infant was in his arms, after struggling for a few seconds, she snuggled against her father's chest. He held her close to him and sighed, and then, inhaling her scent, that of innocence and peace, he smiled.

Early the next morning, as he had been instructed when he had been released from Dachau, Walter reported to the local Gestapo office, where he informed an official that he and his family would be leaving for the Dominican Republic very soon. He was told to report back daily until the day before he actually left the country because the government had to be kept abreast of his whereabouts. When Walter returned to the apartment, he found Margot crying, the letter from the consulate of the Dominican Republic in her hands. Through her tears, she whispered, "Read this," and, holding it up, she pointed to a line which said that the letter was only a landing permit. At the end of her desperate week of running frantically from consulate to consulate, when Margot had finally obtained the letter, she had only skimmed through it, mistakenly believing that it would serve as a visa that would allow her and her family to not only enter, but remain in the Dominican Republic.

Without another word, she and Walter understood that they had to flee Germany immediately, but now they had to find a new destination. When they discussed this newly discovered plight with her parents, Margot's father said that he had heard about a man—surely a disreputable figure—who smuggled Jews over the border into the Netherlands. After a great deal of anxious discussion, they decided that they would approach the man. Later that night, they took two streetcars, after which the four adults, with Margot and Walter taking turns carrying Eva, walked until they reached the address given to them by a neighbor.

The apartment house was located in a rundown section of Duisburg. During a hurried, whispered conversation in a dim, filthy apartment, the man, who, smiling broadly, said that he liked to be referred to as Onkel Kreusen, assured his guests that for a reasonable sum of money he would be able to bring them across the border to safety. Swallowing their fear and because they believed they had no other options, Walter and Margot reluctantly agreed. Margot's parents said that they would remain in Germany so that if she and Walter had to return they would still have a home.

The next day, Walter and Margot traveled to Duisburg-Meiderich, a nearby town to which the elder Isaacsons had moved. Sally Isaacson, a man who had always been exceptionally proud and self-assured, was now a shadow of his former self. After he had lost his butcher shop, he had been hired and then, two years later, rudely dismissed from a low-wage job because he was Jewish. A month later, he was bitterly grateful to find a lowly position in a factory where he sorted rags to be used to fill mattresses.

He and Emma, who had kept in close touch with the Landaus and knew that their son had been released from detention, were delighted to see him. However, they were aghast and broken-hearted to hear that he, along with his wife and baby daughter, would be leaving Germany. They feared they would never see either of their sons again; Walter's brother Heinz, having seen, both literally and figuratively, the hate-filled writing on the wall, had emigrated to Italy well before *Kristallnacht*. Sally and Emma Isaacson, who said they possessed neither the strength nor the will to flee Germany and establish a new life in a foreign land, took turns embracing and kissing their son, daughter-in-law, and Eva, fearing that this would be the last time. After a few hours of small talk and reminiscences and many cups of coffee, they embraced and tearfully said good-bye to each other, trying to sound confident as they asserted that they would all be reunited some day during a period of peace and sunshine. They reasoned that even the worst storm ends, and so, this black whirlwind of hatred and intolerance and disruption of their lives would surely be over one day.

Sally and Emma never saw their sons, Margot, or Eva again.

FIVE

Flight to An Uncertain Freedom

At the end of January 1939, the young couple reluctantly decided that Walter would cross over the border to the Netherlands with Onkel Kreusen before Margot and Eva so that he would be able to find a place in which to live and, hopefully, secure a job. A week after he left, Walter sent word through Onkel Kreusen about where and when Margot should meet him. She took whatever cash she had, as well as what her parents could spare. The next day, she, Eva, and Onkel Kreusen traveled by train to a small town (She immediately forgot its name) in western Germany. She and the smuggler silently waited as the other passengers disembarked at the isolated station. Then, at a word from the man, while the two police officers on duty were busy questioning another passenger, Margot, frantically holding Eva against her chest with one arm and her suitcase in her other hand, slipped off the train and, keeping her head down, walked directly to a nearby wooded area. Concentrating on the instructions that Onkel Kreusen, who remained on the train, had given to her during the rail trip, Margot trudged through what seemed to be miles of damp, cold, shadowy forest, eventually crossing into the Netherlands. She finally exited the forest and reached a secluded inn, where Walter joyfully greeted her and his infant daughter. Holding Eva, he led Margot to his room. The proprietors brought food and even provided milk for Eva.

After they had all eaten, Walter told his wife that even though the Netherlands seemed to be a safe refuge, a number of friendly people had recommended that he and his family continue traveling until they reached Belgium, a country which, with its 600,000-man military, was less likely to fall into German hands during the war which everyone glumly believed was on the horizon. They remained in their room at the inn that evening and for the rest of the next day. At nightfall, a short, tight-lipped man knocked on their door. Saying that he worked with Onkel Kreusen, he admonished the couple to hurry out of the building with him. Quickly gathering their few belongings, they allowed the man to guide them to his car, which was parked out front. He ushered them to the back seat. Then he got in and started the engine. Once the man had scanned the area, he put the car in gear and drove from the inn.

After what seemed to be an eternity of agonizingly slow, cautious driving along rutted country roads, as they approached a Belgian border patrol outpost, Eva, who had been asleep, began crying and then wailing. A border patrol agent put up his hand. The smuggler stopped the car, and the agent pointed a flashlight at the driver. Then he peered into the back seat. The driver, speaking Flemish, told the agent that he was taking the sick baby and its parents to a hospital in Antwerp. The agent shone his flashlight on Walter, Margot, and Eva again and then told the driver to proceed.

Hours later, the man stopped the car in front of an office of the Jewish World Organization, also known as the JOINT Committee or JOINT, in Antwerp. Although it was around 3 a.m., a volunteer who was on duty brought the refugees to a hotel and gave them money for food. After spending a few minutes explaining to the Isaacsons what they should do—and not do—during the coming days, he left, telling them to get some sleep. Two days later, Walter and Margot found an apartment at Klosterstraat 148, which was in a shabby, derelict neighborhood near the harbor, where they met a number of other German Jewish refugees. These newcomers to Belgium helped each other to adjust to the new environment and unfamiliar language.[9] Six difficult months later, during a pleasantly warm day in the middle of August 1939, Ruth showed up at the Isaacsons'

---

[9] Flemish, a dialect of Dutch, is spoken in Antwerp and throughout the rest of the northern portion of Belgium; French and Walloon, which is a Romance language related to French, is spoken in the southern part of the country.

apartment in Antwerp. Margot, not believing what she saw, froze in the doorway. Then, releasing all of the tears and buzz-saw emotions that she had held in check from the time she had fled Germany, she reached out and kissed and clung to her sister. When, still sobbing and shaking, Margot finally released Ruth, her sister said that she was on her way to the United Kingdom; a friend who lived in that country had obtained a permit for her to work there, and that had enabled her to leave Poland. Ruth refused to talk about her dreadful time in exile, saying that she would explain at some point in the future.[10] Then she told Margot that she had managed to visit their parents in Duisburg on her way to Belgium; they had given her Margot's address in Antwerp. In answer to Margot's questions, Ruth said that their mother and father were well, but very lonely and intensely anxious.

Ruth did not know it at the time, but that visit would be the last time that she would see her parents.

A few days later, after Ruth had left for the United Kingdom, Margot realized that she was pregnant again. Although she was nervous at the thought of giving birth in a strange country, she luxuriated in the tingly warmth slowly rising from the center of her body to her face. During this otherwise bleak, disheartening time of evil and uncertainty, when the dark storm of war appeared to be gaining ever-greater strength over Europe, Margot's three precious gifts—her husband, Eva, and now her unborn child—provided her with hope for the future.

Near the end of August, Margot had another reason to feel hopeful and grateful: her parents arrived in Antwerp and moved into the little apartment with her and Walter and Eva. They told Margot that they had decided to use the services of Onkel Kreusen to escape from Germany because, as much as they did not want to relocate, they knew they could no longer remain in their homeland. Laughing, they said that as oily as he seemed to be, Onkel Kreusen had done what they had paid him to do.

---

[10] See the letter from Ruth in Chapter Three.

On September 1, 1939, German ground, naval, and air forces attacked Poland from the west and the north. Two days later, the United Kingdom and France, citing their treaty obligations with Poland, declared war on Germany. On September 17, by prior agreement with the Third Reich, the Soviet Union invaded Poland from the east. On October 6, Polish defenders conceded defeat, and the Germans and Russians divided the country between them. The Isaacsons and the Landaus, although they were relatively safe in Antwerp, listened, with their stomachs tied in knots, to German news broadcasts on the radio. They knew that most of what they were hearing was false.

By this point, Walter had learned how to, in a rudimentary fashion, communicate in Flemish. That allowed him and his father-in-law to earn some money peddling candles to the merchants in their area. Their best customers were the diamond cutters, of whom there were many. That money, along with an allotment provided by local Jewish organizations, allowed them to purchase food and pay the rent for the apartment. Margot and her mother, neither of whom had learned more than a few words of Flemish, spent most of their time taking care of Eva, shopping for inexpensive food, and cleaning the small apartment. On occasion, they visited other Jewish refugees in the neighborhood, sitting for hours sipping tea and talking wistfully about their idyllic lives in Germany before the men with the swastikas came to power.

During the next few months, other than British air raids on Axis ships and fighting in Finland, there was very little actual warfare. In the midst of this relatively quiet period, which was being referred to as the "Phony War," on February 8, 1940, Margot gave birth to her second child, a boy, in the Moederhuis (Literally "mother house," a maternity hospital) in Antwerp. At that time, mothers remained hospitalized for ten days after giving birth. While Margot was hospitalized, Walter, who decided that their apartment was too small for six people, found a slightly larger unit in the same building for only a bit more rent. On February 18, Margot and the newborn came home. Oskar and Jenny took over much of the care of the new baby, giving Margot more time to spend with Eva.

Walter and Margot named the child René Rudolf. The name Rudolf was in remembrance of Walter's younger brother, who had died in infancy; Margot chose the name René because, for reasons she never explained, she wanted the boy to have a French name.

Two months after René Rudolf was born, during the second week of April 1940, a period of time when the Isaacsons and the Landaus felt frozen to the core each time they talked about their future, they heard on the radio that Germany had invaded—and occupied—both Norway and Denmark. The little bit of hope to which they had desperately clung—that the so-called "Phony War" between the Allies and Germany would end in a negotiated settlement—began to fade. They now understood that the United Kingdom and France would be forced to accelerate their military actions against Germany and that other countries in Europe, Belgium among them, would become involved in the bloodshed.

Early on the morning of May 10, all of the people in the little apartment were startled awake by a thundering, ominous sound. As they peered out of a window, they saw swarms of dark-colored airplanes lumbering across a steel-gray sky like so many vultures in search of prey; they knew, based on the markings on the wings, that they were Luftwaffe bombers. Just then, loudspeakers mounted on Belgian military vehicles in the streets announced that the invasion had begun and that all German nationals had to report to City Hall. Oskar Landau, suspecting a trap, announced that he refused to report to the Belgian authorities. Walter, believing that he could trust the Belgians, especially since he was a Jewish refugee, said that he would do as instructed. Although he assumed he simply had to register as a German citizen, he packed a small suitcase with extra clothes—he did not know why he felt compelled to do this—and walked to City Hall, where he was immediately put into a holding cell, along with hundreds of other men. He was told by a guard that the Belgian authorities believed it was necessary to round up and intern all German men to prevent them from acting as spies and from launching a "fifth column" attack. Walter thought it bitterly ironic that Jewish men who had fled their homeland because they were targets of the Third Reich and had sought shelter in Belgium were considered a danger to the Belgian people. This was despite the fact that a number of those men had volunteered to join the Belgian military.

The next day at dawn the men were awakened and, with only a few minutes to prepare, were marched to a staging area outside of City Hall. After a few minutes, a score of decrepit, dirty military trucks with canvas-covered freight compartments pulled to a stop in front of the men, who were directed to climb aboard. There were no benches or seats in the freight area; the prisoners were told to sit on the splintery wood-slat floors. Walter sat on his suitcase. When all of the men had been crammed into the trucks, the clumsy vehicles started moving. Fourteen long, bone-aching hours later, the caravan reached its destination, a squalid refugee and internment camp near St. Cyprien, a Basque village in southeastern France near the Pyrenees Mountains, not far from the Spanish border. The men had been brought to that desolate, windswept location in accordance with an earlier agreement between the governments of France and Belgium involving the internment of all male German nationals in the event of war.

In France and the United Kingdom, shortly after the declaration of war, German men had been rounded up and questioned by the police and security services, at which point they were evaluated in reference to whether or not they were perceived to be threats. Each man was then either released and monitored by the police or interned for the duration of the war.

On the day that Walter reported to City Hall, when, by late afternoon he had not returned to the apartment, Margot, against her parents' advice, hurried out to determine what had happened to him. At City Hall, after several fruitless attempts to make herself understood using her limited Flemish, Margot found an office worker who spoke French.[11] After making inquiries, the man returned and informed her that all German nationals were being held in protective custody for the duration of the war. Dizzy, as the blood rushed from her head and her legs gave way, Margot slumped down to the floor. The office worker helped her to a bench and waited to

---

[11] It is likely that several others spoke French or Walloon, but many Flemish speakers refused to use either of those languages unless absolutely necessary.

see whether she was likely to collapse again. Then he returned to his desk and busied himself with paperwork. After a long while, Margot, her hands wet with perspiration and icy cold, and feeling as if she had been kicked in the abdomen, dragged herself out of the office. She wandered the streets for over an hour, unsure as to what she should do or where she should go.

Eventually, knowing that her children needed her, she returned to the apartment to tell her parents about what had happened to Walter.

SIX

Imprisoned in a Mountain Wilderness

Most of the men who were interned in the primitive mountain camp at St. Cyprien were, like Walter, German Jews who had taken refuge in Belgium or France. A smaller number were German Christians who had been living and working in those countries. Back in Germany, the men from the two groups would not have had any contact with each other. In fact, some of the Christians at the camp may have been fervent Nazis or, at least, anti-Semites, who would have harassed the Jews if they had been at home. However, at St. Cyprien they were all prisoners. While the French guards did not abuse the internees, they did not go out of their way to provide the men with more than the barest necessities of life.

While Walter was learning to adjust to his new, harsh environment in the remote mountain internment camp, the Belgian military was attempting to hold off a massive German assault. Margot, her parents, Eva, and René spent many nights in the cellar of the building in which they lived, holding each other tightly while fighting raged outside. They, along with the other inhabitants of the building shivered each time they heard the thud of a distant artillery shell or a bomb that had dropped from a plane. They vibrated from head to toe and screeched in terror with each nearby explosion. Years later, on the few occasions that Margot chose to talk about those dark times, she would close her eyes, rub her face, sigh deeply, and explain that along with the horror of the bombs exploding and other dangers that her children faced in that dank cellar, she worried about Walter and wondered whether she would ever see him again.

Eighteen days of horrific *blitzkrieg* (lightning war) destroyed the bulk of Belgium's outnumbered aircraft and German tanks decimated its ground forces. On May 28, 1940, King Leopold III capitulated. The harsh German occupation of Belgium began.

It would last for more than four years.

Margot and her parents felt that as dreadful as they believed it would be, they had no choice but to remain in Belgium under German occupation. They asked the old question: "Where could we go?" The Netherlands, Luxembourg, and France, all of which bordered Belgium, had been attacked on the same day as Belgium, May 10, 1940. Tiny Luxembourg had been overwhelmed almost immediately and surrendered to the German invaders; the Dutch had capitulated on May 15, after five days of fighting. The French, with their powerful but inept military, held out until June 4, 1940, at which point German forces entered Paris and installed the swastika flag on the Eiffel Tower.

Another, very persuasive reason why Margot and her parents decided they had to remain in Antwerp was their fear that if they fled, when Walter was released from internment—whenever that would be—he would not be able to find them.

Four agonizing months after Walter had been transported to St. Cyprien, Margot received a letter from him. The International Red Cross—which visited internment, prisoner of war, and concentration camps—had helped to make sure the letter reached its destination. In his note, Walter told about the horrendous conditions at St. Cyprien, and then he explained that the camp had been closed and evacuated because many of the inmates had contracted dysentery and a number of them had died. He wrote that he and the others had been transferred to the newly opened Gurs Internment Camp in southwestern France, also in the foothills of the Pyrenees.

With the fall of the official French government in the northern portion of the country to the Nazis in June 1940, the southern half, under the control of Marshal Philippe Pétain, a Nazi sympathizer, declared itself Free France. Generally referred to as Vichy France, after the city designated as its capital, the political leaders of this portion of the country signed an armistice with the Germans and acted in accordance with all of their dictates.

At this point, Gurs, which had been established in 1939 as a refugee camp for those fleeing the Spanish Civil War, held only Jews and a small number of political prisoners from occupied countries. German officials had ordered the Vichy government to release all Christian prisoners, who were then instructed to enlist in the Wehrmacht so as to "defend" the Fatherland.

While not a concentration camp, Gurs was a hellish place. It was cold and muddy, regularly buffeted by fierce, biting winds and lashed by frequent rainstorms, with drafty, leaky wooden huts for shelter, abominable bathroom facilities, and poor food. Its 382 huts were surrounded by a two-meter-high wire fence. French guards kept watch over the men, but very few prisoners attempted to escape. Looking through the fence, the men could not imagine how they would be able to survive in the mountainous wilderness surrounding the camp or find their way to a town.

Walter was to spend the next two long, dreary years in Gurs. During his internment, he and Margot exchanged weekly letters. He also wrote to his parents, always assuring them that conditions were fine (which, of course, was not true) and that he was well. Since writing paper was, along with many other everyday items, scarce, all of them wrote their replies to each other on the back sides of the original letters. Margot kept all of the letters that Walter sent to her, tied together by a long pink ribbon.

On a bitterly cold day in January 1941, Margot's parents received a letter from the German authorities ordering them to report to the main train station in Antwerp within 24 hours. As with so many other orders and proclamations issued by the Nazis and by European governments during the war in which there seemed to be no rhyme or reason as to why some people, and not others, were targeted, the Landaus wondered why they had been chosen to vacate Antwerp. One of the reasons for this confusing, capricious situation may have had to do with the continuous movement of refugees during those tumultuous times; generally, only those who had registered or had come to the attention of the authorities in other ways received such notices. As far as Margot knew, she and her children were ghosts, invisible in reference to the German occupiers, but then, so were her parents.

The official letter indicated that the Landaus were being transferred from Belgium and would be allowed to bring only 40 pounds of luggage. At one point that evening, Margot paused during the sad task of helping her parents to pack their bags so that she could fill two empty schnapps bottles with water that she had boiled on the coal stove. She corked the bottles, wrapped them in blankets, and placed one in René's crib and the other in his sister's bed. Due to the shortage of fuel, this was the only way to keep her children warm as they slept. A short while later, René began screaming. When Margot checked on him she saw that the cork on the bottle that she had placed in his crib had popped off, causing the water to scald him. He howled in pain. Margot was hysterical with fear and overcome with grief when she saw that her baby had been burned from his knees to his feet. She and her parents ran cool water over his burns, and then Margot rocked him. Because of the nightly blackout and curfew, she was not able to take René to a hospital, so she did her best to soothe him until he finally fell asleep.

Shortly after dawn, Margot and her parents tearfully embraced. Then her father and mother walked out the door and headed to the train station to report as instructed. Although Margot was overwhelmed with anxiety and grief regarding her parents, she dressed her children, picked up René, and took Eva by the hand. Then she exited the building and flagged down a taxi to take them to the nearest hospital, where a doctor said that the baby had suffered third degree burns and had to be admitted. He was hospitalized for close to three weeks. When, many years later, Margot told this story to René, she said that when she visited him in the hospital ward, which she did each day for as many hours as she was allowed, he rocked his head from side to side. He retained that habit for the next few years of his life.

Two weeks after her parents left, Margot, with great effort, was able to find out that they had been sent to a village in the eastern province of Limbourg, Belgium which was being used as a holding camp. Although she felt guilty about going because René was still hospitalized, Margot decided that she had to see her parents because she feared they were in danger and needed her help. Two of her neighbors, women she loved and trusted, said that they would take turns spending as many hours as allowed with René in the hospital each day until she returned.

After a sluggish, uncomfortable train ride, Margot and Eva disembarked at a dilapidated station in a desolate, rural section of Limbourg. When they reached the refugee center, Margot was shocked and sickened to see—and smell—the wretched conditions that the hundreds of Jews who had been evacuated from Antwerp and other places in Belgium were forced to endure. Most of them slept on straw, without mattresses or blankets, on the floor of an unheated school gymnasium. This was in the middle of an extremely cold winter. They were not allowed to use the school bathrooms, and had to relieve themselves in primitive screened-in privies that had been set up in one corner of the gymnasium.

Margot learned that her parents were not there; they had been taken in by a local Belgian family to whom they paid a small amount of money for room and board. The tiny house in which they lived was only a few degrees warmer than it was outside; the water in the washbasin in the room in which the Landaus slept was perpetually frozen, looking like a miniature skating rink.

It was a sad, depressing visit, but as she traveled back to Antwerp two exhausting days later, Margot reassured herself that as bleak as their living conditions were, at least her parents were safe ... for now.

During the following week, Margot received an official letter identical to the one that had instructed her parents to vacate Antwerp. Resolute and unshakeable in her determination to make sure that her hospitalized infant continued to receive the best possible care, she went straight to the local German military headquarters, where she explained the situation to one of the officials. The man listened politely, reviewed the official letter she had received, and told her that he was powerless to act. Then he said that she had to leave the city, with or without the baby.

Later that day, holding René gently because his bandaged wounds were still oozing and very painful, she carried him from the hospital to the apartment, where she packed as many of their belongings as she could fit, along with biscuits and canned milk, into a large baby carriage. The next morning, wheeling Eva and René in the packed carriage, she reported to the train station in Antwerp.

More nervous and fearful than she had ever been, Margot pushed the carriage to the train car to which a police officer, after glancing at the official letter, had pointed. A well-dressed couple, seeing the young mother approach the car, descended and offered to help. The woman held Eva by the hand and René in her other arm while the man and Margot hoisted the loaded baby carriage onto the train. René cried during the entire time they were in transit—whether from the noise of the train, his burns, or fear of the unfamiliar surroundings Margot did not know. She was frightened, as most likely were the other passengers, for they had not been told how long they would be on the train or their destination.

Late that evening, several exhausting hours after leaving the station in Antwerp, just as Margot's children had consumed the last of the food that she had packed, the train stopped and the passengers were instructed to disembark. As she stepped onto the dim, barren train station and looked around, Margot was just barely able to make out the ghostly outlines of what appeared to be ramshackle huts and crudely constructed shacks. She later learned that they were at an abandoned miners' village in Limbourg, the same province where her parents were living, but a considerable distance from them. The collection of dilapidated buildings that she had seen had been used to house Polish miners who had fled their country in 1939, shortly after the German invasion.

Margot and her children, along with Regina Katz, another German Jew who had also been living in Antwerp, were assigned to an unheated, decrepit shack with no running water. Regina had a young son; her husband was also interned at Gurs. The women and their children slept on piles of straw and ate carrots and potatoes that kindhearted farmers gave to them. They took turns walking several miles to a store to purchase additional bits of food and to a dairy farm to buy milk for their children. Since there was no stove, the women improvised: after carefully clearing a spot on the dirt floor and opening a window for ventilation, they lit some straw to make a fire which they used for warmth and cooking and to illuminate their primitive abode after dark. As if their existence was not challenging enough, all of the residents of the makeshift town had to report to the German authorities each day.

Since during this early stage of the war, the leaders of Third Reich had not decided on a comprehensive policy in terms of what to do with the Jews under their control, they adopted a varied approach: monitoring some of them in their homes, pushing others into ghettos, deporting still others to internment camps, and sending increasingly greater numbers to concentration camps, many of which were in the eastern part of Europe. The bored German officials at the old miners' camp simply kept track of the inhabitants and awaited further orders.

Each day was like the others. Only changes in the weather broke up the monotony. Margot worried continuously about her husband and her parents; she also feared that Eva or René would become ill in their cold, drafty hovel and that she would not be able to find a doctor. She worked to push out of her consciousness the nagging idea that, one day, the Germans would tell her that she had to move to another, worse place or that she and her children would be separated. Her only sources of joy were the letters that she exchanged with Walter—although, based on how he did not always reply to questions that she wrote in her letters, she was sure that not all of hers actually reached him, and she assumed that not all of his letters made it to her—and the pleasure of watching Eva and René play and grow and develop. After a while, René's burn wounds healed and were replaced by scars.[12]

In the spring of 1941, because they desperately missed and were consumed with worry regarding their husbands, Regina and Margot decided to travel together to the internment camp in Gurs, France. Even though in his last letter to Margot, Walter had pleaded with her not to chance the long, dangerous journey to see him, she was determined to go. Shortly after she had arrived in the old miners' camp, Margo had sold to guards, for a bit of cash, some personal items and a few of her parents' possessions that she had packed when she had been ordered to leave Antwerp. She had been using that money, along with what she continued to receive from Jewish charitable organizations via the Red Cross to purchase food and other necessary items for herself and her children. She decided that she had enough spare cash to make the trip.

On the same day that she and Regina, to their great relief, each received the *laissez-passer* (permission to cross the border) that they had requested, Margot packed the old baby carriage with supplies, squeezed René into it, and took Eva by the hand. Then she and Regina—with her son in tow—trudged to the rural station, where they boarded a train. During the eight-hour overnight trip to Paris, Margot was repeatedly surprised by the high level of courtesy and consideration displayed by the German soldiers who were her fellow passengers on the crowded train. She thought that perhaps they did not realize that she and Regina were Jewish, or else, she reasoned, they were simply soldiers, and not Nazis. There was a difference.

---

[12] To this day, when René (now called Ron) looks at and touches those scars, he attempts to imagine what life was like during that frightening, harsh winter in that isolated, ramshackle hut.

At the station in Paris, as Margot pushed the loaded baby carriage and held Eva's hand, with Regina and her son walking behind them, she was stopped by a Red Cross officer who asked in German whether they needed assistance. Once Margot had explained the purpose of their visit, the man escorted them to a shelter for refugees in Montmartre. Margot looked around, aghast, thinking that the conditions in the old mining town in Limbourg were better than in this place. Hundreds of women and children, including many infants, were crowded into a dim, dank dormitory-like hall. The sanitary conditions were atrocious; the entire building smelled like sewage. Within a few days, all three children had developed pediculosis. The women repeatedly washed the children's hair in an attempt to comb out lice and eggs, finally resorting to dousing their scalps with watered-down kerosene, which seemed to work, but caused itchy, red rashes on their scalps, necks, and shoulders. When Margot and Regina brought the children to a hospital, as the doctor was treating the inflamed areas, he shook his head disapprovingly and asked, "What are a few lice during war time?" Then he shaved the children's heads, saying that was a sure way of ending the infestation.

Another problem involved food. The only way for the refugees who were housed in the dormitory to obtain decent hot meals was to walk a great distance, with their children, to the other side of the Seine to a *cuisine populaire* (an inexpensive restaurant), something that Margot and Regina did once or twice a day. The women consoled themselves by saying that at least they were becoming familiar with Paris.

Since their passes allowed the women into Paris, but no further, they had to remain in that city until they were able to obtain new ones that would allow them to travel to the far southern part of Vichy France, where Gurs was located. Vichy France—the entire southern half of the country—was exempt from German occupation, but the passes required the approval of the German authorities in Paris, which was in Occupied France. After three long, unpleasant months of waiting in the filthy shelter, Margot learned that she and Regina would be able to move into the Jewish Theological Seminary, whose students had fled shortly after the German occupation of Paris. However, before they could move, they had to obtain the permission of the local

French authorities. After explaining their case to a French official, the women were directed to a bench and told to wait. They were used to this routine: approach an official, smile nervously, politely explain the situation, and then wait and wait and ... . They took comfort in the fact that even though they were in Occupied Paris, they were dealing with a French official. They assumed he would be more sympathetic than a German. Therefore, they were shocked and distraught when, after waiting for two hours, the official approached them to explain that not only would they not be granted permission to move to the seminary, but they had to vacate Paris at once and return to Belgium. They would not even be allowed to retrieve their meager belongings from the shelter at which they had been staying for the past three months.

Margot, Regina, and the three children were directed to a waiting car and driven to the train station, where, without an opportunity to buy food or even take a drink of water, they were told to board the next train for Brussels, which would depart within the hour. While they were waiting, Margot found a Red Cross official who provided them with a bite to eat. The women tearfully told the man of their plight and explained that they knew no one in Brussels. They also said that even though they wanted to return to Antwerp (They did not mention that they had been living in the miner's camp in Limbourg), neither one would have a place in which to live in that city. The official said that he would call the Red Cross office in Antwerp to see what could be done. A short while later, the man returned with a smile on his face and reported that—miracle of miracles—the office in Antwerp had located Margot's parents.[13] The man said that the Landaus had been told at what time Margot and her children would arrive in Brussels; they had said that they would meet their daughter and grandchildren at the station. The official had no way of knowing that the passes that had allowed Margot (and Regina) to enter

---

[13] For reasons that neither Margot nor her parents were ever able to determine, they had been allowed to return to that city.

France specified that they were required to return to Limbourg. Then the man turned to Regina and said that since no one would be meeting her at the station in Brussels, someone from the Red Cross would help her find a place in which to live in that city.

The next morning, when Margot and her children arrived in Brussels, her parents were waiting, as promised. They had traveled by overnight train from Antwerp. The Landaus, who were shocked when they saw their grandchildren, stopped dead in their tracks. Besides the fact that Eva and René had lost weight during their time in Limbourg and then Paris and looked disheveled and tired because of their abrupt expulsion from that city and the tedious overnight train ride, their fuzzy tufts of hair made them look grotesque. Since René was only about a year old—and a boy— he did not look too odd, but Eva, whose long, curly golden locks had been a source of delight to Oskar and Jenny, looked like a pitiful phantom version of herself. After they embraced the children and their daughter, they said that they would take them to their inexpensive one-room attic apartment, which was all they had been able to find when they had been allowed to return to Antwerp.

After Margot said good-bye to Regina, she overheard a Red Cross worker apologetically tell her friend that a German official had checked her papers and declared that she and her son had to return to the abandoned miners' village in Limbourg. Margot's heart broke and she yearned to help Regina, but, of course, nothing she might say or do would be of any use. For whatever reason, no one had checked Margot's papers. She was relieved, but when she looked at Regina she felt guilty.

On June 22, 1941, while Margot and her children had been in Paris, awaiting permission to travel to Gurs, the German military, using the code name *Operation Barbarossa*, invaded the Soviet Union. This was despite the fact that Adolf Hitler and Joseph Stalin—the leader of the U.S.S.R.—had signed a mutual non-aggression pact back in August of 1939. The *Wehrmacht* marched as far into the Soviet Union as Stalingrad, where it became hopelessly bogged down. Margot's father, ever the optimist, assessed the situation by saying, "The deeper they go in Russia, the sooner they will lose the war."

Once she and her children were back in Antwerp, Margot, ignoring the fact that she was in violation of the law by not returning to Limbourg, did what she always did: she worked to create the best conditions under the circumstances for Eva and René. After a diligent search, she located a two-room ground floor apartment at Van Leriusstraat 31 for herself and her children and a small third-floor unit in the same building for her parents. It was a lovely, peaceful neighborhood, much nicer than the rough-and-tumble waterfront area in which she and Walter had lived when they first arrived in Antwerp. Margot and her parents often visited nearby Kievitt Park, where they sat and watched Eva and René play.

Margot was relieved that they were back in Antwerp, and she tried to feel content; after all, she, her children, and her parents were safe in their modest but relatively comfortable apartments. However, she missed her husband; he had been away from her, first at St. Cyprien and then at Gurs, for 15 months. She wrote to him each week. On many a night, she cried herself to sleep.

SEVEN

What He Wanted the Most

At Gurs, Walter was assigned to kitchen work. Although he did not like it, he always put on his best face and did what he was told—all the while managing to put aside an occasional piece of tough meat or a loaf of poorly baked bread or a small handful of just barely edible vegetables, which he later sold to a man from town who regularly waited at the wire fence that surrounded the camp. Walter justified this bit of larceny by telling himself that stealing from those who held him in prison for no reason other than the fact that he was a Jew was neither a crime nor a sin. Besides, he had decided that he needed to save a good deal of money to do what he wanted the most.

The conditions at the camp were horrendous. He and the other men were chronically cold and wet and they were always hungry. Although Walter attempted to get through his long, miserable days with a positive attitude, by the beginning of his second year there he had become quite despondent. Besides missing his wife and his children, he was overwhelmed with grief upon learning, via a letter from his father, that his mother had died in Cologne in June of 1941 due to a complication arising from a surgical procedure. He felt the loss deep in his soul and he suffered great anguish when he thought about how neither he nor his brother Heinz had been there to comfort her at the end.

Although the vast majority of European Jews would be deported to concentration camps in the coming years, at that point in the war, most of the ones who still lived in Germany—such as his parents—or in occupied countries were allowed to remain in their homes. They were regularly harassed, sometimes viciously, and coldly restricted in terms of their everyday movements, both by the government and by civilians, but relatively few had been picked up and transported to camps. Walter's heart ached for his grief-stricken father, who was now alone in the world, and for his wife and children.

In a letter to Margot, Walter wrote of his sorrow:

It is incomprehensible to me. I cannot understand it. My colleagues try to console me, but there is no consolation. One has only one mother, and she cannot be replaced. Now I have only you, your beloved parents and our children. My longing for you is beyond words. I only hope that "Onkel Kreusen" will soon find a way to bring me back to you. I already wrote two registered letters to you and hope that you have received them. If not, it would be a shame. Each one costs five Francs, which is a lot of money for me, especially since I need the money for "Onkel Kreusen."

A few of Walter's fellow inmates had attempted to escape from Gurs. Several had been shot dead and others had been captured and then punished harshly, but one or two, with the help of smugglers like Onkel Kreusen, had managed to get away. That encouraged Walter to take more chances. One day, he talked with an unusually friendly guard who said that he wanted to purchase Walter's gold wedding band. After a moment of inner struggle, during which Walter almost said no because the ring was a warm, tangible bond to Margot, he agreed to sell it for a pittance on the condition that the guard help him to escape. The guard, who had already committed two serious violations—engaging in a friendly conversation with an inmate and attempting to engage in a commercial transaction with him—said that if Walter were to leave his hut late one night when he (the guard) was on duty, he might not notice that someone was walking through the compound and toward the fence. A few days later, Walter talked with the man from town to whom he regularly sold stolen food; the man said that he had recently spoken to a man who worked with Onkel

Kreusen. He whispered through the wire fence that, for a fee, the smuggler would help Walter to escape to Paris. Walter handed a few francs to the man, telling him to set up the plan for late March.

Despite his bone-chilling anxiety and his deep-seated fear that he might be walking into a trap, Walter knew that he had to do what he wanted the most: go home to his wife and children.

Late one night at the end of March 1942, when the other men in his hut were asleep, Walter quietly grasped the small suitcase that he had brought with him when he been evacuated from Antwerp. Then, after shoving his tin drinking cup into a pocket in his coat, he stealthily retrieved a battered cardboard box that he had previously tied to the bottom of his bed; it contained a piece of cheese, a crust of hard bread, and a wine bottle (that had been discarded by the guards) filled with water. He peered out the grimy window at the darkened area in front of the hut.

He had spent close to two years away from his family, first at St. Cyprien and then at Gurs. He hoped he had chosen the right time to escape. He looked around the shadowy cabin. No one moved. The only sound was the ragged snoring of the other men and the howling wind outside. As quietly as possible, Walter opened the rough wooden door and stood in front of the hut. Once he was sure that no one was about, except, he assumed, for the friendly guard who had told Walter that he would be on duty that night, Walter gently closed the door and walked across the central area of the compound to a section of the wire fence that he had examined earlier that day. After looking around again, Walter placed his suitcase and cardboard box on the ground and, using the tin cup, began to dig. Although the evening was bitterly cold and gusty, after a few minutes of frenzied scraping away at the hard soil, he was soaked with perspiration. Once he had dug a narrow, sloping passageway under the fence, Walter stood up and, knowing that his suitcase was too large to fit through the open tunnel, he tossed it over the fence and onto an area of thick undergrowth. Then, after shoving the food box and cup through the passageway, he pushed and grasped and wriggled through, emerging on the other side. Standing up, Walter felt as if he had been reborn. He quickly pushed some soil back onto the cut in the ground. Then he brushed off his hands and clothing, retrieved his belongings, and moved quickly and noiselessly into the dim, frosty woods that surrounded and stood sentry over the camp. Feeling wet and frozen as he walked, Walter hoped the smuggler who worked with Onkel Kreusen was waiting for him.

When Walter spotted the man, he walked over to him and wordlessly handed over half of the agreed-upon fee, after which they continued to move through the dense, wild forest. Briars and vines clung to their clothing as they walked. Thirty minutes later, they reached a rough dirt road, where the smuggler had parked his very small, very old-looking car. The man took Walter's suitcase and, after opening and examining it, placed it in the trunk of the car. Then he opened a rear door and told Walter to lie down on the floor. Once Walter had done that, the man covered him with a coarse, foul-smelling blanket. Keeping the box with his food and water close to him, Walter attempted to make himself comfortable. The space was too short for his body, so he had to bring his knees up to his abdomen and keep his hands at his sides. The surface on which he lay was the uncarpeted, cold steel floor of the car. Each time the vehicle hit a bump or bounced in and out of a rut, Walter winced in pain; with each turn, Walter's body was roughly pushed and uncomfortably pulled. Added to that was the fact that the warm air in his confined space under the blanket smelled of gasoline and burning oil. After a short while, because of the continuous movement of the vehicle, Walter became nauseated; he used all of his inner strength to fight the urge to vomit. He dozed off on two or three occasions, managing to sleep for only a couple of minutes each time. The driver stopped the car four times during the roughly 480-mile journey, once for refueling and three times on dark, lonely stretches of road to allow Walter to relieve himself, flex his body, and eat and drink. At the first stop, knowing that he would not be able to eat, he gave his small supply of food to the man, who greedily devoured it in seconds. Walter sipped his water and waited.

Each time they stopped, Walter had to convince himself not to tell the man that he wanted to walk the rest of the way to his destination— Paris. Besides the fact that he did not have any idea where he was or how to reach the city, Walter understood that the smuggler, who had made this protracted, grueling journey before, knew how to avoid detection by soldiers and border guards. Walter kept telling himself that all of the discomfort and danger were a small price to pay for the great joy and profound sense of relief that he and Margot would feel once they were together again.

The following day, toward afternoon, the driver stopped the car on a gravel road near the border between Vichy and Occupied France. The man helped Walter up from his tight, fetid space and gave him only a minute to stretch and to breathe deeply. Then he handed the suitcase to Walter and pointed to a partially hidden forest path on the side of the road. He gave Walter directions to the nearby train station. Walter peered ahead, knowing that even if the man was telling the truth, and the station lay ahead, the next part of the journey would be even more dangerous than the miles they had traversed. He also knew that he had no choice, so he handed over the rest of the payment and shook hands with the man. All he had left were a few coins for train fare. Once the smuggler had turned the car around and driven off, kicking up a shower of flinty gravel, Walter walked in the direction that the man had indicated.

When, a short while later, Walter reached what appeared to be the clearing at the end of the woods that the smuggler had described, he removed his torn, foul-smelling traveling clothes and changed into the suit, shirt, and tie that were in the suitcase and then, without the benefit of a mirror, he combed his hair. He wished he could shave, but that was impossible now. Taking a deep breath, reciting a silent prayer, and summoning all of his courage, he walked out of the woods.

Although he was exceedingly frightened, Walter puffed out his chest, smiled, and attempted to look confident as he purchased a train ticket to Antwerp at the small rural station. On the train, so as not to attract anyone's attention, he concentrated on staring out a grimy window, pretending to enjoy the scenery. A short while after the train started moving, a group of German soldiers got up from their seats and approached Walter; they asked where he had come from and where he was going. Looking as if he had not a care in the world, Walter calmly explained that he had been ordered to report to his *oberkommando* for his next assignment. The combination of his fluent German, which indicated that he was not a foreigner and not an *Üntermensch* and most certainly not a Jew,[14] his poise, self-confidence, and his blue eyes and blond hair convinced the soldiers that he was a German who was traveling on government business. At that point, they shook his hand, wished him well, and returned to their seats. Although Walter had smiled and attempted to look self-assured during the short conversation with the soldiers, he had feared that they could hear the rapid drumming of his heart. As he stared out the window again, Walter wiped his cold, sweaty hands on his neatly folded pocket handkerchief.

A bit after sundown on April 1, 1942, the first night of Passover, Walter, with a giant smile on his face—an authentic one this time—walked into the apartment in Antwerp and embraced his wife. Eva ran to her father and clung to him. René squirmed in the arms of this strange man and tried to escape, but Walter held him firmly. Despite the fact that Margot had repeatedly shown René photos of his father, the child had no recollection of him and thought that he was an intruder. Walter and Margot knew that, with time, René would learn to accept his father. All that mattered was that the family was intact once more and relatively safe.

---

[14] This was a myth; unlike Eastern European Jews, who, at that time generally used Yiddish as their primary language and spoke the languages of their home countries with accents, most German Jews spoke fluent German.

They did not find out until years after the war that just three months after Walter escaped from Gurs, the German government informed the Vichy regime that the prisoners in the camp were to be transported to the east to "work camps." During the course of the war, a total of approximately 5,500 men from Gurs, mostly Jews, along with a small number of political prisoners, were transported east. Most of them were sent to Auschwitz. Very few survived.

While the members of the family took comfort in each other's arms and were grateful that they were together again, the war raged more ferociously and savagely than before, with the Battle of Britain and bombing raids over Germany killing thousands each week.

At the same time, in towns and cities all over Europe, Jewish men, women, and children were being rounded up in ever greater numbers and transported to concentration camps.

EIGHT

Flight to Brussels

By early 1942, with the United States in the war and fully committed to the defense of the United Kingdom and the defeat of the Axis powers, fighting expanded to North Africa, beginning with Operation Torch, a British-American action. The leaders of the Third Reich now believed that an Allied invasion of Europe was inevitable. That knowledge prompted them to move quickly in terms of their plan to resolve the "problem" of the Jews. At the Wannsee Conference in January of that year they developed their Final Solution whose goal was to make Europe *Judenrein*, that is "clean of Jews."

Unaware of the Nazi mass murder strategy, the Isaacsons and Landaus devoted all of their energy to attempting to live a semblance of a normal existence. That was grimly difficult in Antwerp—and most of the rest of Europe—because so many everyday food items were scarce and those that were available were strictly rationed. Margot and her mother often got out of bed to stand on line at stores at 5 a.m., hours before they opened, hoping that they would have a chance to purchase eggs, butter, milk, bread, or simply marrow bones for soup that day.

Since there were six people in the family, they had a large number of ration coupons for sugar and/or candy, which was, for some reason, readily available. They used almost all of those coupons to buy inexpensive locally produced candy, which Walter and his father-in-law sold from door to door, much of it to local diamond cutters, who seemed to always have money. One afternoon, after spending a delightful couple of hours at the nearby park with her children, when Margot opened the door to the apartment, upon seeing her husband she knew that something was wrong: he was slumped on the couch, clearly upset, his face ashen. "What happened?" she asked. "What is the matter?" He sat up, attempting to display his usual good posture, and told her that he had been stopped by a Gestapo officer who demanded that he open his suitcase and show what it contained. Upon seeing that it was filled with candy, the man immediately concluded that Walter was peddling it. Selling anything outside of authorized stores was illegal, so, after recording his address and filling out an arrest form, the officer instructed Walter to report to Gestapo headquarters no later than the end of the day.

Margot, who had been standing, now sat heavily on the couch next to Walter and took his hands. They both knew that if he reported to the Gestapo as instructed they would never see each other again, so Margot told him to stay home, saying that she would go to plead his case. Upon hearing that, Walter stood up and stated that he would do as instructed; he insisted that Margot remain in the apartment. Just then, Oskar, who had been napping, awakened and asked what had happened. When Margot told him, the older man said that he would go to Gestapo headquarters, where he would demand to be arrested in his son-in-law's place. He was 60 years old and a veteran of the Great War. Surely, that meant something. The Gestapo officers, upon hearing his story, would certainly not arrest him and would not insist that his son-in-law appear. Although Margot was sure that her father's plan would fail, there seemed to be no better alternative. So, grasping at straws, she agreed, saying that she would accompany him, and bring Eva, because her little girl could melt the heart of even the toughest person. Walter, desperate now, reluctantly said that he would stay home and wait for Margot and Oskar to return. If the authorities demanded that he report to them, he would go.

At Gestapo headquarters, Margot, holding Eva, stood beside her father as he talked about the unit in which he had served and where he had seen action during the Great War. Then he explained that his son-in-law had been interned at Gurs for two years because he was a German national. The officer to whom he pleaded his case listened, and then demanded that Walter appear before him no later than 6 p.m. that day.

When Margot, holding Eva, and her father returned to the apartment, Walter instantly knew from their somber expressions that they had not succeeded in convincing the Gestapo to vacate the arrest warrant. As he stood up and prepared to leave the apartment, knowing that he was doomed, Margot held up her hand and said, "No." She told Walter that she needed him and that his children needed their father and that she would not allow him to be taken from them again. Then, after telling her parents to go to their apartment and pack a bag for themselves, she stepped into the bedroom that she shared with her husband and threw some clothing into two small suitcases; Walter joined her and helped to pack.

A few minutes later, suitcases in hand, Walter and Margot looked sorrowfully at her parents, who embraced her, their son-in-law, and their grandchildren, and wished them well. "Please come with us. They will arrest you because we are running away. They may check their files and figure out that you and mother should not even be in Antwerp," Margot sadly told her father. Oskar, attempting to look brave, replied, "We're staying here. I'm 60 years old. I fought for Germany. Nothing will happen to me or your mother." Margot and Walter, holding their children and their suitcases, stood at the apartment doorway for a moment; then they walked out, exited the building, and headed straight to the train station, where they bought tickets to Brussels.

When they arrived in Brussels early that evening, they walked to the headquarters of a Jewish charitable organization called EZRA (The Hebrew meaning of the name is "helps"). The director, Max Chotzen, after making a few phone calls, found a two-room apartment for them at Rue de Merode 82, which was a mostly Jewish neighborhood. The owner of the house, a Walloon, owned a grocery store on the first floor of the building. Margot, making good use of her fluent French, spent many hours talking with the man and his wife.

At about this time, the Jews in Belgium (and in other Nazi-controlled countries) had been ordered to wear a large yellow cloth Star of

David on their outer clothing at all times. In order to avoid notice, as well as harassment or worse, Margot and Walter generally left their apartment only when it was necessary, typically after dark. Since most stores were closed then, Margot shopped only at the one owned by their landlord, even though it was not very clean and the selection of food was neither appealing nor reasonably priced. She felt that was a small sacrifice to make if it allowed her family to remain relatively safe.

The Isaacsons felt secure in Brussels that summer. They exchanged weekly letters with Walter's father and with Margot's parents. Then, in August of 1942, ignoring the risks, Margot's mother and father traveled from Antwerp to Brussels to visit their daughter and her family.[15] After a few short weeks, even though Margot pleaded with them to stay, Oskar and Jenny insisted on returning to their apartment in Antwerp, insisting that they felt safe there.

Over the ensuing years, Margot would look at the lovely note (She kept all of the notes, postcards, and letters that she received throughout her life) that her mother and father had sent to her when they returned to Antwerp. In the note, they explained how much they would always treasure their visit and they expressed the hope that they would be able to see their daughter, son-in-law, and grandchildren again, if not soon, then during a better, brighter time in the future.

Of course, Margot did now know it then, but that visit was the last time she would see her parents and the last time Oskar and Jenny would hold their grandchildren. Two months after the Landaus returned to Antwerp they were taken from their apartment and sent to Mechelen (also known as Malines), a holding camp in Belgium, from which they were eventually transported to the east.

---

[15] For reasons unknown, the Gestapo had not searched for Walter in reference to the arrest warrant or checked to determine why he was no longer at Gurs, something that Oskar should not have divulged when he spoke to the Gestapo on his son-in-law's behalf. Neither had they questioned the Landaus when their son-in-law did not appear in reference to his arrest warrant.

Even though, at that point, the Nazi plan to rid Europe of Jews was first being put into action on a large scale, everyday people had begun to discern the truth about what were euphemistically referred to as "work" or "relocation" camps. People who had witnessed trainloads of captive men, women, and children being herded into the camps and spoken to some of the inmates had told people on the outside that those places were, in fact, slave labor facilities where inmates were treated like beasts of burden and those who were unable to work were routinely murdered. A few captives who managed to escape from the camps provided information about what life was like in the hellish places. It had become an open secret among the Jews in Europe that, little by little, some of the slave labor camps were being converted into factories whose only function was to kill on a massive scale.

NINE

Couvent de la Miséricorde

Throughout 1942, life for Jews in Belgium (and in other occupied countries in Europe) became increasingly more perilous. Since they were required to wear the Star of David on their clothing at all times, they were regularly stopped and questioned. While Jews who were Belgian nationals were generally released after being questioned, increasingly larger numbers of foreign-born Jews were stopped on the street and then taken away—never to be seen again. That was in addition to those who received orders to report to Gestapo headquarters. In order to avoid being picked up, many foreign-born Jews remained indoors as much as possible, but that was not a foolproof plan because the Gestapo often raided entire blocks of apartment buildings in their search for Jewish refugees. Some non-Belgian Jews moved from place to place, nomad-like, keeping their heads down, always looking over their shoulders, often sleeping in abandoned buildings or cellars or, if they were fortunate, in back rooms or the attics of sympathetic gentiles.

After days of agonizing deliberation, a flood of tears, and an overwhelming, choking sense of guilt and desolation, Walter and Margot knew what they had to do. They believed it was only a matter of time before the Gestapo would pick them up while they were out or break down their door to take them and, much more horrifying than that, take their children. They finally made the heart-wrenching decision that some day soon they would have to bring René and Eva to a convent in Leuven, which was about 20 miles away. Margot had heard about the convent from their landlord, who, in the privacy of his apartment, had said he had been told that despite the danger they faced, the nuns never turned away Jewish children who were brought to them. René and Eva would be safe there.

The next evening, the quiet was interrupted by shouting on the street and then the sound of heavy boot steps and thunderous pounding on house doors. That was followed by the angry, guttural command, "Aufmachen!" ("Open up!"). Even though thick, dark drapes covered all of the windows in their apartment because of the mandatory blackout, Walter immediately shut the small lamp next to his chair and closed the book he had been reading. Eva, who was four and a half years old, and René, two and a half, were asleep. A few tense minutes later, when it seemed that peace had returned to the neighborhood, the Isaacsons were startled by heavy hammering on the front door of the building in which they lived. They froze in panic, and then they heard the sound of a man calling out, "Ouvrez, s'il-vous-plait!" It was the landlord; he had locked himself out of his home. The man's wife let him in and then she immediately bolted the door.

Margot and Walter sat quietly, nervously, in the dark for what seemed to be hours. Finally, believing that the crisis had passed, they felt calm enough to prepare for bed. As they undressed and washed, they were tormented by thoughts of what they knew they would have to do to protect their children. They had resigned themselves to the fact that they had to act soon. Now they agreed that the time had come; they could not afford to wait another day. They lay in bed. Neither one expected to sleep. Then the pounding and shouting began again. Margot heard a man bellowing in German an order to block off both ends of the street.

Throughout the rest of that awful evening, amidst the strident voices, brutal hammering, and the heartbreaking cries of people who were being dragged from their homes, Walter and Margot huddled in the dark on the floor of the room that their children shared. They whispered about what they would do if soldiers pounded on the door of their apartment. Walter said that he would fight. Margot, somberly shaking her head in agreement, hissed into Walter's ear, "They will have to take the children out over my dead body and they will have to shoot me or carry me out!"

Time passed slowly. Margot and Walter, still on the floor near their children, waited. Then the street became quiet, so ghostly silent that the couple fell asleep. Walter awoke, startled, confused. He looked at his wife, who was asleep on the floor beside him. The children were safe in their beds. Walter's wristwatch read 6 a.m. He stood up, stretched, walked to a window, and inched back the drapes so that he could see the street. It was empty. The night time roundup was over. By luck or the grace of God or whatever it is that allows one to live and causes another to die, the soldiers had bypassed the building in which they lived.

Relieved that they had made it through that hideously awful night, but shaken and now more convinced than before that their children were no longer safe living with them in Brussels, Walter and Margot decided they had to immediately bring them to the convent, even if it meant they might never see them again.

That morning, September 4, 1942, they dressed René and Eva and hurried to the street, where, after checking for police and soldiers, they boarded a tram for the one-hour trip to the hamlet of Heverlee, which is part of the city of Leuven, in central Belgium. Couvent de la Miséricorde (The Convent of Mercy), contained a school, dormitories, and apartments for the sisters. The vast majority of students at the school were, of course, Roman Catholic. The parents of many of them lived and worked in what was at that time called the Belgian Congo. They had enrolled their children in the boarding school because they believed they would receive a better education in Belgium than in the African colony.

Margot and Walter sat nervously on straight-backed chairs in the dim, plainly furnished office of the mother superior. A nun who was so young that she looked like she might be one of the students stood to the side. After the customary exchange of pleasantries, which were not at all pleasant for the anxious couple, Margot explained to the mother superior that they were German Jews who desperately wanted their children to be enrolled in the school because of the danger they faced on the outside. The kindly sister, who surely had detected the German accent in Margot's fluent French, unhesitatingly agreed to take the children, after which she asked them to fill out some paperwork. She promised that only she and the other sisters would know of the existence of the documents. After Walter had completed and signed the papers, he paid for three months of tuition, using almost all of their cash. The mother superior smiled and tenderly took Eva by the hand. The child, who at four and a half years old, seemed to understand that she was being left with strangers, although she probably assumed it would be for only a short while, was teary-eyed. She had always been an agreeable, obedient child; perhaps that is why, although she began to sob, she quietly accepted this upsetting development in her life. René, at two and a half, was so intensely focused on the large wooden cross hanging from the neck of the young nun who held him that he did not realize his parents were leaving until after they had kissed him and walked out the door.

Years later, when Margot told René about his time at Miséricorde, he remembered it as a dark period in his young life when he was continuously sad and overwhelmed by a dark, nebulous cloud of loneliness and a deep sense of abandonment. That can be seen in the expression on his face in the convent group photograph (See p. 120).

Eva, who was old enough to understand, became used to her new lifestyle after a while. The nuns were always gentle with her and very kind. Although she was never pressured to pray in church or to convert to Catholicism, she recalled attending Mass and being with other children as they prayed. At some convents in Belgium and in other parts of Europe, the nuns and priests attempted to persuade Jewish children to be baptized; some of them wrote letters to parents, asking for their permission. In some cases, this was done to protect the children so that they would more seamlessly integrate with the others. Those nuns thought this to be a necessary precaution for those occasions when German soldiers entered the facility and questioned the children. In other cases, as with Eva, the nuns not only did not pressure Jewish children to convert, but they encouraged them to retain as much of their faith as they were able to under the circumstances. Survivors have reported that sisters at some convents asked Jewish children to explain Yiddish and Hebrew phrases and the meanings of holidays. Other firsthand accounts make mention of Jewish children who had grown comfortable with their new lives and asking to be baptized. Some of those children were brought into the Church, while others were told that conversion would be possible only with the consent of their parents.

While most of the nuns at Miséricorde were Walloons, a few were Flemish, and two were German. All of them treated Eva and René and the other Jewish children who were hidden there with a great deal of affection and respect. Even though German government officials and the Gestapo, understanding the exceptionally close relationship between Catholic Belgians and the Church, generally did not interfere with religious institutions or the clergy, the people who harbored Jewish children were always at great risk. For that reason, all of those involved—nuns, priests, and workers—were under strict orders to never discuss the subject of the hidden children, even in the relative safety of the convent. The Jewish children at Miséricorde were repeatedly told that they were never to leave the compound. This was difficult for some of them to understand, especially when, in nice weather, their Christian classmates were allowed to wander through the nearby countryside or visit the stores in the neighboring town.

Besides the enormous dangers they faced, the sisters at Miséricorde and at other convents throughout Europe had to deal with the critical issue of obtaining food. Even without the Jewish children they were protecting, many of whose parents had no money to pay tuition or had paid small amounts and then never returned (generally, because they had been arrested and transported to concentration camps), providing sufficient amounts of food was a challenging, exhausting chore. Due to chronic shortages and strict rationing, the convents often managed to obtain only bare subsistence levels of bread, cheese, milk, and vegetables—and only occasional pieces of meat. There was usually just enough food for the children and the adults at the convent, but obtaining it was a full-time job.

The parents of hidden children were allowed to visit only on Sundays because this was thought to be the only day during the week when the Gestapo was unlikely to search for Jewish children and other contraband that might be hidden at the convents. It was also the safest time to travel, not that doing so was ever really safe. The first time Walter and Margot visited Miséricorde, two months after they had left their children (because the mother superior had asked them to give Eva and René time to become accustomed to their new situation), they brought enough candy for all of the students at the school. When the children were brought to see their parents, René, ignoring the candy, said "Le pain," which is the French word for "bread," although he did not appear to be hungry. At the end of the visit, when René realized that his mother and father were leaving, he became agitated; despite their efforts to calm him, he cried and screamed for them and held out his hands. Walter and Margot both wept as they held their younger child one more time before leaving. Although Eva was most certainly quite upset too, she remained calm, smiling weakly and kissing her parents good-bye.

On the way back to Brussels that day, Margot, overwhelmed with sadness and guilt, consoled herself by saying over and over again that keeping their children at the convent was completely necessary. Walter assured her that Eva and René were being properly taken care of, and he added that, more likely than not, all of the other children at the school, Jewish and Catholic alike, were sad when their parents left after a visit. Enveloped in a heavy, dark cloud of wretchedness and remorse, Margot somberly nodded in agreement. Then she closed her eyes and pretended that her children were seated next to her on the tram.

Years later, Margot would wipe tears from her eyes as she told her children that she and their father had thought about them every minute of each of the days that they were in the convent. She explained that if the four of them had stayed together in Brussels, even if they had not been arrested and transported to a concentration camp, it would have been a very unpleasant life for them (Eva and René) and they may have become seriously ill. She went on to explain that during that horrid period of time she and their father had spent a great many days and almost every night hiding in damp, dirty, unheated cellars (even in winter) and other dreadful places, mostly in gentile neighborhoods, where it was unlikely the Gestapo would be conducting searches for Jews. They ate what they could buy when hunger drove them out of hiding (with their required Stars of David out of sight). Many days, they survived on barely edible scraps of food; on others, they went without eating. She said that she and their father had taken comfort in the fact that in the convent their children were protected by warm-hearted women who provided them with enough to eat; just as important, she and their father were pleased that they (Eva and René) were able to be with other children, attend an excellent school, and live a normal life, such as it was. A life on the run, she said with a sigh, would not have been good.

She added that even though she and their father were always careful when they walked the streets—mostly at night—and in terms of where they hid, they were never really safe. Each and every time they heard a noise they thought the Gestapo was only a few steps away from them. No, she repeated, as lonely as Eva and René may have been and as much as they had missed her and their father, at least at Miséricorde they were out of harm's way and with people who shielded them from harm and provided them with love.

During that dark period of time, since Margot and Walter did not have a fixed address they made weekly trips to the local post office, where they mailed letters to and received replies from the mother superior of the convent. At one point, Margot received a letter from her father; in it he wrote that, strange as it may seem, because of all of the misery and heartache that he and her mother had endured, his faith in God had become stronger and more unshakable than ever.

Part of his letter reads as follows:

... and again, we are approaching the holiest day of the year—Yom Kippur. We are glad that our beloved grandchildren are in good hands and can play with other children. Dearest children, have a good fast and pray we will be soon together in peace and happiness!

A few days later, Margot received a postcard from him and her mother. This bleak message was the last contact she would ever have with them:

We are here at the train station together with a lot of our Jewish friends and acquaintances on our way to Mechelen. Many little children are here also. May G-d bless you and our beloved grandchildren. We are sure that we'll see each other again. Our love will always be with you.

In a corner of the card, her father had scribbled "transport #287." After reading that card, Margot and Walter fell into a deep trough of silent depression and dark grief and began to believe that all was lost. A few days later, Margot did what she had not done for weeks: she brazenly walked the streets in broad daylight, her large yellow Star of David openly displayed on her coat. During the previous few months, she and Walter had always made sure that their stars were obscured when they sneaked out of their hiding places at night, and they kept their heads down as they desperately searched from store to store for inexpensive scraps of food that they could purchase without ration coupons.[16] Surprisingly, as Margot walked this day, no one on the street seemed to notice her or care about the yellow six-pointed image on her coat. When Walter, who had been sleeping when his wife had left their hiding place at the back of an abandoned store, awakened and was not able to locate her, he

---

[16] Because they no longer lived at a permanent address, they did not have ration books.

was overcome with fear. He shivered as icy fingers of panic ran up and down his spine. He immediately went out to the street to look for her. After a frantic search, he found Margot standing at a rubbish-strewn street corner, her hands in the pockets of her long coat, looking down at the ground. After a moment during which she seemed to be confused about where she was and what Walter wanted her to do, she allowed him to lead her back to their temporary shelter.

After Margot cried for several minutes, which Walter, holding her tight, found to be excruciatingly painful, she composed herself. Then, as she listened to her husband's warm, encouraging words, she promised that she would not take chances again and said that they both had to live so that, one day, when all of the horror was over they would be able to bring their children home.

TEN

Judenrat

Millions of people suffered unspeakable personal tragedies during that dreadful time in Europe. Many years after the war, Margot told her children about one calamity, the memory of which had reached the inner depths of her heart and settled there like a leaden weight. During the period of time that they lived in Antwerp, while Walter was interned in Gurs, she became friends with a woman named Ceil Wangrow, whose husband was also in Gurs. One day, when Ceil returned with a bottle of milk and some bread that she had bought for her twin sons, she found the apartment empty. As she looked around, she froze and her knees became jelly-like. Even before she spotted the handwritten note ordering her to report to Gestapo headquarters, she knew what had happened. Howling in despair and agony, Ceil ran through the streets to Margot to ask what she should do. Margot held her and cried with her, but said she did not know. The distraught woman then dragged herself to Dr. Ullman, the chief rabbi of Brussels, who sadly told her that she should not report to the Gestapo because there was nothing she could do for her children; they were lost. He told the hysterical woman that she had to be strong and survive for her husband.

Ceil was frantic and hysterical for days, after which she fell into a deep, dark state of hopelessness during which she lay in bed, motionless for hours at a time, refusing to eat or drink or even use the bathroom. Rabbi Ullman kept her hidden in his apartment during that agonizingly painful time. Then, after a few more days, she ate a bit of food and drank some water. Months later, Ceil was able to just barely function in a dull, semi-awake manner. She seemed to accept what had happened to her children; perhaps she believed she would see them again some day. That hope, which almost always resulted in bitter disappointment and a lifetime of heartbreak and guilt, was prevalent among many of those whose loved ones had been taken from them by the Nazis.

Dr. Ullman employed Ceil in his household, a ploy which afforded her protection from the Gestapo. Her husband Rudy, after spending months on the run after he had escaped from Gurs, returned to her in 1944. They never saw their children again. After the war, Ceil and Rudy emigrated to Cleveland, Ohio. Margot kept in touch with Ceil throughout the rest of her life. At some point during each telephone conversation, there would be a moment when they both fell silent and the very air surrounding them seemed to become heavy and dark with painful memories.

Walter and Margot (along with Jews throughout the occupied countries) were now convinced that the rumors were true: those who had been transported to the east had been brought to concentration camps at which they had been killed. They were overwhelmed with constant, cold fear, not just for themselves, but for their children. For months, they agonized over the thought that René and Eva, just like Ceil's children, could be taken away during a Gestapo raid and then sent to a death camp. As much as they trusted the nuns at Miséricorde, they were constantly on edge at the thought that those kind women would not be able to protect their children from a Nazi roundup. For that reason, they desperately wanted to take René and Eva out of the convent, but they hesitated because, besides the danger inherent in their children living in Brussels with them, the trip to and from the convent would be perilous. However, they wanted René and Eva with them because they knew that, should the Gestapo come, they would fight like tigers to protect them. Walter and Margot went back and forth in terms of what they should do. Both choices, leaving their children at Miséricorde and taking them out, seemed equally hazardous. They continued to discuss their choices as fewer and fewer Jews appeared on the streets of Brussels.

Then fate intervened, parting the oppressive, heavy clouds that seemed to always be overhead and allowing a thin streak of sudden, miraculous golden sunlight to shine on Walter and Margot Isaacson. In mid-November 1943, Max Chotzen, the director of EZRA, the Jewish assistance organization, located Margot and Walter and sent a message to them. In it, he said that he had been trying for a month to reach them because the *Judenrat* in Brussels needed a cleaning person, and he had suggested that Walter be hired to fill the position. The *Judenrat* was a community council that the Nazis required Jews in all occupied cities and rural areas to form. Those committees were responsible for helping the Jewish population in whatever ways they were able, such as finding housing and food, providing medical care, etc. They also acted as unofficial arbiters of disputes among the Jews in their areas.

The councils, or *Judenräte* (the plural of *Judenrat*) were (and continue to be) a source of bitter debate and controversy because, out of necessity, they cooperated with the Germans. Of course, it was better for Jews, rather than the Gestapo, to have jurisdiction over Jews in occupied areas, at least in reference to minor civil matters. In addition, it goes without saying that the Germans did not provide services to Jews in occupied countries or to those who had been sent to concentration camps, so, without the *Judenräte* most of those services would not have existed.[17] One of the special services provided by the *Judenrat* in Belgium was to send "care packages" containing soap, ointments, towels, toothpaste, toothbrushes, etc. to the Jews who were interned in Mechelen while they awaited transport to the east.

The members of the *Judenräte* and the ones who worked for the councils were provided with identity cards which purportedly exempted them from Gestapo raids and roundups. The Nazis allowed that kind of protection because the councils made it easier for them to maintain order in Jewish communities in occupied areas. The Germans believed that allowing those in the *Judenräte* to be exempt from roundups encouraged them to perform their communal duties; in addition, the seemingly cordial business relationship between *Judenrat* leaders and German officials helped to make the occupiers appear to be somewhat benevolent in the eyes of the Red Cross and the world at large.

---

[17] Other Jewish organizations and the Red Cross did provide services, but the local *Judenrat* was often the place to which Jews went for assistance.

However, by virtue of the fact that the *Judenräte* had to cooperate with the Germans, they were constantly subject to harsh criticism. The most scathing condemnation involved the fact that when the Nazis decided to transport a particular number of Jews from a city or a rural area to concentration camps they instructed the local *Judenrat* to compile a list of names. In some cases, members of the *Judenrat* refused to do as they were told; others threatened to resign from the committee. Those choices generally resulted in the arrest and incarceration and, ultimately, the death of those individuals. The attitude on the part of *Judenrat* members who stayed on the job and compiled the lists was, "If we don't do it, the Nazis will simply choose some other Jews to sit on the council, and *they* will put together the lists, and, if no Jews help them, the Germans will compile the lists themselves."

Some historians have compared the behavior (and level of culpability) of members of the *Judenräte* with that of prisoners (Jews and gentiles alike) in the concentration camps who took on the role of *kapo*, or *funktionshäftling* ("prisoner functionary"). The origin of the term *kapo* is subject to debate. Some say that it derives from the Italian word *capo*, meaning "head" or "head person" or "boss." Some historians have come to believe it is a corruption of the German word *kameradschaftspolizei*, which can be translated as "comrade police officer," while another theory is that it is a variation of the French word *caporal*, which means "corporal." In any case, the *kapos* were chosen by German guards to act as the unofficial security force within the concentration camps. In addition, they were sometimes the ones who had the responsibility of taking bodies from the gas chambers and transporting them to ovens or to mass graves. Those who filled this position relied on the belief that as long as they did the bidding of the German guards they would be given better food and lighter work than the other prisoners. They also hoped that they might be perceived as so useful that they might be able to avoid being sent to the gas chambers.

Some *kapos* were brutal, at times, harsher in their treatment of their fellow prisoners than the German guards; some were chosen by the Germans because they were known to have violent or criminal backgrounds. Others fulfilled their repugnant duties as sympathetically and compassionately as possible under the circumstances.

While some of the members of the *Judenräte* may have been guilty of abuses, comparisons with those who served as *kapos* in the death camps is problematic. Most *Judenrat* members attempted to help their fellow Jews. The issue of their cooperating with the Nazis by compiling lists of names for transport will probably be debated forever.

The Brussels *Judenrat* was housed in a mansion that had been donated by a philanthropist named Hertz who also ran the day-to-day operations of the organization. Most of its many large rooms had been converted into offices; there was also a kitchen, a stockroom, and a mailroom/packing room. Since Walter had been hired to be the custodian/cleaner of the building, he received an identity card and an official letter which allowed him to walk the streets without fear of being picked up by the Gestapo. Once he had obtained those documents, he asked Mr. Hertz whether his wife could be hired by the *Judenrat*. Mr. Hertz sighed, and then he replied that he wished he could hire every Jew in every occupied country in order to protect them. Then he said that he would need some time to talk to a German official regarding the request.

Two days later, Mr. Hertz told Walter that he would be able to hire Margot to do some menial work in the building, but that according to rules established by the German authorities, husbands and wives employed by Jewish organizations had to have "intact families," meaning their children had to live with them under the same roof. That meant that the Isaacsons would have to remove Eva and René from Miséricorde. Although Walter and Margot longed to be reunited with their children and wanted the relative safety that the ID cards would afford them, they were not the least bit confident that the Germans would consistently respect that insubstantial umbrella of protection. They wondered, what if the Allies actually were to invade Europe, as so many captive people had hoped for so many years? What if the fighting reached Brussels and an artillery shell were to hit the building in which they lived? What if the Germans began to lose the war and had to evacuate Belgium? Would they ignore the rules they had established, and start to arrest the small number of Jews with official identity cards? What if, through a clerical error on the part of the Gestapo or simply a horrific twist of fate, as had happened to Ceil Wangrow, the Germans were to enter the apartment one day and take away their children? Were they willing to take that chance? Wouldn't René and Eva be safer in the convent?

On the other hand, Walter and Margot believed that this opportunity for both of them to work for the *Judenrat* was a one-time gift. Also, by this point, Eva and René had been at Miséricorde for over a year. That was such a major slice of their very young lives that they had grown quite accustomed to living there without their parents. Margot and Walter wondered whether their children would ever be able to feel close to them again. After the war, Eva often talked about life at the convent, especially in reference to how she had looked out for her little brother. She said that although she had missed her parents at the beginning, she had not been unhappy there. Although René had been so young, he remembered his time at Miséricorde, retaining in the recesses of his memory cloudy feelings of unhappiness and abandonment. Years later, when he asked about it, his parents told him that during their visits he seemed to be happy and clung to them, and that he cried bitterly when they left.

Of all the stomach-churning decisions that Margot and Walter had been forced to make from the time they had fled Germany, this one, the question of whether or not to withdraw Eva and René from the convent, was the most frightening. Ultimately, because they wanted their children with them and because they hoped that by establishing an "intact family" they would all be protected by the rules covering members and staff of the *Judenrat*, they decided that they had to take the chance. At the end of November 1943, after expressing their heartfelt gratitude to the nuns for all they had done over the course of 14 months to protect and nurture Eva and René, the Isaacsons withdrew them from Miséricorde.

The *Judenrat* was able to afford hiring Margot by assigning her to work some of Walter's hours; he put in only six hours per day, instead of the agreed-upon eight, and Margot worked the other two. Together they earned enough money to rent a one-room apartment and purchase food. They ate very little, so there was always enough for Eva and René. Although Walter and Margot went to bed at least a bit uncomfortably hungry many nights, they took solace in the fact that they all had identity cards which, theoretically, protected them from Gestapo roundups.

During the previous year, the German occupiers, who had been taking into custody and transporting only foreign-born Jews who had entered the country illegally,[18] now began to arrest and deport Belgian Jews. The Isaacsons, of course, as German nationals who had entered the country without permission, should have been rounded up and transported long before. Margot often wondered whether it had been their skill in terms of hiding from the Gestapo or just plain luck that had allowed them to avoid being picked up and sent to concentration camps during the years they had lived in Belgium.

One evening in March of 1944, their *Judenrat* exemption was put to the test. As the Isaacsons were preparing to turn in for the night they were startled by pounding on the apartment door. Cautiously opening it, Walter came face to face with two Gestapo officers, one of whom pushed him aside and, after taking a few steps in, examined the tiny apartment, while the other man stood just inside the doorway, blocking it. After the one scanning the apartment spotted Eva and René asleep in a cot in the kitchen (near the coal stove, the only source of heat), he looked at Margot and Walter, who held out their *Judenrat* identity cards. The man took the

---

[18] A policy with which many Belgians heartily agreed.

cards and after carefully reading them and holding them up to the light, he politely handed them back and, standing stiffly, said, "Gute Nacht. Schlafbrunnen" ("Good night. Sleep well"). Then he and the other officer walked out of the apartment.

A minute later, Walter and Margot heard knocking upstairs. They later learned that the Gestapo officers had arrested two men who lived on the next floor who were not even Jewish.

Even though the fighting raged far from Belgium, on occasion the deadly consequences of the war reached into the heart of Brussels. One night, a V-1 rocket whose target, like all of the others, was England, went astray, falling very short of its intended destination, and hitting a home for children in Brussels, badly damaging the building and killing several people. Margot was shocked to learn the next day that two of the victims were the children of a woman she knew who had placed them in the home to protect them from the Germans. A few days later, Margot visited the woman. She was, as would be expected, devastated by the loss. She was so emotionally impaired that, weeks later, after having slept very little and eaten only what friends and neighbors fed to her by hand, she had become a despondent, emotionally bereft dry shell of a human being, an empty husk who blamed herself for the death of her children and prayed that she would die.

That tragedy occurred over and over again in those days: parents who were not able to protect their children, who watched in horror and desperation as their offspring were torn from them, had to live with the guilt of having survived.

ELEVEN

Liberation

The June 6, 1944 Allied invasion of Normandy was a golden day for the millions of people throughout Europe who were in the chokehold of the Nazi occupiers. Walter and Margot stared at a neighbor's radio for hours as they listened intently to news reports of the fighting. They did not know how long it would be before the American or British Army would reach Belgium, but they were hopeful that it would be soon. Of course, they knew that they and the other Jews remaining in occupied countries might be in even greater danger now than they had been before; perhaps the Germans would decide the time had come to transport to concentration camps the handful of Jews who were left in Brussels and the rest of Belgium, even those with *Judenrat* passes, or simply murder them in their apartments. For that reason, they stayed indoors and kept their children close to them at all times.

On August 25, 1944, the German garrison in Paris surrendered. The City of Lights was free. The Isaacsons, hearing the news, waited, hoping each and every day to see Allied troops marching triumphantly down the streets of Brussels. The days seemed endless, the nights longer. The glimmer of sunshine and warm freedom that they had sensed began to fade as the weather cooled and the calendar read September. Then they heard that British troops had crossed from France into Belgium in a few distant places. Two more long, dreary, frightening days passed. Fewer and fewer German soldiers and Gestapo officers were on the streets.

Then the glorious day arrived: on September 3, 1944, the 2nd British Army, commanded by General Sir Miles Dempsey, entered the city of Brussels first, followed by American troops. One of Walter's and Margot's fondest memories, the one that made them feel excited and unfettered and hopeful for the future, was the sight and sound of British and American military vehicles rumbling down the streets of Brussels. However, even though by December 1944 British and American forces were marching from the west and the Russians from the east, intent on neutralizing the lair of the Nazi vipers—Berlin—the war was far from over. Adolf Hitler ordered his best troops to fight to the death and hold off the Red Army. At the same time, he committed close to 200,000 soldiers to the Ardennes Forest in eastern Belgium in an attempt to stop the American troops in their tracks and obliterate them. The costly, bloody one-month counteroffensive that took place there became known as the Battle of the Bulge. For a while, it seemed as if the Germans might actually not only push back the Allies, but retake some of the ground that those forces had gained since the D-Day landings. If that were to occur, the Gestapo would be back in Brussels, and they would surely round up the few Jews who had not been transported to death camps.

At the height of the battle, fearing the worst, Walter and Margot brought their children back to Miséricorde and asked for refuge. The mother superior took Eva and René, but said that men were not allowed to stay at the convent. Then, looking at the concern and fear on the faces of the young couple, she said that she would make an exception to the rule. She asked only that the Isaacsons not leave the room that she assigned to them. Margot, Walter, and their children remained in hiding in the convent for four days. During that agonizingly tense period of time, the sisters shared their meager supply of food with their guests and kept them informed about the battle raging in the Ardennes. It is to the great and everlasting credit of the nuns who lived at Miséricorde that they repeatedly, at great personal risk, sheltered those in need.

By the middle of January 1945, the formidable German counteroffensive in the Ardennes broke and American and British forces resumed their relentless march toward Berlin. At roughly the same time, the Red Army finally beat back the German divisions blocking their way and moved into East Prussia, with the taking of Berlin their ultimate goal. Hitler, vowing to never surrender, ordered all German forces to protect the capital. It was to be a fight to the bloody end.

On April 30, 1945, as intense fighting raged on the outskirts of Berlin, Adolf Hitler and Eva Braun, who he had married only hours before, committed suicide in their underground bunker. One week later, May 7, 1945, Germany's military commanders surrendered to Allied forces. The war in Europe was over; all of its captive peoples were free. Margot, Walter, and their children had survived, but six million other Jewish men, women, and children, along with millions of gentiles who were also enemies of the Reich had perished, the vast majority of them in Hitler's death camps.

A few weeks later, with the city of Brussels in tumultuous transition and its citizens still wildly celebrating, the Isaacsons, feeling free and at ease for the first time in many years, moved from Rue de Merode to a small, clean apartment at Dieweg 92 in the suburb of Uccle. It was a beautiful neighborhood that the war seemed to have bypassed. That may have been one of the reasons Margot and Walter chose it for their new home. They transferred Eva from the Catholic school in Brussels that she had just begun to attend to a public school within walking distance of the new apartment. At the same time, René, now six years old, was hospitalized for a tonsillectomy. Although it is a vague memory, he recalls having had a sore throat, which his mother treated by administering almost unlimited amounts of ice cream.

In August of 1946, the Isaacson family went to the seashore for a few days. Although the beach was littered with war-blasted vehicles, empty, rusted ammunition boxes, and cruel-looking shards of jagged shrapnel, once the Isaacsons found a relatively clear spot on the sand, they had a good time. After the extended period of crushing fear, dislocation, and death that they had endured, dating from *Kristallnacht*, Walter, Margot, Eva had become used to seeing ugly hunks of shattered iron and steel, broken bricks, and smoldering ruins. René, who at six and a half did not clearly remember all that had happened during the past few years, was not surprised to see the ruins on the beach. That was a familiar landscape.

That fall, René began first grade and Eva entered third grade in the local school, where French was spoken. Even though their parents spoke German at home, both children had grown up using French as their primary language.

René was unhappy in school and often misbehaved. On one occasion, he was reprimanded by a teacher for a minor infraction of rules and was told to wait in the hallway outside of his classroom. After a few minutes of sitting uncomfortably on a hard wooden bench, and overcome with boredom, he stood up and walked down the hall to where the students' coats were hanging. Because he had nothing else to do, he put his hands in a coat pocket, and then another, and another. In a few of them he found coins, which he put in a pocket of his pants. While René did not think of what he had done as stealing, neither did he tell his mother about the coins. Later that night, when Margot hung up his pants, a few coins fell from a pocket, and so she asked him about the money. When he did not answer her questions, she was convinced that the child had stolen it. The next day, Margot handed the money to René and then walked him to school to speak to his teacher about the issue. After figuring out what René had done, the women confronted him. He immediately apologized and handed the money to the teacher.

During the harrowing years when Margot and Walter had moved from place to place, always looking over their shoulders and never staying long in any location, they spent whatever money they had on food, and nothing else. Before Walter landed the *Judenrat* job, he had been able, on occasion, to find part-time menial work where no questions were asked. When the war finally ended, he found steady, low-wage employment as a handyman and as a helper at a soup kitchen. Since Belgium did not issue work permits to those who were in the country illegally,[19] he accepted whatever jobs he could obtain, regardless of how little they paid. The Isaacsons did not mind their poverty because they were together and safe.

---

[19] The Isaacsons had entered Belgium without visas in 1939.

In the confusion of those early months after the war, it was close to impossible to determine what had happened to loved ones who had been taken away, but Margot and Walter, hardened by their years-long traumatic experiences, were under no delusions about the fate of the Landaus and of Sally Isaacson. The reality of those deaths were open wounds on their hearts. Feeling that it was too much to think about, they attempted to smile and look to the future. They knew they had to be strong and optimistic and make plans, if only for the sake of their children.

By the end of 1946, it had become clear to Walter and Margot that, for economic reasons alone, they had to move from Belgium, but they could not stomach the thought of returning to Germany. The nation that they and their parents had thought of as their homeland had not only passed laws against them because they were Jewish and officially denied their citizenship, but it had publicly classified them as *Untermenschen*, and worse, had developed and carried out a beastly plan to exterminate them, as if they were disease-carrying vermin.

The Isaacsons decided they had to leave Europe. Moving to the United States was their first choice, but because of the Immigration Act of 1924, also known as the Johnson–Reed Act (which was revised in 1952), during the post-war years, emigration to America was a lengthy process involving waiting for a number to come up on a list. Since Margot and Walter did not have anyone in the U.S. to sign an affidavit indicating that they would not be a burden on the country, which would have speeded up the process, they would have to find another destination. After weeks of asking questions and sending numerous letters to friends and relatives who had fled to other countries, they got in touch with Helmut Isaacson, a cousin of Walter's who had emigrated to La Paz, Bolivia in 1939. With his help and that of another cousin, Wilhelm Isaacson, who also lived in Bolivia, Walter and Margot managed to obtain visas to travel to that country. They were excited and relieved, but they were not quite ready to travel to the New World.

At the same time, they were overjoyed to read a letter from Walter's brother Heinz informing them that he was living in London, and that he had married and had a baby girl. In addition, two other cousins of Walter's, Ernst and Susan Jacob, had moved to that city. That miraculous news was followed by a letter that left Margot unable to speak or even move for a few seconds: her sister Ruth, now married with twin boys, named John and Alan, was also living in London.

When they made inquiries in reference to emigrating to the United Kingdom, they were told that it would take years to gain permission to do that, but they would be allowed to visit.

In April 1947, the Isaacsons traveled by train to Calais, France, where they boarded a ferry to cross the English Channel. A few hours later, they were in London. During the course of the next week, they visited Ruth and Heinz and their families, along with some of the few survivors of what had been an extensive clan of Isaacsons, Landaus, and other relations, both close and distant. It was an emotional, bittersweet reunion. All of them had suffered a great deal and had experienced much deprivation during the years leading up to the war and throughout its duration. They held each other and laughed and reminisced about their wonderful life in Germany before the tyranny of the Nazis had changed everything, ushering in the monstrous years that followed. At the same time, they attempted—not always successfully—to contain their tears as they thought about relations who they had not been able to locate.

Margot and Walter, who were sure that her parents and his father were no longer among the living, wondered, "Where are their bodies?" Would they be able to locate them and arrange for proper burials? At this point, after having read in the newspapers and after having seen newsreels at movie theaters that showed the piles of bodies—the ghastly evidence of Nazi genocide—that Allied troops had found when they liberated the death camps, Margot and Walter knew the answer to that question.

TWELVE

Leaving The Darkness Behind

Two years after the guns had fallen silent and the appalling reign of terror and death that had been planned and prosecuted with detached efficiency by the Third Reich—the so-called "Thousand-Year Reich"—had ended, Walter and Margot were still haunted by hazy, unnamed fears and cold, dark dread. That was (and is) true of many, perhaps most of those, Jews and gentiles alike, who lived through that ghastly time in Europe. Those years had been defined by fear and pain, heartache and hunger, and the persistent presence of violent death. Margot and Walter were grateful that they and their children had avoided being transported to death camps and had survived the war in relative good health, but the emotional scars caused by those years were real and palpable and had become a permanent part of their lives. Those deep wounds to their psyches and souls served as lasting reminders of all they had lived through and seen during that era of government-authorized ethnic and religious classification, vile hatred, and mass murder. They would never be able to forget the years of unrelenting vilification and persecution, the official loss of their German citizenship, the terrifying escape from the country of their birth, their sojourn in a foreign land, the years that Walter had spent as a prisoner at Gurs, the cold fear of the heavy knock on the door, the continuous need to hide, and the anxiety and choking guilt that they experienced when they had to place their children in the hands of people they did not know.

Despite the heavy weight on their hearts and souls, Walter and Margot were able to carry out their responsibilities and be good parents. Some victims of the Nazi atrocities, especially those who had been squeezed into the squalid, human-jammed cattle cars and had managed to still be alive when the Allies liberated the death camps, lived out the rest of their days in cold darkness, unable to break free of the suffocating nightmare in which they had dwelled for so long. How many of those tortured souls, even the ones who emigrated to America or Palestine— now Israel—and who managed to live seemingly normal lives in their adopted countries had to resist the impulse to keep their blinds drawn and drapes closed and reside in the shadows? How many of them, to this day, feel vulnerable, believe that what happened then and there can (and will) happen again? Those damaged survivors live with their unremitting pain, deep sense of loss, and heavy guilt because they survived when the ones they loved did not. Even in the midst of joyous occasions, surrounding by cheerful loved ones, at least a part of the very essence of those permanently injured survivors remains in the time and place where unspeakable crimes were committed.

Margot and Walter, perhaps because they had Eva and René and each other, gradually relearned how to live their lives and how to experience joy, but from time to time they had nightmares involving their children. Perhaps those bleak nocturnal images, those terrifying mind-scenarios were fueled by Margot's and Walter's lingering sense of guilt arising from their decision to leave Eva and René at Miséricorde. Yes, they knew that they had made the correct decision—in fact, the only possible one under the circumstances—and for the rest of their lives they were profoundly grateful to the nuns and priests and others who, at great personal risk, concealed and shielded and loved Eva and René. However, they had difficulty coming to terms with the fact that they had, in a sense, abandoned their young children.

René (Who is now known as Ron) says that he will feel in debt to the kind nuns of Miséricorde for the remainder of his life. Although he cannot say that he clearly remembers any of those good people,[20] he has a

---

[20] Margot often spoke about Sister Thérèse, with whom she had exchanged letters about the children during their time in the convent.

kind of sense memory of his time there and he is profoundly grate   ...o the nuns who protected him and his sister, along with dozens of other Jewish children. Those good women never asked anything of the young ones in their care; in fact, they always respected who the children were: young Jewish brothers and sisters in need of shelter from the ravenous beasts lurking outside the walls of the convent.

In May of 1947 the Isaacsons said good-bye to their relatives in England and prepared to return to France. During their stay in the United Kingdom Walter and Margot had told Eva and René that within a matter of weeks they would be able to emigrate to Bolivia. Before they had left Belgium a few weeks earlier, the Isaacsons had received from the Jewish organization JOINT a small amount of money to help them to establish themselves in Bolivia. They added that sum to the meager amount that they had left from the jobs that Walter had performed after the war.

They took the ferry from Dover, England to Calais, France and then traveled by train to Bordeaux, where they boarded a derelict freighter called the St. Croix. It was a massive, reeking, rusty ship which regularly transported beef from Argentina to Europe, and then brought half-starved refugees from war-ravaged countries to South America on its return trip. The cooling system in the mammoth-sized freezer in the hull of the ship that usually contained raw meat had been deactivated; the giant room had been cleaned (not very well) and then divided into two dormitories: one of them held hundreds of men and adolescent boys; women, girls, and small boys slept in the other. Both sections contained frail, wobbly cots with fraying canvas for use as blankets. There was virtually no privacy anywhere on board. In addition, the bathrooms were filthy and the food was appalling, but those accommodations were all that the Isaacsons could afford. They knew they had to save as much money as possible so that they would be able to set themselves up in Bolivia, where they and their children would start a new life, one that would not include the dark, bitter hardships that had defined their lives for so many years.

From Bordeaux, the ship headed to Dakar, Senegal, which is the westernmost city in Africa. After a one-day layover, the St. Croix steamed slowly and laboriously across the Atlantic Ocean to the New World, docking in Rio de Janeiro, Brazil. The voyage had taken three wretched, uncomfortable weeks.

When they arrived in Rio de Janeiro, Margot, Walter, and their children went straight to the airport, where they boarded a small airplane—their first flight[21]—for Santa Cruz de la Sierra, Bolivia. After a restless night in a run-down hotel in that town, they boarded another airplane to complete the final part of their journey, to La Paz, the capital of Bolivia, which is 11,975 feet above sea level in the Andes Mountains. Most of the people they saw at the airport and as they traveled by taxi through the streets of La Paz were Native Americans, either Quechua or Aymara. Although most of those people spoke at least a bit of Spanish, the three main languages used in that part of the country were Quechua, Aymara, and Guarani. None of the Isaacsons knew how to speak those languages, or Spanish, for that matter.

Eva and René were nervous and more than a bit fearful, but also tingly with excitement to find themselves in La Paz, which was different in every way from any other place they had ever seen. The crumbly pale-hued stucco buildings were unlike those in Belgium, England, or France and the shops and streets looked different. Even the sounds were unfamiliar; the rumbling of ancient, patched-together automobiles, the honking of geese, the braying of donkeys, and the conversations they heard—in Spanish and in native tongues—were so foreign to their ears that they almost believed they had landed in a place not of this world.

Margot and Walter's fears and anxieties and their sense of dislocation at finding themselves in that very alien environment were tempered by the powerful and uplifting knowledge that they were away

---

[21] In truth, at that time, 1947, relatively few people, except for those in the military, had flown in airplanes.

from the misery and gloom and stink of Europe. At the same time, it was with profound sadness that they thought about that doomed, cheerless continent where tens of millions had died and where disconsolate survivors walked, downcast and zombie-like, past ravaged, burned-out buildings and the ruins of once-great centers and symbols of culture, learning, and art. Walter and Margot knew that throughout that vast, grim graveyard dark nightmares held sway and very few inhabitants dreamed of a bright future.

The elder Isaacsons believed they were in a place where there *would* be a future, hopefully, a luminous, prosperous one. They had always been hard workers; they had never expected success to just fall into their laps. They assured Eva and René that they would all quickly learn to speak Spanish and would come to love their new land.

The taxi took them to the home of Helmut and Flora Isaacson, Walter's cousins. Flora's parents, who Eva and René came to know as *Opa* ("Grandpa" in German) and *Oma* ("Grandma") Gumpertz, lived with her and her husband. Flora and Helmut, who had two children, Leon, six years old, and an infant named Ruth, had wisely fled Germany with her parents and emigrated to Bolivia in the summer of 1939, shortly before the start of the war, and had established a pleasant, comfortable life for themselves. They provided Walter and his family with a modestly furnished room in their small, tidy home and insisted that the Isaacsons stay with them for as long as they needed.

During their short lives—Eva was nine and René was seven—most of which had involved hiding, privation, and war, they had never had an opportunity to practice their faith. For that reason, they were fascinated by the Friday night Sabbath services conducted by their father's cousins. Their little eyes glowed and they listened attentively to the *berachot* (blessings) intoned over the candles, wine, and the challah. They felt warm and happy and very much at home during the lovely meals that followed. During one of those Sabbath dinners, Eva solemnly said, "When I grow up, I want to marry a rabbi."

Besides language and cultural differences, Walter, Margot, and their children had to get used to life at the chillingly high altitude of La Paz with its "thin" air. At almost 12,000 feet above sea level, there are fewer molecules of air than at sea level, which translates into less oxygen. Walter found this to be an immense problem during their first weeks in La Paz, as he tried to earn some money by peddling to the indigenous people who lived in the rural areas outside of the city socks that he had purchased at wholesale prices. Walking for miles from cabin to cabin and shack to shack each day, up and down dusty, hilly roads and rutted pathways with a load of socks on his back would have been challenging under any circumstances; however, the relative lack of oxygen in the air left Walter exhausted and aching each night. Another difficulty was that the only way in which he was able to communicate with potential customers was by virtue of simple hand gestures and facial expressions.

A few weeks after their arrival, as Margot and Walter became progressively more worried about money and the future of their family, they met two men who had emigrated from Germany years before. Mr. Wurzel and Mr. Parker,[22] who produced cold cuts from locally raised cows, wanted to open a store across from the marketplace in La Paz where Native Americans sold coffee, cocoa, fruit, vegetables, and grains, all of which came from the outlying area. The men said that they would sell the meat to Walter and Margot at wholesale prices; in addition, the men would furnish and pay the monthly rent on the store. The Isaacsons, selling at retail prices, would be able to keep all of the profits on the sale of the meat and any money they made selling other products they thought the local people might want. Margot and Walter, who had very little money to invest, readily agreed.

In addition to "carne fria" (cold meat), they sold sandwiches, hot coffee and cocoa that Margot prepared, and ice cream that she purchased

---

[22] There is no information about their full names.

from a local wholesale business. After a few weeks of struggling to make even a slim profit (and seeing that the small amount of seed money that they had brought with them from Europe was diminishing), they realized that their only reliable seller was ice cream, so they borrowed a small home ice cream maker from Walter's cousin and began making and selling a single flavor whose base was a vanilla pudding that Margot had made during their years in Belgium.

Not far from the store was a commercial bakery called Figgliozi from which they regularly bought fresh bread for the sandwiches they made and a few other items. One day, when Margot was in the bakery purchasing a box of ice cream cones, the owner, Max Bieber, asked why she needed so many. When Margot told him about their homemade ice cream, Max explained that, in a few days, he would be installing a machine that he had ordered from the United States that was capable of producing large quantities of ice cream in 12 different flavors. He offered to sell to her, at wholesale, as much ice cream as she wanted. At the same time, believing that Margot would be an asset to his business, he offered her a job in the *heladeria* (ice cream parlor) that he planned on opening. She accepted both offers.

The Isaacsons were relieved that they no longer had to make their own ice cream and were pleased that they would have a reliable supply of mass-produced product to sell at the store. Of course, as an added benefit, Margot's position at the *heladeria* provided them with an additional source of income.

Despite the fact that Walter, with Margot helping when she was not at the *heladeria*, worked from early in the morning until the native market across the plaza closed in the evening, at the end of each week, when they counted how much they had taken in and then deducted what they owed, they saw that their earnings were paltry. They knew that despite the fact that they had added a number of new products to their shelves, their offerings were still too limited to generate as much business as they would need in order to earn a decent income. In addition, there was a problem with the meat. When it was delivered to them each morning by Wurzel and Parker, fresh from the oven, it was hot and moist. However, by the time it had cooled down enough to be sold as cold cuts, it had lost a great deal of weight due to evaporation. What that meant was that even though they may have paid for 10 pounds of meat, after it had cooled, they had only nine pounds to sell; since they sold the meat by weight (except for what they put in sandwiches), they lost some profit with each sale.

As they began to look around for other opportunities, they saw that a vacant store at another plaza, this one across from a prison, was available for rent. Every day, people congregated there to visit relatives and friends in prison, most of whom were being held on political charges. At that time, Bolivia was a seething cauldron of vying political groups. Governments fell or were overthrown, sometimes peacefully and sometimes after blood had been spilled, over and over again; during the six years that the Isaacsons lived in Bolivia there were at least a half dozen government turnovers.

Taking a gamble, the Isaacsons told Wurzel and Parker that they were going to vacate the store. Then they signed a lease for the new store, and named it *Fiambrera Buena*, which literally means "Good Lunchbox Pail," but was used to mean "Good Delicatessen." Like the previous business, this one specialized in the sale of cold cuts (from a different wholesaler) and a variety of sandwiches. Once they saw, to their great relief, that they could count on steady business from the people visiting the prison across the street, they began stocking their shelves with soap, canned fruit and vegetables, soup, powdered milk, chocolate, cookies, and a variety of other commodities. After a while, they had a cooler and a freezer installed, which enabled them to stock butter, milk, and ice cream. Eventually, they sold bottles of wine.

The Isaacsons always attempted to abide by the letter of the eccentric and ever-changing laws of Bolivia, for example, by making sure their profits never exceeded 20% over the wholesale price of goods. However, the laws and those who enforced them were capricious, and the bribing of public officials was not only common, but a regular part of conducting business. On a weekly basis, someone from the Policia de Sanidad (Health and Sanitation Police) would inspect the store for cleanliness. Even though the Isaacsons kept their place of business immaculate, each inspector who visited found a violation, which seemed to disappear as soon as they offered some money to the man.

When it seemed as if the store would be able to sustain them— that is, pay for itself and provide a small but adequate income—Margot resigned from her job at the ice cream parlor and resumed working full-time with her husband. Walter desperately needed her to help him because he found that at the end of each day, dozens of small items were missing from the shelves. Their margin of profit was so slight that the loss of those articles hurt them.

They worked from 7 a.m. until 10 p.m. every day of the year. After a while, for reasons they were never able to determine, fewer people were patronizing their store. The Isaacsons were keeping their heads above the floodtide of debt, but they worried about losing the money they had put into the store[23] and about paying rent on their tiny apartment. Even though Walter's cousins had wanted him and his family to stay with them, if not indefinitely, then for a while longer, the Isaacsons felt that they had relied on Helmut and Flora's generosity for long enough. Besides that, they wanted their own place, so a few weeks after opening the new store they moved into an apartment. It was divided into two rooms: a large one that served as a sitting area/bedroom for all four of them and a small kitchen. The outhouse (There was no modern bathroom.) was in the rear of the building, at the far end of a scrubby, untamed backyard where chickens were allowed to roam freely and scratch the dirt for insects.

---

[23] Which came from the small amount they had left from Walter's jobs and what had been provided to them by JOINT before they left Europe.

A few months later, Walter and Margot found a larger apartment that was only a short walk from the store. It cost a bit more than the previous one; however, it had a bathroom and tub—but no hot water. To bathe, the Isaacsons had to heat water using a petroleum burner (called a *primo*). Because of the low air pressure at La Paz's high altitude, it took much longer than at sea level for water to boil for bathing and for cooking. A neighbor suggested that they purchase an electric heater that they could immerse in the tub, explaining that it would warm the water more quickly than would the petroleum burner, but Margot was reluctant to use that piece of equipment. She smiled as she looked at the tub, fondly remembering the one that her parents had purchased for their apartment in Duisburg when she was young.

Since the Isaacsons spent so many hours at the store, Margot hired, for a trifle, a young local woman, who arrived each day with her baby tied to her back, to clean, do laundry, cook meals, and take care of Eva and René. Margot felt guilty because she paid the equivalent of pennies for this service, but that was the going rate, and the woman seemed to be grateful for that small income.

Margot learned to speak fluent Spanish by attempting to communicate with customers; Walter struggled, and learned just enough to get along. They hired a tutor to teach the language to their children; with the man's help and by talking with neighbors, Eva and René transitioned from French to fairly good Spanish within a few months.

There were a number of schools in their neighborhood in La Paz, including the American Institute, a Jewish school, one started by German immigrants, and one organized by people who spoke French. Margot was thrilled to enroll Eva and René in the Jewish school. Eva adjusted to it immediately, but René experienced problems from the very beginning. He was inattentive, did poorly in his subjects, and often violated class rules. This was probably due to the fact that he was shy and found it difficult to make friends, mostly because, unlike Eva, he felt that he was different from the other children, all of whom spoke fluent Spanish. In addition, he acted out because he missed his mother, who spent most of her time working. After a few incidents involving minor instances of unacceptable behavior, Margot was told that unless René learned to follow the rules, he would be asked to leave the school. She patiently counseled her son, who promised to stay out of trouble. However, his behavior did not improve; in fact, he began brawling with other students and getting into other kinds of mischief going to and coming home from school. At that point, Margot decided that she would escort him both ways each day.

Despite Margot's best efforts, René continued to misbehave and fight. Finally, she reluctantly withdrew him (and Eva) from the school and enrolled them in the local public school. A few weeks later, Eva asked to go to the French school, and Margot consented. At that point, she found a place for René in the American Institute.

Although he still acted in a rebellious manner and continued to get in trouble on occasion, René adjusted to his new school. Little by little, despite the fact that he still spoke Spanish out of school and French at home, he began to communicate in passable English. After a while, he began to enjoy his subjects and feel comfortable with his teachers,.

And he discovered Superman.

One of René's fellow students allowed him to read his well-thumbed *Superman* comic books and they went to occasional *Superman* movies. In what can only be described as a kind of super attraction, René developed an overpowering hunger to read and reread each of those magazines and devour the magnificent illustrations until he was able to mentally replicate each and every one of them. He loved the colors—floods of vivid reds and rich blues and sweeping areas of white—and he felt as if he was taking part in the action of the bold, heroic, truly American stories. This figure, this man, this being, this Superman was, to the young boy, the personification of utmost bravery and honor and righteousness. René began to associate Superman with the United States, which he perceived as a land of courage, high principle, and justice. He spent hours dreaming of being Superman and performing great deeds in the United States of America.

He also dreamed of becoming an American.

During the next few months, at least partially due to the wildly chaotic and continuously changing political situation, with government after government falling—sometimes peacefully, at times violently—Bolivia's economy plummeted from its chronic sluggishness to a low point at which inflation rose to astronomical heights. The cost of the basics became more than the average person could afford. Helmut and Flora, who had planned on emigrating to the United States at some point, decided that they could not wait any longer. As soon as their papers were in order, they sold their lovely house and belongings, said good-bye to Walter and his family, and, with their children and Flora's parents, left the country. Max Bieber, Margot's former employer at the ice cream parlor, had moved to Argentina a few months earlier. At that point, Walter and Margot had begun to accept the fact that not only were they not managing to save money, but that sooner or later, they might not even be able to afford to pay rent on the store or on their modest apartment.

Reluctantly accepting the reality that they had to make plans to move once again, the Isaacsons thought about what it would be like to live in Argentina or the United States. Even though the latter was their first choice, as stated earlier, the main obstacle to emigrating to America was that they would need a sponsor in that country. At the same time, they had heard from several people who had moved to Argentina that life there was very good. Gerda van Leuven, a childhood friend who had attended Margot and Walter's wedding, had followed her fiancé, Otto Heidelberg, to Argentina, where they married. Margot had maintained her relationship with Gerda via mail, so now she wrote to her friend to explain their extremely shaky economic situation and the political turmoil in Bolivia. Gerda immediately replied, saying that although Argentina was under the control of right-wing dictator Juan Peron, it was a stable, safe place in which to live. She offered to help the Isaacsons gain entry and said that she would do whatever she could to help them to adjust.

Margot had also kept in touch with Elli Wallner, another old friend who, with her husband Sami, had moved to the United States in 1949. For several years before that, the Wallners had lived in Capinota, Bolivia, a beautiful tropical hamlet with very few Europeans. Sami had loved his job as a highly esteemed and very appreciated doctor in the little town, but Elli, who was from Berlin, intensely disliked the primitive conditions of Capinota, and so they emigrated to the United States, where Elli had a brother and a sister. Once the Wallners had settled in the peaceful village of Middletown, New York, Elli wrote to Margot, encouraging her and her family to join them in America, where, she said over and over again, the air smelled sweet and everything was grand. In this safe and prosperous land, she promised, the future was bright.

As the Isaacsons tried to decide about what they hoped would be their final move, they continued to work seven days a week at their store. The children attended school during the day and René, but not Eva, went to Hebrew school in the afternoons. In early 1953, René became bar mitzvah. After the service, his parents hosted a small party for friends. Helmut Isaacson, Walter's cousin, had flown in from New York to attend. That special occasion was the only time that Margot and Walter did not go to work in their little store, which was, day by day, draining their paltry savings and burying them in what seemed to be a dark, bottomless hole of debt from which they might never be able to emerge. Each time they examined their finances they felt more and more desperate.

Inflation rose each day, and with it the prices that Walter and Margot had to pay for merchandise. In 1947, when they had arrived in Bolivia, one boliviano had been worth $.70 in U.S. currency; in 1953, it was worth one tenth of that, $.07. There was a limit to how high Margot and Walter would be able to raise their prices to keep up with inflation before customers stopped buying and they were left with a failed business that would pull them down and drown them in red ink.

Desperate, the Isaacsons decided they had to leave Bolivia as soon as possible. Another of Walter's cousins with whom he had maintained steady contact over the years, Herbert Albersheim, who lived in Baltimore, Maryland, sent a letter in which he said that he would gladly take in the Isaacsons and help them to settle in the U.S. He enclosed a copy of an official affidavit stating that he would make sure the family would not be a burden on the country. Walter and Margot greeted Herbert's letter with a sigh of relief and were able to smile for the first time in weeks. They applied for visas to the United States; however, by the time the documents arrived in the mail, because the Isaacsons had spent so much money keeping the store operating, they did not have enough left to cover their traveling expenses. Even if Walter and Margot were to sell everything they owned, they would still be $800.00 short in terms of what they would need to travel to the United States. For that reason, even though it was their second choice, they decided to accept Otto and Gerda Heidelberg's generous offer of help, which involved moving to Argentina, a destination that was considerably closer and, therefore, less expensive to reach than the United States.

During that dismal and worrisome period of time, a letter from Elli Wallner arrived. In it she once again asked Margot and Walter to seriously consider moving to the United States. Margot allowed the letter to sit for a few days before she replied, sorrowfully telling Elli that because of the disastrous rate of inflation in Bolivia, they did not have enough money for travel to the United States. A week later, another letter arrived, this time from Sami Wallner. Skipping the customary pleasantries, he had simply written, "How much money do you need?" Although Walter and Margot were uncomfortable with the thought of taking money from a friend, after looking at Eva and René and thinking about their future—how limited it was in Bolivia and how expansive it could be in the

United States—they swallowed their pride and wrote in reply that if they chose the most economical travel route, they would need $800.00.

One week later, a check from Sami for that amount arrived in the mail. Margot and Walter wasted no time: they immediately notified the man from whom they leased the store and the landlord of their apartment of their plans and they put all of their possessions up for sale. Eva and René happily helped their parents to pack their clothing and a few belongings. They were all overjoyed at the thought of their new life in America, that land of endless opportunities, that shining beacon on a hill. For Margot, Walter, and Eva, America represented safety and freedom and prosperity. René was happy to go because the United States was the home of pastel-colored skies and of Superman.

Then a dark cloud abruptly blotted out the sunshine above René's head. His father took him aside and said that they should go for a walk. After a while, he stopped and then he put his big hands on the boy's shoulders. Then, looking sympathetically at his son, Walter gently explained that before they could travel to the United States, they had to perform a painful duty: since they would not be able to take Blanco, the little white dog that René had found on the street and brought home months before, they would have to have him "put to sleep."

René, crying uncontrollably, felt sick to his stomach at the thought of what was to happen to his friend. At the clinic, he held Blanco until the veterinarian tenderly took the little creature and carried him down the hallway and into a room with a heavy door. René stared at the door, hoping, praying that, any second now, Blanco would run out and jump into his arms. Of course, the door never opened.

René cried on the way back to the house. He grieved silently for most of the next two weeks. It was months before the boy was able to accept the fact that his gentle companion was gone, and for a long time he felt weighed down by guilt because he had agreed to and been a party to Blanco's untimely demise.

The painful lesson that René learned from that experience was to help him many times during the years to come. Even though he had to remind himself of it over and over again, he came to understand that, at times, the most wonderful opportunities and the greatest achievements in life come at the cost of profound sacrifice.

An astonishing transformation in René's attitude came on the heels of that understanding. He made a promise to himself, one that he did not reveal to his parents: if he and his family actually were able to move to America, he would do whatever would be necessary to put an end to his rebellious behavior and he would do his utmost to help his struggling parents to become financially stable.

As they prepared for their journey, René changed, seemingly overnight, from a difficult adolescent to an ideal son who appreciated his parents for making his dream come true: allowing him to go to America where, perhaps, he might meet Superman.

THIRTEEN

Going to the Land of Sunshine and Warmth

Walter calculated that the least expensive way of reaching the golden land—the United States—involved traveling by train, then ship, and then airplane. The first leg of the trip would be from La Paz to Antofagasta, Chile, where Reni Leeser, the former Reni Schneider, Margot's girlhood friend from Duisburg and sister of Margot's first love, Martin, lived with her husband Julius. Walter and Julius had played soccer together in Germany when they were young boys.

Besides all of the usual reasons for maintaining contact with people from their past, Margot and Walter desperately needed to stay in touch with them so as to preserve a sense of normalcy in their lives. During the first few years following the war, as they were forced to accept the truth—that Margot's parents, Walter's father, dozens of other relatives, and a heart-breakingly large number of friends were never coming home—they reached out to those who had survived. They cherished each contact with a relative, no matter how distant, or with a friend or even just an acquaintance from the time before the Third Reich, when life had been sweet and normal and the boundaries between Jews and Christians had been inconsequential.

From time to time, they took refuge in a serene inner life, a cerebral existence whose setting was an idealized image of lovely Duisburg before the skies darkened and the people they thought they knew began to applaud the brutish acts of the men in power. That is not to say that Walter and Margot hid from reality. On a daily basis, they resolutely took on each and every challenge that served as an obstacle to their success and the safety and happiness of their children. In point of fact, they had always resolutely attempted to cope with the bleak circumstances of their lives, first in Germany after the rise of the Third Reich, and then in Antwerp and Brussels, both of which proved to be unreliable places of refuge; in La Paz, which was a desperately difficult place in which to live for its native population and harshly challenging for the Jewish refugees who had settled there, Walter and Margot had struggled every day.

Margot and Walter hoped that America would be the country that they and their children would be able to call home, the place where they would not be outsiders, the sweet sanctuary in which they would have the opportunity to work hard and build a life for themselves and for Eva and René. All that they had ever heard about the United States led them to believe that they would not only be able to make a comfortable life there, but that they and their children would, in time, have the privilege of becoming American citizens.

The train from La Paz to Antofagasta, a city on the coast of Chile, ran once a week. Since it was a 36-hour trip, the Isaacsons booked a sleeping coach for the four of them. The first stop, 10 hours later, was a town in western Bolivia called Oruro. Eva and René were in their berths and their parents were preparing for bed when there was a knock on the compartment door. When Walter opened the door, he was confronted by three brawny police officers. Both Margot and Walter instinctively moaned and shrank at the sight of these men, looking so much like Gestapo officers. Without an explanation, the man who appeared to be in charge instructed Walter to come with them. When Walter explained that their destination was Antofagasta and that if he disembarked now he might not make it back before the train left the station, the lead officer said that he had to accompany them to the police station and that, no, he would not make it back to the train in time. When Walter asked for an explanation, the officer in charge replied that all would be explained at the police station. Concerned and anxious, but knowing that he had to do as he was being instructed, Walter told Margot to go on, promising that he would meet her and the children in Antofagasta. Margot refused, saying that they had all spent too many years apart from him and they would not do it again. As she walked into the corridor so as to remain with Walter, she turned back to the compartment and told Eva and René to quickly dress and pack the bags. While they all waited for the children to be ready, Margot held Walter's hand and stared defiantly at the police officers.

In the street, the officers refused to allow Margot and the children to accompany them to the police station, saying that she should appear there in the morning to learn about her husband's situation. One of them drove her and the children to a dank, grimy hotel that smelled of onions and garbage; it was in a rundown, dimly lit part of town. Before he left, the police officer handed to Margot a card with the address of the station house.

Even though Eva and René were frightened and worried, they eventually fell asleep. The next morning, they knew by their mother's drawn, pale appearance and the fact that she wore the same dress from the day before, that she had not slept at all. She said they had to get out of bed, dress immediately, and then have a quick breakfast. As Eva and René ate buttered rolls and drank milk at a nearby cafe, Margot, who sipped a cup of black coffee, assured them that they would be on the next train to Antofagasta—with their father.

At the police station, to which Margot and the children were able to walk, an officer read from a sheet of paper the crime with which Walter had been charged: non-payment of taxes. After asking a few questions, Margot understood what had happened: after the Isaacsons had left La Paz, their bookkeeper, Mr. Friedman, had reported to the authorities that his clients had not paid the required 42,000 bolivianos ($60.00) in taxes for the liquidation of their business and the sale of their belongings— money they had not known they owed. He also had told the police that their destination was Antofagasta. Even though the amount they owed was small, at that point the Isaacsons had just enough money to get to the United States. After discussing the dilemma with Walter, Margot, who had their traveling money in her pocketbook, said that they should pay the fine, even though that would leave them with less than they needed to continue on their journey. Then she told Walter her plan for obtaining the amount they needed to reach America. Walter agreed; after Margot paid what they owed, he was released from jail.

An hour later, while Eva and René waited in the grimy hotel in Oruro with their father, Margot took a taxi to the airport, where she boarded a plane to La Paz. Her plan was to ask a man named Tepperberg, who was the business partner of Walter's cousin Helmut, to lend her the money they needed. Even though she and Walter realized it was a long shot, Margot reassured herself by thinking that on the one or two occasions in the past when she and Walter had opportunities to talk to Mr. Tepperberg he had seemed to be a kind, sympathetic soul.

When Margot arrived at Mr. Tepperberg's place of business and asked to speak to him, she was ushered into his small, cluttered office. Margot got right to the point: she calmly and unemotionally explained their plight, and then she asked for what she considered a princely sum. She explained that to be able to continue on their journey to the United States they would need the 42,000 bolivianos that they had just paid for the taxes they owed, plus an additional amount to cover the cost of her airfare to and from La Paz, cash to pay for food and lodging in Oruro during the week that they waited for the next train, and what it would cost to purchase four new tickets to Antofagasta. Mr. Tepperberg shook his head to demonstrate that he understood; then, reaching into his wallet, he handed the cash to her.

That evening, Margot returned to the foul-smelling hotel in Oruro. She smiled widely as she told Walter how Mr. Tepperberg had unhesitatingly given her the amount of money they needed and said that they could wait to pay him until they were settled and had jobs in America. This was one of many occasions when people within the community of Jewish refugees helped each other without a second thought—or, perhaps, with many thoughts, many bitter memories of the time in the recent past when so many others had turned their backs on their persecuted neighbors.

As stated earlier, Margot and Walter always remembered the kindness of the nuns who not only did not turn their backs, but at great personal risk, sheltered their children. Years later, Ron (René) said that even though he has only partial recollections of that time in his life, he frequently thinks about those compassionate people who took in his sister and him in their time of need. Those brave women risked their safety to protect children who were strangers to them and who were not of their faith. The intense bonds that women religious in various parts of Europe developed with the Jewish children whom they sheltered are strong and have remained indissoluble over the decades.[24] The next morning, after the Isaacsons had eaten breakfast, they walked to a cleaner, nicer hotel that the waitress who had served them at the coffee shop had recommended. Oruro, an old mining town, is, like La Paz, situated at a high altitude; the temperature was comfortably cool during the day and hovered near freezing each night that week. Although they spent much of their time in the confines of their cramped hotel room, the Isaacsons made sure to take a long walk each day. They bought food from local grocery stores and ate most of their simple meals in their room, but, on occasion, they dined in inexpensive nearby restaurants. They had books to read because Walter, after explaining their frustrating situation to the man who was in charge of the miniscule local library, managed to acquire temporary borrowing rights.

The following Tuesday, as the Isaacsons boarded the train to Antofagasta, they felt, for the first time in a week, unfettered. Even though the children had found the first 10 hours on the train—from La Paz to Oruro—to be a plodding, hopelessly boring grind, now, after their forced

---

[24] Some of those bonds developed many years later, when the children had become adults and first began to understand how much the nuns had sacrificed for them.

stay in that town, they thoroughly enjoyed the remaining 26 hours of the journey. René and Eva looked out the window at the ever-changing countryside, ate food their mother had packed, and slept soundly, relieved that their family was intact.

Reni and Julius Leeser met the Isaacsons at the station in Antofagasta and took them to their house. Margot had telephoned Reni the week before to tell her that Walter had been taken into custody, and then before they boarded the train a week later. The Isaacsons spent two days with Reni and Julius. Even though the Leesers provided their guests with an abundance of delicious home-cooked food and very comfortable accommodations, René fell victim to such an overpowering need to keep moving—toward the United States—that he had trouble sitting still and hardly slept a wink.

At the port of Antofagasta, the Isaacsons boarded a ship which, while far from luxurious, was much more comfortable than the one on which they had sailed from Bordeaux to Brazil six years earlier. After a slight delay as last minute repairs were made, the ship steamed into the Pacific Ocean, reaching the Panama Canal three days later. It glided through the canal and docked at the eastern terminus, the city of Colon on the Caribbean Sea, where the Isaacsons boarded a small airliner which took them to Miami, Florida.

As Margot, Walter, and their children descended the stairs down to the tarmac at the airport in Miami, they looked at each other with a combination of great joy and equally great fear. After all they had been through, they knew that something could still go wrong, but each of them quietly rejoiced in the fact that they were in the glorious United States of America. As it turned out, there *was* a snag: despite the fact that Margot and Walter were meticulous planners, they had missed the connecting flight to New York.

During the time that they had to wait for the next flight, they decided to see the sights in Miami, their first American city. They liked just about everything they saw. Although none of them was fluent in English—Ron had learned English at the American Institute in La Paz and they had all taken some language lessons from Seventh Adventist missionaries—they made themselves understood. They were pleasantly surprised to meet so many very friendly people who smiled at them and seemed to be more than happy to help them find their way. All four of them were sure they were going to like living in America.

However, they did find two aspects of Miami unpleasant: the first was the super-humid heat, which crept into their underwear and kept them uncomfortably moist all day; they felt as if they were locked in a steam room. They had left La Paz in the middle of what passes for winter in Bolivia, and now found themselves in the midst of a typically hot, clammy Florida summer day.

The other, highly distasteful feature of Miami—which they later learned was the situation in the rest of Florida and the other states in the south—involved the way in which black people were treated. The Isaacsons were horrified and felt sick to their stomachs when, as they traveled in buses that day, they saw that black people were required to sit in the rear. They also saw the words "White" and "Colored" on signs outside of public bathrooms and above water fountains. In La Paz, all people, fair-skinned Europeans and dark-skinned Indians, were treated alike in terms of everyday rights and accommodations. The Isaacsons were not able to understand why black people were treated in that degrading way in America. Walter and Margot, visibly upset, shook their heads sadly and muttered to each other in German about something that René did not understand. Walter and Margot had always spoken to René and Eva only in French and had discouraged them from learning German. They had not wanted their children to have any associations with that now-distasteful ancestry. A consequence of that decision was that they were able to talk to each other in German without their children understanding most of what they were saying, which they sometimes found to be advantageous.

Eva, who had, over the years, picked up on her own much more German than René had, whispered to him that they were talking about the signs in shop windows and other places throughout Germany, Belgium, and other countries during the time of the Third Reich that read, "Juden sind unerwünscht," literally, "Jews not wanted." Walter and Margot sighed, shook their heads again, and said they hoped New York did not have those kinds of hateful racial restrictions.

Hours later, tired and overheated, the Isaacsons ate in a diner, where they enjoyed a technological marvel: air conditioning. Then, since they did not have money for a hotel room, they returned to the airport, where they sat on hard plastic chairs. After a while, as the terminal became quiet, the Isaacsons stretched out. First the children, then Margot and Walter dozed off; they slept deeply during their first night in America.

Early the next morning, they boarded their flight to New York. Walter's cousin Helmut met them at what was then called Idlewild Airport, today's Kennedy Airport. He drove them to his apartment in Manhattan, where Flora fed them. Then, as they had done when Margot, Walter, and the children had arrived in La Paz six years before, Helmut and Flora provided their guests with a comfortable room in which to sleep. Since Margot and Walter were exhausted, they did not ask to visit any of the sights in Manhattan, but the next day they did take a short walk through Helmut and Flora's lovely Upper West Side neighborhood. Everything they saw pleased them.

Two days later, August 2, 1953, a Sunday, Helmut drove Walter and his family to the Port Authority Bus Terminal, where they boarded a bus for the two and a half hour ride to their final destination, Middletown, New York, in Orange County, where Margot's friends Sami and Elli Wallner lived. At the bus station in the center of the sleepy town they boarded a taxi and asked the driver to take them to what was then called the Middletown State Homeopathic Hospital (which closed its doors in 2006), where Sami worked as a doctor and where the Wallners lived. At that time, the hospital, which treated patients with mental disorders, had 4,000 beds. It also had houses on the grounds for doctors.

At the main building, Walter, with Margot and the children at his side, told a receptionist that Dr. Wallner was expecting him and his family. A minute or two later, Sami rushed down the hall and embraced the Isaacsons. Then he walked them out of the building and drove them in his car to his stately red brick house, which was situated on a magnificent wooded lot just off one of the quiet side roads of the hospital grounds.

Margot, Walter, Eva, and René stood on the grass of the front yard, looking up at the elegant, beautifully maintained house; Margot whispered to Walter and the children, "I am glad for them, but a house like this, we will never have." They walked into the sun-filled foyer, where they were warmly greeted by Elli, who was holding the hand of her shy five-year-old son Harry. As she held tightly to Elli, Margot was suddenly overcome by a fiercely powerful wave of joy that radiated up from her feet to her chest and then to the top of her head; she imagined she was being lifted into the air, and she felt weightless, as if all of her concerns and worries had evaporated. Then she sank down heavily onto Elli and, for a few seconds, was not able to catch her breath.

Later, when they were alone, Margot told Walter of her sense of exhilaration and lightness as she stood in the sunny foyer. She said it had been obliterated almost immediately by a heavy surge of anxiety so intense that she had not been able to breathe. Walter confessed that he had felt similar conflicting emotions, and then he told her not to worry; after all, he said, they had been through so much and had been lifted up and dropped down so many times for so long that what they had just experienced was perfectly normal and to be expected. Then he said that they had to think of this place, the United States, as their new home. There was no other place for them, and they had to learn to adapt and they had to be strong so that they would be able to overcome the many obstacles that would surely block their way in the years ahead.

Margot continued, saying that she was not sure, at that very moment, as they talked in hushed tones in the room that Elli had prepared for them, whether she was relieved to be in America or more frightened than she had been in years. Walter said that he believed it would all work out for them. After all, he whispered, everything they had seen that day on the bus ride from Manhattan and in the taxi in Middletown and here with Sami and Elli had been lovely. Then he asked, was it all *too* wonderful to be true? Was it real or was it a fantasy? Was what they had seen an introduction to a lovely life in America or was it only the good side of the coin and a prelude to disappointment? Would living in the United States turn out to be as difficult and sour as had been their life in Bolivia?

Later, as Elli proudly took them on a tour of her house and as Margot and Walter looked through the large windows at the trees and grass and blossoming flowers that surrounded it, they hoped that Middletown would be the place where they would finally be able to settle. They wanted America, the land of sunshine and warmth, to be their home.

Eva, 11 and René, 9 in La Paz, Bolivia

**Sally Isaacson's butcher shop;
"Wurstfabrik" means "Sausage Factory."**

Jenny Landau

Oskar Landau

Miséricorde; René is fourth from the right in the front row

Ron and a nun at Miséricorde, 1985   **Ensign Ronald Isaacson**

Walter, Margot, Eva & René in La Paz, Bolivia

Sally and Emma Isaacson

Lucy and Susan, 2003

From Darkness Into Light

Part II

Light

FOURTEEN

Middletown

For the first few dizzying days in Middletown, as the Isaacsons attempted to acclimate themselves to their new surroundings, they practiced speaking English to each other and to the Wallners. It was Margot and Walter's fourth language, after German, French, and Spanish. They felt most comfortable with German, using it when they spoke to each other and to people who were from Germany. As is typical in reference to language learning, the youngsters, who were fluent in French and Spanish, made more progress and acquired greater fluency in English in a shorter period of time than their parents.

As the four of them wandered through the neighborhood, they were amazed and delighted by the abundance of food and varied household goods on display in magnificently colorful arrangements at the local A & P, the first supermarket they had ever seen. Strolling down the immaculate sidewalks along North Street in the center of Middletown, they admired the fine-looking homes with their neatly manicured lawns and they marveled at the number of shiny cars parked on the street and resting on the tree-lined driveways.

Walter and Margot, who always endeavored to teach Eva and René how to meet and overcome life's challenges, explained to them that while it was wonderful that they were living in a large comfortable house with *two toilets* and with access to lots of food, they could not depend on the generosity of their friends indefinitely. Margot said that she and their father hoped to find jobs immediately. Then she told Eva and René that they would have to help out in every way possible: by doing well in school, by acting properly at all times, and by working at part-time jobs. René, remembering his promise to himself, said that he would immediately look for a job too; Eva said that she would do likewise. Then Walter pointed out that once they had enough money to move out, they would, by necessity, have to live in a small, inexpensive apartment with very few furnishings, and not a luxurious house such as the one owned by the Wallners.

During that first week in town, Elli introduced Margot to Mrs. Levine, whose husband owned a shoe factory; she explained to the woman that her friends had just arrived from Bolivia and desperately needed jobs. Mrs. Levine told Margot that she and her husband should go to the factory the next morning. That day, after a brief interview, Mr. Levine hired both of them to work at minimum wage, $.75 per hour. Walter was trained to operate a cutting machine and Margot was assigned to move materials and partially fabricated shoes from station to station within the factory. While Walter's job was repetitive and boring, Margot's chores were physically demanding. Although they talked about it, they ultimately decided not to ask whether they would be allowed to switch tasks. That was because even though women had worked in just about every kind of manufacturing position during the war years, during the post-war period machine jobs were almost always assigned to men.

Once the Isaacsons had accumulated some cash, they mailed to Mr. Tepperberg the amount that he had given to Margot when she went to his office in La Paz. Then, when they had saved more money, they offered it to the Wallners to pay back part of the $800.00 they had borrowed and to compensate them for their generosity. Of course, their kindhearted hosts refused to take any of it, telling their friends to use the money to build up a "nest egg," a phrase they had to explain to them in German.

In the evenings and on weekends, while Eva and René read or completed their homework—René was in the seventh grade in junior high and Eva was a freshman in high school[25]—Margot and Walter looked for an apartment to rent. They ran into two problems over and over again: their awkward English and the fact that they had no references; those

---

[25] Both had been placed one year behind in terms of their ages.

issues seemed to worry each of the landlords to whom they spoke. After the first couple of occasions, they understood that people perceived them as "foreigners," or worse, as "intruders."

After three weeks of searching, they settled on a run-down, ground floor furnished apartment that was a short distance from their place of employment and very close to the schools that their children attended. It consisted of a kitchen, a combination living room/bedroom, a miniscule bathroom without windows, and a large walk-in closet. The landlord installed two cots in the closet, and that served as a bedroom for Eva and René. Despite the fact that they were both teenagers, the Isaacson children were not overly upset by this arrangement because they had always shared sleeping spaces. Even though it was not much of an apartment, Margot and Walter decided that they had relied on the generosity of the Wallners long enough, and had to have a place of their own.

Among the technological advances that were entirely new to the Isaacsons was the gas oven; all of their lives they had used wood-burning or coal stoves for cooking (and occasionally for heat). One afternoon, while her parents were at work, Eva, as instructed, placed food that Margot had prepared the night before in the oven. She turned the knob to light it. When she did not see a flame, she bent down and looked into the open oven. Just then, the gas jets ignited, enveloping Eva in a *whoosh* of scorching heat. She jumped back and howled in pain and ran to the sink, where she repeatedly splashed water onto her face, neck, and hair. When she turned to look at René, who had bolted from his chair in alarm, he saw that Eva's eyebrows and eyelashes had been singed and her face was beginning to turn red and to swell like a balloon. As he gently held a damp kitchen towel against her face, Eva cried, mostly out of fear.

When their parents arrived home from work a few minutes later, Margot ran to Eva and removed the damp towel from her face; seeing how red it was and how Eva's lashes and eyebrows were almost completely gone, Margot began to whimper, which caused Eva, who had finally become less agitated, to start to wail again. Then, telling Walter to stay with René, she escorted Eva out of the house to a neighbor, who drove them to the nearest doctor.

Fortunately, Eva had suffered only a minor burn, as if she had been exposed to the sun for too long. The doctor said that her eyebrows and lashes would grow back in time. He charged five dollars, which Margot arranged to pay in weekly installments.

During the course of the next few months, although Walter and Margot continued to look for a more spacious apartment, they did not feel compelled to move, at least for the time being ... until, one morning at breakfast René said something which caused them to devote more energy to their efforts. Walter was talking about the furious thunderstorm which had lashed and pummeled the house the evening before. When he said that the storm had been so loud he had not been able to hear anything else, René said, with a smirk, "I heard everything last night, and I don't mean the storm." After a long moment of deathly silence, the two embarrassed parents smiled weakly; then Walter said that it was time they looked for a larger apartment.

Two days later, Walter announced that the owner of the building in which they lived had said that an apartment on the second floor with more rooms had just become available. The good news was the rent was the same $60.00 per month that they were currently paying; the downside was that the new place was unfurnished. The next day, after determining at Sears the price for the minimal amount of furniture they would need, Margot and Walter decided to take the larger apartment.

They returned to Sears, where they ordered a kitchen table, four chairs, a studio couch that could be converted into a bed, and two cots, for a total of $400.00. They agreed to make a down payment on delivery day and pay the rest in installments. On the day before the scheduled delivery, the Isaacsons went to Sears to touch base with the sales person in the furniture department. He told them he was glad they had come in because they had to speak to the credit manager, a tall, skinny man who bluntly informed them that he could not deliver the furniture without full payment first because the Isaacsons had no credit references. Margot and Walter, embarrassed and upset, told the man that they had always paid in full for whatever they needed, but were new to the country and did not have $400.00. He repeated to them that they had to pay in full before the furniture could be delivered.

As Margot and Walter walked down the street, flustered and concerned about how they would be able to live in their new, empty apartment, which they were scheduled to move into the next day, they stopped in front of a small furniture store on North Street that they had passed dozens of times without really noticing it. After staring longingly for a moment at the beautiful display in the window, they resumed walking toward home. The owner of the store, a man named Rosenstein, came out and asked, "Can I help you?" The Isaacsons, unsure about what to say, just stood where they were until the man invited them in. They felt a combination of excitement and dismay as they admired the kitchen and dining room sets, the living room sofas and chairs, and the beds. Finally, deciding that it would not hurt to talk to the man, Walter sadly explained their dilemma. Without a moment's hesitation, Mr. Rosenstein said, "Select whatever you need, and don't worry about the money now." Not understanding or, actually, not believing what they had heard, the Isaacsons continued to forlornly stare at the furniture. After Mr. Rosenstein repeated what he had said and assured Walter and Margot that he meant it, their spirits lifted and they quickly picked out the few items they would need to make the new apartment livable. They arranged the same terms with the man as the ones they thought they had with Sears. Rosenstein told the couple that he could tell just by talking to people how credit worthy they were; as far as he was concerned, he said, Margot and Walter had perfect credit.

Margot's drudge job was exhausting and depressing her, so

Walter told her to quit and find something else. After a long period of reflection, she finally did as he suggested, and quickly obtained a position as a governess of two children. She enjoyed taking care of the children, but was distressed to find out that even though she had never agreed to it, she was also expected to clean the house. She kept at this job for a few weeks, at which point she gave notice and then registered at a private employment agency. The owner of the agency told Margot that he might not be able to find a position for her because even though she was able to read and write in English fairly well, she spoke the language slowly and with a pronounced accent. After she had rattled off the other languages with which she was familiar, he checked his files; then, with a smile, he made a phone call during which he arranged an interview for her with the owner of a company that imported essences from South America. An hour later, Margot was hired to maintain the purchasing and shipping files in the office; her new salary was $45.00 per week, $15.00 higher than what she had earned at the shoe factory.

Even though she liked the job and was thrilled to be earning what she considered to be a great deal of money, Margot found the complicated filing system, which relied on numbers and letters, to be confusing. In addition, even though her fluent Spanish, both written and spoken, allowed her to communicate with South American distributors, which was a major aspect of her job, she felt that her English language skills were not satisfactory when she had to talk to the people in manufacturing plants in the United States over the telephone; try as she might, she did not always fully understand what was being said to her, and she knew that was causing her to make shipping errors. After two frustrating weeks, the boss asked her to come to his office, where he sorrowfully explained that he would not be able to keep her on the job. He added that once she had perfected her English language skills he would love for her to reapply for the position.

Instead of falling into a state of hopeless depression over this development, Margot, decided that she and Walter should register for English as a Second Language classes at the local high school, figuring that not only would they both be better equipped for the labor market, but that improved language skills would help them with their everyday contacts with people. That was important to her because, by now, she was very happy to be living in Middletown.

A few months later, with considerable improvement in her ability to speak, read, and write English and with greatly renewed confidence, Margot applied for a number of new jobs; remembering the complicated filing system at the import company, she did not reapply for that job. She eventually obtained a position in the Glue Department at Classy Leather Goods, which manufactured plastic handbags. Even though she was disappointed that she had not been able to land a job that involved the use of her improved English language skills, she put all of her energy into her new position. Almost immediately, she found the repetitive assembly work numbingly boring. In addition, her hands and arms broke out in a blistering rash caused by the glue that she had to use. Despite her discomfort, she kept at her job.

A few months later, Walter left his position at the shoe factory and was hired at Classy Leather Goods too. Besides the fact that the per hour pay was better, they both were able to work on Saturdays at overtime rates, which significantly increased their weekly salary.

Several months into the academic year, Eva and René had come to accept the fact that they were different from the other young people they had met. For one thing, although most of the people their age used their time out of school to complete homework, watch television, play sports, and socialize, Eva and René spent much of their time working. Of course, a few of the students who they knew also had part-time jobs, but they used their money to buy phonograph records or clothes or to go with friends to restaurants and the movies. René's and Eva's earnings were used only for the very important purpose of supplementing their parents' income. Eva washed floors for one of her teachers and worked as often as possible as a babysitter. René was hired for a newspaper delivery route, for which he purchased a used bicycle so that he could make his rounds. He also worked at a service station in town on weekends, washing cars.

Another way in which they did not seem to be like the others was in reference to their manners. The other people their age were clearly *American* in terms of their casual conversations and their solid self-assurance. Eva and René, on the other hand, were obviously foreigners. Their faint accents were not the problem. It had more to do with what their parents had told them about their terrifying experiences in Europe during the Holocaust and the sense of dread which seemed to be the backdrop of their otherwise agreeable life in America. Their mother and father frequently talked about what had happened to them in Germany, where they had lost their citizenship and most of their rights; they repeatedly told of their lives in Belgium: the constant fear of the knock on the door and the transports to the east and how most of those they held dear had been taken away and had never returned. They often reminded René and Eva about the difficult, bitter years in Bolivia, where even though the Isaacsons were not hated or abused, they were always perceived as strangers. Then they reminded their children that, "Even though the people here are nice—and why shouldn't they be? They were born here; they never had to hide and run from the men who would take them away—and they treat us well, you must always *remember* that you are Jews because if *it* happens again at some point in the future, in this place, people who you think are your friends will not allow you to *forget* that you are Jews."

Because René felt different from the others, from the Bobbies and the Tommies and the Billies and all of the other boys with nice American names and since people seemed to think that his name was a female one, he renamed himself. No longer would he be called René. Now he was Ronnie, a name he had heard in the schoolyard one day.

During that period of transition, Walter and Margot, who were not worried about fitting in, devoted all of their energy to work. They put in exhaustingly long hours at their manual labor jobs, which were far below their education and skill levels, and never complained; they were relieved and grateful to be earning enough money to pay for food, rent, and other necessities of life. On occasion, they spent some of that money to take Eva and Ronnie to the movies or for ice cream. They also were able to do that most American thing: open a savings account, which allowed them to set money aside for the future.

Most nights, when they had finished dinner, after Eva and Ronnie had been excused, Margot and Walter remained at the kitchen table, sighing and drinking tea and talking in soft tones. Ronnie used to think they were just too tired to get up and go to bed. He also assumed they were talking once again about how much they missed their charming old way of life in Germany before the rise of the Third Reich. However, one evening, he lingered in the doorway as his parents murmured to each other in German. Even though, over the years, Ron had picked up only a smattering of words in that language, he understood that they were discussing how content they were with their new life in America; he realized that their sighs were not expressions of sorrow and regret, but articulations of relief and satisfaction with how their lives had changed.

They had endured so many dreadful years of running, looking over their shoulders, hiding, internment, leaving their children with strangers—all the time living with bone-chilling fear—and then, once they had left the horror of Europe behind, they had moved to Bolivia, a place where they had always felt like strangers.

Finally, they were where they belonged.

FIFTEEN

Something Lost, Something Gained

As soon as Margot looked at the man's troubled face, her stomach lurched; she knew that something bad, maybe horrific, had occurred. The foreman, a warm-hearted fellow who always tried to help the workers, simply said, "Margot, You have to come with me now." She left her workbench and anxiously followed the man to a stockroom. As the foreman opened the door, he said, "Your husband got hurt." Margot stood frozen in the doorway of the small, unkempt room, unable to enter. There he was—Walter—slumped forward on a folding chair, his face ashen and wet with tears, his mouth taut with pain and fear. A man in blue coveralls was crouched down in front of him, tightly squeezing a blood-soaked cloth against Walter's left hand; the red puddle on the linoleum floor between them was sickeningly large. Margot cautiously approached on what felt like rubbery legs. The man looked up and told her that her husband had cut himself badly. The man did not tell her that Walter had, in fact, severed three of the fingers of his left hand on the cutting machine that he operated. Margot, forcing herself to gain control over her panic, knelt before Walter and, nudging the other man aside, grasped the blood-saturated cloth and squeezed it. Even as she realized that fingers were missing, she thanked the man, who told her that Mr. Ash, the owner of the factory, had called for an ambulance and that it would arrive shortly. Struggling to calm herself, remembering other frightening times in their lives, Margot told her husband that he would be fine and that she would go in the ambulance with him.

At the hospital, a doctor cleaned and stitched the wounds and vaccinated Walter for tetanus. After he had bandaged Walter's ravaged hand, he went out to speak to Margot. He regretfully explained to her that the severed portions of the fingers, which one of the factory workers had wrapped in a clean handkerchief and given to Margot before she stepped into the ambulance, had been too severely damaged to be reattached. Then he told her that her husband had been admitted to the hospital because there was a chance that the site of the injury could become infected and he wanted to keep Walter under observation for a few days.

Since the accident had occurred right after Christmas, Eva and Ron[26] were home from school, and so they, along with Margot, visited Walter on each of the seven days that he was hospitalized. During his stay, Walter became increasingly upset, disheartened, and worried. He was overwhelmed with dread because he feared that he would never be able to earn a decent income again. At the beginning, he attempted to ignore the throbbing pain that shot from where his fingers used to be to his elbow, and do without the pain-killing medication that had been prescribed for him, but after a few hours, he always had to ask for it. However, by the end of that long, gloomy week, he felt a bit less uncomfortable and found that he no longer needed much medication.

At home, Walter read and he slept a great deal. He did not have much of an appetite. Margot thought that because he was not working he was trying to save money by surviving on starvation rations; she talked to him and repeatedly encouraged him to eat. The New York State Workers' Compensation Board agreed to pay him $50.00 on a bi-weekly basis, which was much less than he had been earning at Classy Leather Goods. He and Margot considered hiring an attorney and suing, but in the end, they decided that they did not want to engage in a long, tedious, probably pointless legal battle; besides, they needed the compensation money immediately.

In February of 1954, two short months after the accident, much to his relief, Walter was asked to return to work at Classy Leather Goods. He was assigned to the Expediting Division. Not only did his mutilated

---

[26] By this point, he was referred to as Ron and as Ronnie.

hand not cause difficulties, but Walter thoroughly enjoyed his new position. In truth, he would have been pleased to work at any job.

Much more at ease now because he was employed, Walter began eating normally and acting more like his old self. He never complained about his grievously damaged hand.

One evening a month after Walter had returned to work, Margot, who had been attending night school, rushed into the little apartment to announce that she had just passed her High School Equivalency Test and now possessed a high school diploma. Walter and the children congratulated her. As her sparkling eyes beamed with pride, she said that the diploma was a stepping stone for her, one that would be good for the entire family.

The next time Margot saw Mr. Ash she told him about her newly acquired diploma and asked whether she would be able to move into an office job at the factory. After considering the matter for a few seconds—and possibly remembering the gruesome injury that her husband had suffered—he smiled and told Margot that he would be pleased to have her working in the office. He continued by saying that, regretfully, there were no vacancies now, but if she were to pass a test of her typing skills she would be able to move from the Glue Department to the office to fill the next job opening. He escorted Margot to the office, where he asked the manager to administer the test. Margot thanked the man, sat at a typing desk, and stared at the keyboard. Her heart sank. She immediately knew that she would fail; the letters on the keyboard of this American typewriter were arranged differently from those on German typewriters. A few minutes later, the office manager reported to Mr. Ash that Margot had typed slowly and made numerous errors. Mr. Ash suggested that she purchase a typewriter and practice at home, saying that she would be able to take the test again in the future.

Since Walter and Margot were making regular, timely payments on the furniture that they had purchased, they now had a good credit history. That enabled them to purchase a full-sized Smith Corona typewriter, for which they agreed to make weekly five-dollar payments. Margot practiced on that typewriter each and every night after dinner, stopping only when Eva and Ronnie had to get to sleep. On weekends and days off, she sat at the kitchen table for hours, banging away on the keyboard. When she was sure that she was proficient she took the typing test again. This time she passed. A few weeks after that, a position in the Billing Department became available, and she was hired for it. Even though Margot earned only a couple of dollars more per week in this new position than she had in the Glue Department, she believed it to be a step up in the world of work, one that would benefit her family.

As the year progressed, Ron studied hard and attempted to do his best at school, in addition to putting in many hours each week at his part-time jobs. Eva, always an excellent student, did well in her studies and resourcefully juggled her jobs. They now spoke English with only a shadow of an accent, one that would fade in time; their parents, despite their stubborn German accents, were now quite competent in English.

During the summer of 1954, Eva and Ronnie were able to escape the heat by working in the cool, hilly hinterlands a few miles out of town, she as a counselor at a summer camp run by a family named Goldsmith and he as a kind of all-around helper at a bungalow colony near a bucolic town called Bullville. Although neither one earned much money, they both enjoyed their jobs and delighted in the sweet air and thick sun-dappled woods of what they considered to be "the country." They also made friends with other young people with whom they worked.

One of the people with whom Eva became friendly was the lifeguard at the camp, a young man named Victor Mallenbaum; he had just completed his first year of college. As their friendship developed, Eva became completely captivated by the older boy. Whether or not she was conscious of it, one of the reasons she felt so strongly about Victor may have been that his oft-stated long-term goal was to become a rabbi. The moment Eva told her family about Victor and his plans for the future, they remembered what she had said at dinner one Friday night during the period of time they had lived with Helmut and Flora Isaacson in La Paz, Bolivia: "When I grow up, I want to marry a rabbi." Was it fate? Was it coincidence? Or, as they suspected, did Victor's planned career just seem to strike an agreeable chord in Eva's consciousness? They never asked, and she never talked about it.

Margot and Walter liked Victor very much and, despite the age difference—Eva was sixteen and a half years old, while Victor was close to nineteen—they approved of the friendship. Once it became clear that this was more than a friendship, they counseled their daughter to be cautious and smart. Then they told her that they trusted her and believed that Victor was a fine young man. He was actually a very positive influence on Eva. When she told him that she had scored 40 on an IQ test, he said that was ridiculous because she was obviously very intelligent, and that her poor English language skills when she took the test, shortly after enrolling at the school, must have been the reason. That was very common in those days: very little thought was given to the connection between the test taker's skill in the language in which the test was administered and his or her score on that kind of test. Margot and Walter, who knew about Eva's low score, never considered pointing out to school officials that Eva's English language deficits may have been a factor. They had grown up in a culture and during a period of time in which education and educators were revered. They would never have even thought about questioning teachers or administrators in reference to Eva's score, or any other academic issues, for that matter.

Victor was not constrained by those traditional sentiments. At the beginning of the new school year, he told Eva that despite her low IQ score she should take academic classes, and not the home economics courses for which she was scheduled; he insisted that she should prepare for college, something that she had never considered. When Eva tearfully said that she was too uncomfortable and anxious to approach the counselor, Victor went to the high school and insisted that her schedule be changed to one that would prepare her for college.

That year, Eva excelled in all of her academic classes, including English Language Arts. In fact, she won first prize in the school's essay contest, writing on the topic "Speaking for Democracy." Shortly after a news article about the contest and a photograph of Eva appeared in the local newspaper, she was invited by the Middletown radio station to read her essay on air during one of its weekly programs.

Her essay, which was greatly influenced by what her parents had repeatedly told her, reads, in part, as follows:

> ... I have more than I have ever known before. For today, I walk down a street and am not afraid of a policeman asking me for my passport. I go to a beautiful school. My parents will soon be able to vote for those whom they want to govern them. I do not have to fear speaking freely, nor do I have to hide or be ashamed of my religion. I read a newspaper which will, without fear, one day praise and the next day denounce something done by the president.
>
> In one year here in America, I have risen from a nothing, a slave to tyrannical rulers, to a human being with rights and dignity. It is because of this I can now have the pleasure to speak for democracy ...

The Middletown Chamber of Commerce, saying that they were proud of Eva's accomplishment, presented her with a portable radio. She was pleased with her achievement, as were her parents and Ron. The words and themes of her essay caused Margot and Walter to marvel, yet again, at the magnificence of their new home, their land of endless possibilities, America.

At the beginning of 1955, Walter and Margot decided that they could afford to move to a larger, more comfortable apartment, so, after a short search, they signed a lease for a three bedroom second floor apartment in a two-family house at 26 Lake Avenue. It had a spacious living room, a dining room, and a sunny, modern kitchen with, of all things American, a dishwasher. They moved on February 1, 1955, just a few days before Ron turned 15. Margot and Walter were happy and proud. Ronnie and Eva were even more delighted because, for the first time in their lives, they did not have to share a bedroom. The only gloom on this chilly but sunny new day involved the fact that, for reasons she never explained, Eva's relationship with Victor had ended. Although she smiled in an attempt to appear happy and unconcerned, her parents and Ron knew that she was grieving.

Just two months after they had relocated, Margot told her children—to their great (and embarrassed) surprise—that she was pregnant. She sadly stated that she was worried that they would not be able to support another child, especially since she would have to take a leave from her job. She asked Walter, Eva, and Ron what they thought she should do. Without hesitation, they unanimously agreed that they wanted her to have the baby and said that they would willingly work more and spend less to make sure there was enough money.

On November 2, 1955, almost exactly nine months after they had moved, 15 years after Ronnie had come into the world, and 17 years after Eva had been born, Margot gave birth to a girl. She and Walter named their American-born daughter Susan Janie. Margot said she had always liked the name Susan and had chosen "Janie" in memory of her own mother, Jenny. As soon as Eva and Ron saw the tiny bundle in their mother's arms, they fell in love with her. Since they were so much older than their baby sister, they—especially Eva—quite naturally took on the role of parents, her second, more playful set of parents.

Ron and Eva took turns holding and admiring the beautiful

infant, who was wrapped securely in a soft pink blanket. Their proud, happy father looked on, taking great comfort in the fact that this child would never experience the cold, dark trauma of having to run or be hidden away because of her heritage and religion. She would never have to be dragged from one country to another and another, always an outsider, perpetually seeking safe haven and acceptance. No. This child, Susan Janie, would call only the United States home. She was a natural-born *American* Jew; that was a proud, durable identity and a birthright that could never be denied her.

Due to the fact that Margot had taken a leave from her job right before she gave birth and was not yet ready to resume working, the Isaacsons had just enough income to make ends meet. Ron worked diligently at his part-time jobs and Eva began working at the local newspaper, *The Record*. An additional problem that they faced involved the time they all spent traveling to and from school, jobs, doctor appointments, and other places due to the fact that they either walked or had to rely on spotty public transportation. After giving the matter a great deal of thought, Ron decided to use $400, money that he had saved from his various jobs—which his parents had told him to keep for the future—to buy a car for the family. The used black Pontiac that he bought was the first car the Isaacsons had ever owned. Walter, Margot, and Eva passed their written and road tests on their first attempts; Ron was one year too young for a permit.

One month later, after a few slow, deliberate drives through the neighborhood, Walter nervously drove the family to Manhattan so that they could visit Helmut and Flora Isaacson. As he tensely moved the car at a snail's pace along suburban roads and highways from New York to New Jersey and across the George Washington Bridge into New York City and then along the busy city streets, Margot, Eva, and Ron enjoyed themselves immensely and felt that they had ... arrived, that they could finally say they belonged. After all, what is more American than owning a car and having the freedom to travel from town to town and state to state?

Even though Margot knew that the borders between states were as inconsequential as the breeze and that people did not have to ask for permission to cross from one to another or show identification to an armed guard, she still marveled. That was just another wonderful aspect of the freedom that they all had begun to take for granted in America.

The car gave Margot the ability to return to work at Classy Leather Goods because now she was able to drop Susan off in the morning at a babysitter's house far from home and still make it to the office on time. That is not to say that she felt good about leaving her baby with the woman—who was reliable and kind. In fact, the thought of Susan spending the day with someone else made Margot quite unhappy, but the family needed the money that she earned.

Ronnie took a part-time job as an usher at the Paramount, the only theater in Middletown. When the manager asked whether he knew someone who might want to work as a cashier from 6 p.m. until 10 p.m. on a regular basis, Ron told the man that he would ask his mother. Margot jumped at the chance. The next day, after she had landed the new job, she handed in her notice at Classy Leather Goods. Even though she earned less money as a cashier than she had in the office at Classy Leather Goods, working this new job allowed her to spend the entire day with Susan; in addition, she no longer needed to pay a baby sitter. Eva and Ron arranged their work schedules so that one of them was always available to watch their little sister while their mother worked at the theater. As a bonus, the owner of the theater gave free passes to Margot. That made it possible for the family to see dozens of wonderful films—something they had previously done only on very rare occasions—such as "The Ten Commandments," "Ben Hur," "The Court Jester," and the incomparable classic "Gone With the Wind." Just sitting in the darkened movie theater, regardless of what was projected on the big screen, provided the four of them with a warm sense of excitement and pleasure.

During the four and a half years that Margot worked at the Paramount she attended Orange County Community College one night each week. She devoted a great deal of time during the day, as well as some evenings after she returned from work, to intensive studying. She labored for hours on each of the papers that she had to submit. She began by writing a draft copy by hand, checking her sources and references as she worked; after she had proofread and corrected the entire manuscript, she sat at her typewriter and, concentrating mightily, produced her final version. Since Margot had become a skilled typist, she rarely needed to retype any portion of her papers.

Margot hoped that once she had earned a college degree she would be able to obtain a much better job, perhaps as a teacher. Even though she knew that she would not be able to apply for that kind of job until Susan began attending school, Margot smiled as she thought about the future. To her way of thinking, a teaching position was high on the ladder of success and would allow her to earn a respectable income, which would help her family to prosper.

SIXTEEN

Dwelling in the Here and Now

In early 1956, Eva happily informed her parents and her brother that Victor Mallenbaum had called her and that they had talked for a long time via telephone. Over the next few weeks, she and Victor renewed their friendship, which quickly evolved into a very serious relationship. A few months later, right before Passover, Victor proposed marriage to Eva. She immediately and blissfully said yes. Since Eva had just turned 18, her parents suggested that she and Victor agree to a long period of engagement. Eva, looking thoughtful, said that they would think about it. A week later, Victor, accompanied by his father, his brother, and his brother's wife, visited the Isaacsons. Although they were from different backgrounds—the Mallenbaums were American-born Jews who observed Orthodox traditions, while the Isaacson were German-born and not religiously observant—the two families got along well and spent a long delightful afternoon sharing their stories and growing close to each other.

During the next few months, each time Walter and Margot picked up Eva at the train station in Middletown after one of her weekend visits to New York City, where Victor lived with his family, they hoped she would tell them that she and her fiancé had decided to put off the wedding for a couple of years, or at least until she had completed high school.[27] However, the young people were too much in love to wait another year. On January 27, 1957, four weeks before Eva turned 19, she and Victor Mallenbaum, with only a few family members and friends present, were married. After a small reception, they moved into a furnished apartment in Brighton Beach, Brooklyn.

Since Victor had grown up in an observant household, Eva had

---

[27] See Footnote # 25.

to learn how to maintain a kosher home, which involved, among other obligations, using one set of dishes, utensils, etc. for meat meals and another one for dairy (non-meat) meals and buying food that was certified kosher. Eva worked in an office during the day and completed high school at night, while Victor pursued his rabbinical studies.

During the two winters that Margot and Walter had lived in their roomy apartment on Lake Avenue, they had repeatedly complained to their landlord that it was always a bit chilly. No matter how much they implored the man, he never provided them with what they considered to be a sufficient amount of heat. After all they had been through, Margot, Walter, and Ron had learned how to adapt to unpleasant situations, in this case, by wearing sweaters when they were in the house during cold weather. However, their little Susie had been sick over and over again during each of those two winters. Margot and Walter, convinced that was due to the low temperature in the apartment, decided they had to find a new place in which to live. After a brief search, they found an attractive, modern first-floor apartment with a backyard that they would be allowed to use. A major attraction was that the apartment contained its own thermostat, which the new landlord showed them how to use.

Walter and Margot signed a lease and gave the new landlord a security deposit, after which they notified the owner of their old apartment of their intention to move. Before they vacated on March 15, 1957, they paid the man rent up to that date, not understanding that they were obligated to pay for the remaining time on the lease or until he found a new tenant. A few weeks after they relocated, they received an official notice to appear in municipal court; the former landlord had filed suit for the remainder of the rent due to him until the date of the expiration of the old lease. Walter and Margot thought that they probably should pay what the landlord said they owed, but that would have amounted to a great deal of money. In addition, they were upset that he had never provided sufficient heat, which was why they had to move, and that he had filed suit, rather than informing them that they owed the money. For those reasons, they hired an attorney, Jane Gilman, to contest the lawsuit. In court, Ms. Gilman contended that the Isaacsons had moved because the lack of heat in the old apartment had made it impossible for them to live there. She called Dr. Romain, Susie's pediatrician, to testify. He stated that he had made several house calls to the old apartment during each of the past two winters, and that each time he had been there the rooms had been uncomfortably cold. He then explained that the low temperature in the apartment had caused the baby to become ill. After listening to both sides, the judge ruled against the Isaacsons.

The attorney advised Margot and Walter not to pay the amount owed, saying that she would file a motion. A few weeks later, when Walter saw that his paycheck was less than he had expected it to be, he asked the bookkeeper at Classy Leather Goods about it. She explained that his pay was being garnished because of a court order. The next day, Margot, outraged, went to the courthouse, where she was told that their attorney, Jane Gilman, had missed the hearing regarding the motion that she had filed; for that reason, the judge had ruled that the former landlord could apply to have Walter's paychecks garnished until all of the rent money owed had been paid.

Other than that annoying, expensive financial setback, for the next few years, life for the Isaacsons seemed to take place under sunny skies and peaceful moonlit nights. Walter and Margot were both employed and satisfied with their jobs; Eva and Victor were happily married and very busy; Susie had grown into a beautiful, happy toddler who, while she kept everybody on their toes, was quite obedient; and Ron was doing well in school and dutifully working his part-time and summer jobs. During his junior year in high school, Ron joined the Naval Reserve, traveling to the Naval Training Facility in Newburgh, New York one weekend each month for classes. In August 1958, Ron traveled by bus for 18 hours to Great Lakes Naval Station in Illinois for boot camp, an experience he thoroughly enjoyed. He said that he looked forward to active duty in the Navy at some point in the future.

Two exceptional events occurred toward the end of that year. The first one, which was characterized by the conflicting emotions of boundless joy and echoing sadness, involved a visit by Margot's sister Ruth, her husband, and their twin boys. Once the sisters, who had not seen each other since 1947, had desperately embraced for a full minute and drenched each other's faces with rivulets of tears, they pulled away and laughed. The two families spent a happy week together. Parting was painful, but Margot and Ruth promised they would not allow so much time to elapse before they saw each other again.

Just a few weeks after Ruth and her family had returned to the United Kingdom, Margot received a letter from her sister in which she said that they had decided to emigrate to Australia.

The other great occurrence that year was marked by absolute pleasure and unrestrained feelings of pride and exultation. On a bright, chilly day in December of 1958 that they would always think of as one of the most satisfying and thrilling of their lives, Walter, Margot, Eva, and Ron became United States citizens.

As proud and delighted as Ron and Eva were, this life-changing event was of even greater significance to their parents. Margot shivered and Walter frowned as they whispered about the harrowing, dark years in Germany once the Nazis had come to power. That had brought to an abrupt end a wonderful, sunny period of their lives and ushered in a bleak, all-too-real nightmare. Once more, they talked about how dismal and downcast they and their parents had been when they read about the Nuremburg Laws; they shook their heads sadly as they made mention of the signs on store fronts and on street corners that warned Jews to stay away; and then they started to, and then they stopped reciting the names of "friends" who had coldly and abruptly abandoned them because it was "inappropriate" for them to continue to associate with Jews. They remembered the horrors of *Kristallnacht*, which was followed by deceitful government radio broadcasts that blamed the Jews for the nationwide pogrom; then Walter and many others had been taken away, and ... then so much more happened, but they did not want to dwell on the wretched past. They knew they could not pretend it never happened. It had been one of the defining times of their lives. How could they push out of their minds Walter's long internment in Dachau and then Gurs or their constant, choking fear that the Gestapo would pound on their door and take them away or the miserable 14 months they had spent sleeping in cellars at night and trying to be invisible during the day while their children were far from them, hidden—they hoped safely—in a convent?

Then, emotionally spent and limp because of the cold, gloomy, painful memories that they had dredged up, Margot and Walter just stopped. They sat silently at their kitchen table and reverently moved their fingers over their certificates of naturalization. Those fragile paper documents were not just proof that they were American citizens; they were emblems of their new life.

As a means of confirming the fact that he was also beginning a new, very different life, when Ronnie had filled out the application for naturalization, he had written "Ronnie Rudolf Isaacson," the name that he had been using since shortly after the family had moved to Middletown, and not René Rudolf Isaacson, which was a vestige of his former, now defunct identity. Just as with his mother and father, Ron held official documents in high regard. This glorious one, his naturalization certificate, was tangible, undeniable proof and a testament to the fact that he was now an American, and proud of it.

By this time, Margot and Walter had finally begun to receive small reparations payments from the government of West Germany.[28] This was due to a law that had gone into effect in 1952. They had applied

---

[28] And then, beginning in 1990, from the newly reunited country, which was renamed the Federal Republic of Germany.

147

shortly after the program had been announced, but bureaucratic red tape had delayed their payments. Their compensation payments were intended to make amends for their suffering and because of the fact that Margot had lost both parents and Walter had lost his father in the death camps of the Third Reich.

They used some of that money as a down payment on their first house, a small, rather ancient two-story model in a lovely neighborhood in Middletown. The first floor contained a living room, a dining room, and an antiquated kitchen; the second floor held three bedrooms and a tiny, old-fashioned bathroom. One nice feature of the house was its front porch, complete with rocking chairs. Despite its many poor qualities, the Isaacsons were proud of their home. They moved into the house at 24 Commonwealth Avenue at the beginning of April 1959.

During the summer of 1959, Victor and Eva returned home from a six-month stay in Israel. Of course, the Isaacsons, all of whom had missed the couple, gave them a joyous welcome. Victor, who had to complete one more year of rabbinical study before he could be ordained, found summer work, along with Ron, as a waiter at Brookside, a small boarding house in Middletown.

During the next year, 1960, the Isaacson and Mallenbaum families celebrated two significant and joyful events: Victor was ordained a rabbi and almost immediately obtained a position in Milford, Connecticut and Eva gave birth to a boy who she and her husband named Sidney. Margot and Walter were delighted with Victor's accomplishment, especially since it meant that he would be earning a fairly good income in the prestigious position of rabbi. They were pleased that Eva would have an easier life because of her husband's position. Even though Margot and Walter considered themselves secular/cultural Jews who celebrated only the major holidays, worked, drove their car, and went to the movies on the Sabbath, and did not keep a kosher home, they respected Victor's piety and his observance of traditional Jewish laws.

As is to be expected, more than Victor's success, the birth of their first grandchild filled Margot and Walter with an instinctive, overwhelmingly cheery warmth, a powerful surge of joy and feeling of renewal the likes of which neither of them remembered ever having experienced. They knew that this child, Sidney, was going to be a source of great pride and *naches* (Yiddish for "joy and gratification") for his entire family, but his birth meant more than that. It was infinitely greater than a blessed event; it was an affirmation of the continuation of the life of their family, of Victor's family, and of the Jewish people.

That September, Susan started kindergarten. Margot missed her youngest child terribly during the few hours that she was at school each day. Then, after a week of loneliness, Margot decided to turn the situation upside down, and look for a job—ideally in an office—at which she would be able to work during those hours. Margot approached Ben Gilman, who was Jane Gilman's husband and law partner; the Isaacsons had kept in touch with the couple from the time of the lawsuit regarding the rent that they owed. After a few minutes of discussion, Ben hired Margot to work at his office for a few hours each afternoon. She liked her new part-time position, but she kept her evening cashier job at the Paramount.

In 1961, when Susan began first grade, Margot resigned from the movie theater job and began to work full time as a secretary for the principal of Memorial School in Middletown, which was a short distance from the Isaacsons' house. She was now earning more money than she had at any of her previous positions and working at a job that she thoroughly enjoyed each and every day.

SEVENTEEN

The United States Merchant Marine Academy

In the fall of 1958, during Ron's senior year of high school, he had applied to three United States service academies, hoping to be accepted by his first choice, the Naval Academy, or his second, the Coast Guard Academy. He was confident that his SAT scores in math met the grade for all three, but was concerned about his verbal ranking. Besides high test scores and good grades, a requirement for acceptance at a service academy is the written recommendation of a member of the United States Congress. A few weeks earlier, during a conversation with Ben Gilman, Margot had mentioned Ron's long-term goals and how he needed that letter of recommendation. Ben said that he was a close friend of Katherine St. George, the Congressional representative from their district.[29] He arranged for Ron to meet Representative St. George, who, without hesitation, drafted a letter of recommendation for him.

Late one sweltering afternoon the following summer, as Ron walked into the house, his mother handed an official-looking letter to him. It was from the United States Merchant Marine Academy. He tore it open and, in great excitement, read that he had been accepted for admission. Even though it was his third choice, Ron was delighted and immensely proud. For the next hour, he sat in the kitchen and listened as his mother called dozens of friends and relatives to inform them of the wonderful news. In addition to being proud, his parents were overjoyed and relieved to know that their son would receive an excellent education at virtually no cost, become a U.S. Coast Guard-licensed marine engineer, and earn a bachelor of science degree in marine engineering.

Ron entered the United States Merchant Marine Academy at

---

[29] She was also a cousin of the late President Franklin Delano Roosevelt.

Kings Point, New York—which is on the north shore of Long Island—in July of 1959, a month after graduating from high school. That was the beginning of a very demanding, but rewarding year. Ron, who was used to being independent and making his own decisions, at first found it difficult to follow the dozens of rules and regulations of the Academy, but he was obedient and highly motivated.

First-year students, known as plebes, were forbidden to leave the Academy grounds until the Thanksgiving break. Although Ron would have liked to visit his family during those first few months, he understood the culture of the Academy and knew that he had to accept the rules. Deciding that he was not only going to do well in his classes, but fully immerse himself in life at the Academy, he tried out for the school varsity soccer team, and was accepted.[30]

Ron enjoyed playing soccer and, as an added benefit, was able to leave the campus during those first few months when the team participated in away-games. One game in 1960 in particular—against the fearsome SUNY Maritime College at Fort Schuyler, located in the northeast Bronx at Throggs Neck, where the East River meets Long Island Sound—maintains a place of honor in Ron's memory. Playing right wing striker, Ron scored the winning goal and was carried on the shoulders of his teammates at the end of the game as they shouted, "Yay, Ike!" "Ike" became his nickname for the rest of his time at the Academy. Besides the fact that having a nickname assigned to him allowed Ron to feel accepted and liked, he was proud of the appellation because he revered President Dwight David Eisenhower, who was known as Ike.

Ron loved the Academy and was proud to be in attendance. For that reason he put a lot of effort into acclimating himself to the school's

---

[30] He had been on the varsity team in Middletown High School, developing friendships with teammates that would last for many years. Paul Vignola was Ron's best friend for decades after they had graduated from high school. When Ron attended his 25th class reunion, he was thrilled to see some of his old friends again, such as John Howell, Bob Krivicich, Sal Martinez, Tom Clark, and Jan Decker.

military-style culture, which included being monitored by upperclassmen. One of the responsibilities of the upperclassmen was to teach the plebes to be obedient and to respect rank and seniority. In order to do that, they regularly approached plebes as they walked through campus; after stopping them and staring malevolently at them, one of the upperclassmen would demand, "Plebe candidate, what is the mission of the United States Merchant Marine Academy?"

The plebe had to give the expected reply:

Sir, the mission of the United States Merchant Marine Academy is to graduate outstanding young Americans with definite ambitions to serve as leaders in the United States maritime industry, to impart to them the necessary academic background and fundamentals of a nautical and military education essential for a successful maritime career, and through effective teaching, training, and guidance, to send them forth to their calling with a deep respect and affection for the United States Merchant Marine Academy and its corps, sir!

Plebes were also regularly stopped and commanded to recite the honor code and the school motto. At other times, they were instructed to describe the specifics of the Academy flagpole and the base on which it rested. They were required to state, among other details, the latitude and longitude of the pole and the fact that it is 172 feet tall and topped by a sculpted eagle. Plebes who did not provide the correct answers to a variety of questions, most of which involved Academy minutiae, were issued demerits. In addition, failing to walk in the prescribed military manner (chin down, alongside the nearest walls, and turning square corners), failing to salute upperclassmen, and not maintaining one's room or/and uniform according to the written and unwritten rules of the Academy were among the infractions that could cause a plebe to be written up and given demerits. Those who accumulated a certain number of demerits during the term were assigned to unpleasant cleaning details. Ron made sure to follow all of the rules and not suffer the fate of some of his classmates who, either due to laziness or defiance, racked up demerits.

Ron was surprised to learn that he and two other men, Barry Rosenberg from Hartford, Connecticut, and Barry Deutsch from Far Rockaway, New York, were the only Jews among 326 plebes. Out of more than 1,200 cadets in the Academy that year, only 10 were Jewish.

Ron was assigned to 4th Company in Rogers Hall. His roommate was a young man from the midwest who was, from the start, cold and astonishingly unfriendly toward Ron. He ignored each of Ron's attempts at conversation by turning away from him. Ron had heard other plebes complaining that the man was chronically aloof. Knowing that they would be sharing a room for at least the rest of the year, Ron attempted to be cordial to the man. However, while his roommate simply kept his distance from the others in his class, he made it clear that he intensely disliked Ron.

The man had the upper bunk and Ron had the lower one. At around 6 a.m. one morning, upon awakening, Ron saw that the door to the room was ajar and, while the door to his locker was closed, his combination lock appeared to be open. At first, Ron assumed that he had forgotten to lock it the night before, but when he opened the locker door he saw that a crude, jagged swastika had been scrawled with black marker onto the surface of the small mirror that he used during shaving. Once Ron got over his shock, he knew that his unfriendly roommate had to have been the perpetrator of the vile act; somehow, the man had learned the combination to the lock. Instantly hot and furious, Ron's instincts and hormones took over: he scrambled up the steel ladder to his roommate's bunk, jostled him awake, and, when the man sneered at him, Ron punched him on his jaw over and over again, each blow squarely hitting its mark. Then Ron stopped. Still standing on the ladder, he looked at the startled, injured man and called him a "Nazi bastard." The stunned man held his face with one hand and kept the other one up to fend off any additional punches. He did not ask Ron why he had attacked him. Ron, keeping his hands on the ladder now, told the man that he was going to report him to Captain H.O. Travis, the rigid, demanding, universally feared regimental commanding officer, but even as he said that, Ron knew that he would not tell anyone. Besides the fact that Ron was sure that would lead to his being expelled from the Academy for fighting, he did not want to report the man. It was not sympathy for his roommate that held Ron back, but a sense that he had defeated the man and that he was now in a position of power over him, one that would be diluted if he called anyone else's attention to the anti-Semitic act. *Besides*, Ron wondered, *would anyone do anything?* How much understanding would any commanding officer have in reference to this incident? Perhaps he would think of this act of vandalism as just a type of hazing, a kind of prank that should be ignored.

Later, when Ron thought about the episode, he remembered that as he was pummeling his roommate, a couple of upperclassmen had looked into the room through the open doorway. Ron had seen the men out of the corner of an eye, but he had been so intent on punching the man that he had not thought about how they were witnesses; at that moment, those men had been incidental. Later, he worried that they would report the tussle. When a few days passed and it was clear that neither the witnesses nor the roommate had reported what had occurred, Ron began to relax.

With time, Ron came to believe that his roommate, who was from a rural area in the midwest, had probably never seen a Jew before. Whatever the young man had learned or heard about Jews, along with Ron's slight trace of a foreign accent, was likely what motivated him to develop such deep loathing for his roommate that he scrawled the swastika on the mirror. The man never talked about the pummeling that he had received, which made Ron all the more sure that he had committed the act of vandalism.

That first year, besides dedicating himself to his studies and to soccer, Ron fell in love. He had not been looking for a girlfriend or even a date. In fact, he had been in search of something else on that Friday night when he met a young woman whose face and voice and essence captivated him and warmed him to his very core.

It was October 16, 1959. Even though Ron had never felt much in terms of religious devotion, he decided to attend the Friday night service and *oneg shabbat*[31] held at the Academy chapel. As one of only 10 Jewish cadets, Ron found himself, for the first time in his life, interested in embracing his religious heritage. He had always found it grimly ironic that even though his parents, Eva, and he had been persecuted by the Nazis for their Jewish heritage and three of his grandparents had been murdered by agents of the Third Reich, no one in his family had ever been devout. (Of course, now that Eva was married to a rabbi she was living the life of an observant Jew.) Perhaps because he was one of a very small minority on campus and because he was a bit homesick Ron wanted to do something that made him feel Jewish—connected to other Jews—even if it was only to attend an occasional synagogue service ... and enjoy the sandwiches and cookies provided at its conclusion.

Later, Ron was grateful for the fact that he arrived a few minutes late to the service, which was sponsored by Temple Beth El of Great Neck, the town in which the Academy is located. When he walked into the chapel, he saw that two seats next to a few of the other Jewish cadets in attendance were available; he sat on the one closer to the other fellows. Then, as he looked toward the *bimah* (altar) at the front of the chapel, Ron saw that a young woman was reciting the traditional Hebrew blessings over the candles. Finding her very attractive, he focused on her face and on her lovely, melodious voice. When she had concluded the blessings, she smiled, and then she made her way from the *bimah* to her seat, which happened to be the vacant one on the other side of Ron. At first, flustered, he stared straight ahead and did not acknowledge the woman. Then,

---

[31] A gathering with refreshments following a Friday night Sabbath service.

realizing that he was being rude and because he wanted to get a good look at her, Ron said hello and whispered that he had enjoyed her recitation of the blessing. They exchanged pleasantries, but when Ron sensed that she was uncomfortable to be talking during the service, he smiled and turned away from her.

Once the service ended, Ron accompanied the young lady, whose name was Lucy Deborah Wachter, to the table holding sandwiches, cookies, coffee, and wine. As they ate and drank, Lucy told Ron that she lived in town and was a senior at Great Neck North High School. She said that Great Neck was a wonderful place in which to live and that it was (and still is) predominantly Jewish. Then Lucy explained that she and her family belonged to a local conservative synagogue and that this had been the first time she had ever attended a Jewish service at the USMMA chapel. She added that she had agreed to come because her best friend, Bonnie Geller, whose father was the Academy physician, had invited her.

Lucy said that she found Ron's trace of an accent intriguing. She listened with great interest and sympathy to his story of his parents' life in Germany and the difficult years that the family had spent in Belgium. He told her a bit about his time in Europe after the war and how challenging life in Bolivia had been. In turn, Lucy said that she had just returned from a wonderful trip to Israel and parts of Europe. Then she added that she had met a boy while she had been in Israel, but that relationship had ended before she left for home. At that point, Lucy, looking at her wristwatch, said that she had to leave. Ron, who had known that she would have to go home soon, suddenly felt anxious because he wanted to talk to her for a while longer. With the words catching in his throat, he asked whether he would be able to speak with her on the telephone from time to time. After hesitating for a moment, Lucy gave Ron her number. Then, explaining that he did not have much spending money, Ron asked Lucy whether she would be willing to call the pay phone in his dormitory and ask for him. After pausing for a few seconds, Lucy frowned and said that it would not be proper for her to do that, explaining that she believed boys, and not girls, should be the ones calling. Thinking quickly, Ron proposed a solution to the dilemma: he would call her and then hang up after three rings, at which point she would call him. Lucy agreed to that, and he gave her the number.

After Lucy and her friend left, Ron returned to his dormitory. Lying on his bed, he thought about the evening ... and, with his heart beating rapidly and blood rushing to his face, he pictured Lucy. Ron thought Lucy had liked him, but he was not sure. Of course, she may have just been acting friendly to an obviously lonely, homesick young man. It did not matter. He had enjoyed talking to her. At the very least, they could be telephone friends. Maybe he would see her at another Friday night service. Perhaps, once the three-month period had passed and Ron would be allowed to leave the Academy grounds, they would be able to go to a movie or for a bite to eat. Maybe, with time, the friendship would blossom and grow.

For the rest of that weekend, Ron tried to keep at bay thoughts of Lucy. He knew that he had to spend as much time as possible studying because even though he was attentive in all of his classes and always kept up with required readings, he was at a significant disadvantage in comparison to the other cadets: after only six years in the United States, even though Ron was fluent in terms of spoken English, he was deficient in his ability to comprehend complex textbook language and write competently in English. Each and every day, he devoted a gargantuan amount of time and energy to his studies—and he improved—but it was a struggle. Most of his grades were only fair; however, he excelled in calculus, chemistry, and Spanish, which, of course, he had spoken in Bolivia. Those grades enabled him to maintain a respectable grade point average. He had heard, over and over again, that the standards at the Academy were so high that, typically, only half of the entering students managed to graduate. He worried about that and sought to convince himself that, with hard work, he would succeed where others had failed.

Ron called Lucy's home number on Monday night, allowing the telephone to ring three times before hanging up. He waited by the wall phone in the dormitory hallway, nervously telling himself that she would not return the call. After all, why would she? What did he have to offer her? On the other hand, he thought ... he was pretty sure she had liked him. It was also possible, Ron reasoned, that Lucy was not home ... or maybe she had lost the paper on which he had written the phone number. Then he had a worrisome new thought: perhaps her mother or father, seeing Lucy attempting to make a phone call right after the three rings, would be suspicious and ask whether she knew who had called and then hung up. The seconds dragged on, pulling him down, as if he were sinking, drowning. He held his breath; he felt chilled and wet. As he stared at the phone, he waited, telling himself that she might not call. Turning his eyes from the phone, he looked around and then down the hall. Any second, another cadet might want to use the phone. Ron knew what he would do: he would hold the handset against his ear and, leaning against the wall and keeping his other hand on the wall phone, he would hold the button down. Of course, if Lucy were to call back while Ron was depressing the button, the cadet who was waiting to use the phone would know what he was doing. He thought he should not do that because it would be a dishonest trick. On the other hand—the strident jangling of the telephone shot through him. He was surprised; then he was surprised that he had been surprised because, after all, he had been waiting for the phone to ring. He picked up the handset and mumbled something—he was not sure what he said. It was Lucy. He was no longer sinking. He was pleased and felt comfortably warm and very content and buoyant. They talked for a long time that evening and then several more times during the week.

On Friday, Ron invited Lucy to the next Sunday Tea Dance. She said she would be there. When Lucy exited her car in the parking lot Ron, who had been waiting for her, decided that she looked even prettier than he remembered her to be. As they walked into the social hall, they chattered away as if they had been good friends for years. After Ron had introduced her to a few of his classmates, he asked her to dance. He was a fairly good dancer; Lucy was exceedingly graceful and nimble. His heart beat rapidly as they moved across the dance floor. Holding Lucy close, he sighed as he inhaled her fragrant warmth.

Later that night, as he lay in his bed with his eyes closed, Ron thought of Lucy and realized that he felt happier and more satisfied with his life now than he had since he had arrived at school.

One day that November, after a soccer match at a nearby college, Coach Barber granted liberty to the members of the team, with the understanding that they return to the campus by 10 p.m. Without even a nod to the other players, Ron ran to a phone booth and called Lucy. After explaining that he was free and able to stay out for a few hours, he said that he wanted to see her. Lucy said that she would like to see him but she was not sure she would be able to do so; in her role as the president of the local Junior Hadassah she had invited a guest speaker for that evening's meeting to dinner at her house, and he was sitting in her living room at that very moment talking with her parents. She knew she should tell Ron that she would not be able to meet him, but she did not want to do that. Of course, going out and leaving her guest was an irrational thing to do, but feelings for Ron had managed to find their way into her heart. After asking Ron to stay on the line, Lucy returned to the dining room, where, out of earshot of her guest, she explained the situation to her mother. Much to her relief, her mother told her go to, at which point Lucy apologized to her guest, saying that she had to run an errand. Then she picked up the keys to her parents' car and quickly walked out the door.

When Lucy met Ron a few minutes later, she was breathless with excitement, as was he. They talked for a short while in the car, and then Ron suggested that they drive to a park near the Academy. When they reached a dim, secluded spot, Lucy parked. After a few more minutes of small talk, Ron took Lucy's hand and held it. Then he kissed her. To his delight, she returned his warm expression of affection. For the next hour, they talked, kissed, and held each other. Then, telling Ron that she had to leave so as to make it back to the Hadassah meeting to introduce the guest speaker, Lucy drove him to the Academy entrance. When she returned to her house and opened the door, she was mortified to see that the meeting had already started.

Despite her great embarrassment, Lucy was pleased that she had spent some time alone with Ron and that they seemed to have come to an unspoken understanding about their relationship or, at least, about the direction it might take in the future.

Since Ron was not allowed to leave the Academy grounds until Thanksgiving, Lucy made the short drive from her house to the nearby campus once or twice each week. Sometimes they talked as they strolled along the leaf-strewn walkways; at other times, they sat in one of the common rooms, where Ron could not help but notice the envious stares of other cadets.

Ron's time at school moved along at a snail's pace until, finally, the Thanksgiving break was just around the corner. Sitting in his stark dormitory room, staring at the open textbook in front of him, Ron attempted to concentrate, but his head was filled with random thoughts. He smiled as he pictured his parents and his sisters. For a split second, he thought he could almost smell the savory aromas that would permeate the air of his mother's kitchen as she prepared the holiday meal. His face felt flushed and tingly as he imagined the cheery conversations and the laughter they would share at the dinner table. He knew his parents were exceedingly proud of his accomplishments and were looking forward to seeing him; he felt warm inside when he thought about being with them.

He always derived a deep-seated sense of satisfaction when he did things that pleased his parents. Their sacrifices during the years in Belgium and what he knew were scars on their souls were never far from his thoughts. Occasionally, over the years, when he and Eva were alone, they talked about that time in their lives. Eva said that she remembered dribs and drabs of their life in the convent. Ron had a cloudy memory of living there—particularly the sensation of having been abandoned. In addition, he had listened so attentively each time his parents and Eva made mention of his time at the convent that he was, at times, able to clearly picture himself there and then. He sometimes had hazy memories of smells from Miséricorde and of being hungry. They were not as discernible as the astonishingly wonderful Thanksgiving aromas that he could almost believe were languidly drifting into his nostrils as he sat at his desk in his dorm room at the Academy, but they were there, somewhere in the deepest, least accessible parts of his memory.

Accepting the fact that he was not in the proper frame of mind to study, Ron closed the book and thought of Lucy. Even though they had not actually spent much time together, he was beginning to believe that she was the one, the only one. He wanted to ask her to come with him to Middletown for the Thanksgiving weekend. Besides the fact that they would have four wonderful days together, he wanted his family to meet her. When he called Lucy's house—he did not follow the usual procedure of calling, letting the phone ring three times, and then hanging up—and asked her to go to Middletown with him for Thanksgiving, she said she wanted to, but would have to clear it with her parents. They talked on the phone for a while. He told her what he was studying and she talked about her plans for college. He hesitantly said that he had been spending a great deal of time thinking about her. Lucy, who was less reserved in terms of revealing her feelings, said that she was pleased and that she thought about him sometimes.

Later that evening, Lucy called the telephone in the dormitory, and when someone picked up, she asked for Ron. When Ron got on the line, she happily announced that, after a long, serious discussion with her parents, they had agreed to allow her to travel to Middletown with him for the Thanksgiving break. She said that, at first, they had been taken aback to hear that Ron had invited her to visit his home. They were not concerned about their 17-year-old daughter keeping company with a man who was two years older than she was or the fact that she would be sleeping under the same roof as him—they trusted Lucy's good sense and moral character—but they feared that the relationship was moving too quickly. Lucy did not tell Ron that they expressed the opinion that she could do better than become serious about a young man from what appeared to be a relatively poor background. In the end, despite the fact that Ron was not their first choice for Lucy, they had given her permission to go to Middletown with him.

During their four days together, Ron and Lucy took long walks during which they talked non-stop, held hands, and used every moment that they were alone to kiss. As they traveled around Middletown, Ron showed her the sights. He also proudly introduced her to several of his former high school soccer teammates.

There was one sour note: although Ron's parents were polite and gracious and repeatedly told Lucy that they hoped she felt welcome in their little home, she could not help but believe that they did not approve of her. When she told Ron that they seemed to be kind of stiff and distant, he said that was just their way. After all, she was the first girl he had ever brought to meet them and they were not sure how to act. In truth, ironically, Walter and Margot felt just as Lucy's parents did: that Ron and Lucy were from different worlds and would never be happy together. When Ron had first breathlessly told his mother and father about the astonishing young woman from Great Neck who had captured his heart, they sighed and then, in sad, dark tones, said that a girl like that, from an affluent family, was surely used to the finer things in life, things that Ron would never be able to provide for her. They counseled him against continuing the relationship because, at some point, she might decide that Ron was not able to meet her expectations. Ron, who had grown up respecting his parents and deferring to their opinions and dictates, knew that they were mistaken this time. He said that not only was Lucy not overindulged or pampered, but she was the most genuinely down-to-earth and even-tempered girl he had ever known. He resolutely repeated that he wanted to bring her home with him for Thanksgiving. Despite their grave misgivings and apprehension regarding Ron's relationship with the young woman, they had acceded to his wishes.

Before the weekend was over, Ron, who had never felt this strongly about a girl before, asked Lucy to go steady with him. She smiled, shook her head, and said yes.

The next few weeks at school, as his first term at the Academy was coming to an end, were busy and stressful for Ron. He applied himself with increased vigor to his studies and managed to pass all of his courses with reasonably good grades.

At the end of the day on December 23, the cadets were granted the traditional Christmas leave. As they jubilantly cheered their way off the campus, Ron proudly fixed in his mind the day and time during the break that he would have to return for special duty. Since Ron did not celebrate Christmas, he, along with a few other Jewish cadets had volunteered to take 12-hour watches over the Academy's complicated steam boiler system, which required 24-hour surveillance; this would free the maintenance staff from having to perform the task during the holiday. Ron had been told that his job would be to monitor and then record temperature and pressure readings into a log book to ensure that fuel was being efficiently fed to the boilers and that steam was flowing at the correct pressure to all of the buildings on campus.

Early in the evening of Christmas day, Ron, who was pleased and excited to be fulfilling this important responsibility, traveled by bus from Middletown to the Port Authority Bus Terminal in Manhattan, at which point he walked to Penn Station to board a Long Island Railroad (LIRR) train to Great Neck, and then he got on a local bus to the

Academy. As he eagerly walked into the boiler room after his four-hour trip, he was shocked to hear the cadet on duty sourly ask, "Where the hell were you?" Looking at his watch, Ron said that he was not late, explaining that he had been told to report right before midnight on Christmas Eve to relieve the cadet who had been assigned to fill the previous 12-hour shift. The man told Ron that he was late by exactly 24 hours. He added that the cadet who had been expecting Ron to relieve him the night before had been forced to remain on duty for Ron's shift, meaning that he had kept watch for 24 hours straight. Now Ron was perplexed. Why had that other cadet expected him the night before? Ron was sure he had been instructed to report a few minutes before midnight on Christmas Eve.

As Ron was pondering that question, the young man who had been talking to him was relieved by another cadet. Ron watched the first cadet gather his belongings and exit the building. Feeling deflated, baffled, and agitated, Ron followed in the footsteps of the cadet. It was not until he was on the local bus back to the LIRR station that Ron, with his head pounding as if he had been struck by lightning, overheard a conversation that explained what Ron had done wrong: he heard a man tell another person what he and his family had done on Christmas Eve—the night before! Since Ron had never celebrated Christmas or ever paid much attention to it, he had thought that Christmas Eve was the evening of Christmas day, December 25. Only now did he understand that he should have reported for duty for his 12-hour shift right before midnight on December 24, the previous evening.

Besides feeling stupid and utterly ashamed, Ron felt guilty about the cadet who had been forced to endure a 24-hour watch. Then it hit him: his dereliction of duty would result in official censure or some other repercussion. As he looked out the window of the bus, he began to feel numb; his head spun and his stomach churned as he thought about the dreadful fallout coming his way.

When Ron returned to the campus at the end of what had been a tense, depressing break from school during which his brain had been held captive by sharp-edged thoughts of what punishment he would suffer, he was immediately summoned to the office of the regimental commanding officer, the fearsome and unapproachable Captain H.O. Travis. The always impressive commander coldly informed Ron that due to his shameful dereliction of duty, his utter disregard for his assignment, and his obvious lack of respect for his fellow cadets, he was now on probation and restricted to Academy grounds until further notice. As if that were not dreadful enough, Captain Travis informed Ron that he would be required to appear at a formal disciplinary hearing that was scheduled for the following week. An official letter regarding the charges against him, as well as the range of penalties, including possible dismissal from the Merchant Marine Academy, had been mailed to Ron's home.

Ron's mother, upon reading the letter and after speaking via telephone to her son, rekindled the long-dormant fire that had blazed in her soul during the dangerous years, first in Germany and then in Belgium. That passion for survival had helped Margot to do whatever was necessary to protect her children and to save her husband. They had all suffered years of indignity, pain, dislocation, and gnawing, ever-present dread. Now that they were living in the sunshine of the United States and had all worked so hard, she was not going to allow her son to be expelled from the Academy, especially since his error had been caused by his lack of understanding regarding a holiday about which he knew very little. Once more, she would do whatever she had to do to protect her family. She called the Academy and requested permission to attend the hearing.

Margot took off from work on the day in January 1960 on which the hearing had been scheduled and drove to Kings Point. She was ushered into Captain Travis's office and sat on one of the hard wooden chairs. With Ron sitting nervously a few feet away from her, Margot listened to the captain's recitation of the charges against her son. When he concluded, the cadet who had been forced to cover Ron's shift spoke. Then, looking at Ron, Captain Travis asked whether he wanted to testify. Ron stood up, cleared his throat, and said that he had, indeed, not shown up for duty at the appointed time, and he apologized. Then he said that he had misunderstood the day on which he had been told to report. As Ron sat down, Captain Travis continued to look at him. It was clear that he did not believe Ron's explanation about why he had not fulfilled his duty.

Then Margot asked whether she might testify. Captain Travis said that she would be allowed to speak only if she had information pertinent to the incident. She said that she did. Standing up, Margot introduced herself. Then she explained that Ron had not ignored his responsibilities. He had, in fact, repeatedly told her and her husband how proud and pleased he was to have been assigned the important task of monitoring the Academy heating system. Although she was respectful and exceedingly polite as she spoke, she was not the least bit intimidated by the formidable regimental commanding officer. Looking him straight in the eye, she went on to tell how from the moment Ron had gotten up that morning until the time he left the house to travel to Kings Point he had beamed like sunshine with pleasure and anticipation and had been so excited that he checked his watch over and over again. Then, smiling gently, as if she was about to explain a difficult concept to a child, she told Captain Travis that he surely understood that not all people celebrate Christmas; after all, that is why the Jewish cadets had been willing to take the 12-hour shifts to monitor the heating system during that holiday. At that point, in her unhurried, heavily accented English, she said that just as the captain probably did not know that Jewish holidays always begin at sundown, Ron had not known that Christmas Eve was the night *before* Christmas. Then, softening a bit, she said that Ron's so-called dereliction of duty had been due to his lack of understanding of a Christian concept, the time that Christmas began. She concluded by imploring Captain Travis to allow Ron, who had an unblemished record, to remain at the Academy.

Captain Travis was clearly impressed by the articulate and well reasoned explanation given by this obviously fearless, loving mother. After a moment's reflection during which he stared gravely at Ron, he presented a short narration regarding what was expected of cadets in terms of carrying out responsibilities. Then he wrote on a yellow legal pad for a full minute. When he had concluded that task, the captain, focusing on Ron, said that he would not call for his expulsion. However, he continued, Ron would be restricted to the grounds of the Academy for the next three months and would be assigned extra work details in order to reduce the demerits that he had accumulated as a result of his not having discharged the duty that had been assigned to him. Margot nodded and Ron, greatly relieved, thanked the captain.

Ron intensely disliked the duty assigned to him, which involved cleaning rooms, raking the school grounds, and emptying waste containers, but not because the work was hard. What preyed upon his mind was that it was punishment duty. Each day, over and over again during his three-month period of restriction, Ron thought about the error that had gotten him into this situation. He did not do that to chastise himself. In fact, he brought to mind the mistake he had made on that fateful night for the opposite reason: he wanted to remember, to reach into the synapses in his brain, the chemical pathways that controlled his decision-making and planning, and create a permanent memory of what went wrong so that he would never make that kind of mistake again.

Ron knew that many sets of eyes at the Academy were on him. That knowledge encouraged him to fulfill his punishment duty as well as he was able and to apply himself more than ever to his studies. He set for himself the goal of excelling in all of his classes, including the ones that he found most challenging. He could not help but find it vexing that his unpleasant roommate, who looked right through him as he walked past, always achieved high grades in his classes with what appeared to be a minimum amount of studying. Ron perceived that as one more example of how inequitable life can be. Even though he attempted to flush from his mind all thoughts regarding his disagreeable roommate, he could not help but feel uncomfortable whenever the man was in the room with him. Some nights, the man's presence made Ron feel so edgy that he lay in bed for hours before he was able to fall asleep.

When he was not attending classes or studying or carrying out his punishment duty, Ron spoke to Lucy on the phone. Since he was not permitted to leave the campus, she visited him every Sunday. He hoped—he was pretty sure—that she was as happy with him as he was with her.

By the end of March 1960, Ron had worked off the last of his demerits, and his restrictions ended. At about the same time, Lucy happily informed him that she had been accepted for entrance to Boston University in the fall. Ron was pleased for her.

Ron's plebe year, generally believed to be the most difficult one, was over at the end of July 1960. Out of a class of 326 cadets entering the Academy in 1959, only 192 had made it to the end of their plebe year.

Each plebe had to spend one full year at sea aboard a U.S. flag vessel under the supervision of a chief engineer (for marine engineering cadets, such as Ron) or a chief mate (for nautical science cadets).

In order to accommodate cadets participating in fall varsity sports, such as football, soccer, and wrestling, the Academy split their sea year of training into two six-month segments separated by six months of academic studies. For that reason, Ron would complete his sea training in March 1962 as a second upper classman, and not at the end of 1961.

Besides having been allowed off the Academy grounds during that initial period to play soccer at other schools, another benefit of playing a varsity sport was that now all of the athletes were housed in the same dormitory. That led to an even greater than usual sense of camaraderie among those cadets. Ron became close friends with all of the other varsity players, regardless of the sports they played. He had wonderful roommates, such as Ron Jordan, Bob Foster, and Phil Pelletier.

EIGHTEEN

Sea Training

In late July 1960, as Ron began his second year, the campus of the Merchant Marine Academy was eerily quiet. Besides the large number of students who had resigned and those who had been scrubbed because of low grades or/and disciplinary infractions, most of the upperclassmen were at sea. As a soccer player, Ron would have a split year: the first half on campus, and the second half at sea. Ron's unpleasant roommate, who was at sea, had been replaced by Bob Foster from Brockton, Massachusetts, a member of the wrestling team. Unlike his former roommate, Bob was an exceptionally friendly, helpful companion. He and Ron became friends immediately.

The term moved along at a pleasant but lively clip.

Beginning in February of 1961, the cadets who had spent the first half of the year on campus were assigned to merchant ships. The ones who were majoring in nautical science were assigned to deck officers, and the ones, like Ron, who had decided to major in marine engineering were assigned to assistant engineers or chief electricians. In March of 1961, Ron was ordered to report to the SS American Producer, a cargo vessel owned and operated by the United States Lines,[32] which was based in Brooklyn. He was assigned to be trained by the chief electrician under the supervision of the ship's chief engineer.

Although Ron attempted to look—and feel—at ease as he boarded the ship, his stomach was in knots. After reporting to the captain and then the chief electrician, Ron was coldly instructed to take a self-guided tour of the engine room so as to familiarize himself with the propulsion system, which consisted of two high pressure steam boilers,

---

[32] The company no longer operates under that name.

two steam turbines which operated two shafts connected to two propellers, and all of the auxiliary equipment needed to run the ship. As he descended the dark, narrow metal stairway to the hellishly hot and foul-smelling engine room, Ron felt queasy. After just a few seconds of breathing the acrid air, Ron knew that he was going to be sick. He ran to a dark corner, where he lost the contents of his stomach. Then, before anyone found him, using a bucket and mop and water from a slop sink, he cleaned up the mess as well as he was able. Ron did not know it then, but that would be the only time he would ever be sick on board a ship, even when he was in rough seas.

A few days later, the ship set sail for Marseille, France. During the seven-day voyage, Ron was under the supervision of the chief electrician, who was supposed to provide training to the young cadet. From the onset, rather than instructing Ron in reference to the operation of the ship's systems, the chief electrician assigned him to dirty menial chores, such as using a scalding solvent to clean buckets filled with filthy electrical components. At first, Ron assumed that the chores to which he had been assigned were a typical part of the training. However, after a few days, during which the chief electrician made a point of speaking to Ron in a harsh, authoritative voice, and only when he had additional dirty jobs for him, Ron decided that the man was a crusty, hard-nosed professional who did not want to be bothered to train him. However, as time passed, as much as Ron did not want to believe it to be true, he came to believe that the man objected to his lingering accent and his religious background. He wondered when ... if ... the bigotry would ever end.

Despite Ron's belief that he was the victim of prejudice, he knew he had to do whatever the chief electrician asked. His twin goals were to learn about the mechanical workings of the ship—which, he realized, might never happen because the man was unwilling to teach him—and complete the cruise with a good rating from the man. He told himself something that he already knew but found painfully difficult to accept: at times, he simply had to keep his mouth shut and ignore people's preconceived notions, even on the occasions when they caused him to be the victim of offensive behavior.

One balmy evening, as Ron, who was off duty, stood on deck admiring the ink-black sky with its tiny pinpricks of far-off illumination, he was startled by the stealthy approach of the chief electrician. Without offering a greeting of any sort, the man, spitting out his question, asked why he, a Jewish boy (Ron was surprised the man didn't say "Jew-boy."), was attending the Merchant Marine Academy and why he would want a career as an officer on a ship. When Ron, who was shocked and intimidated by the query, remained silent, the chief electrician continued by saying that Jews have no place on ships. Finally finding his tongue, Ron, with great restraint, explained that his maternal grandfather had been born on a ship and had spent a lot of time on them; then Ron added that he had always loved ships and had always wanted to go to sea.

Ron understood that his worst fears regarding the electrician had been confirmed, but he did not know what to do about the dreadful situation. Not only was he not receiving the training that the obviously bigoted man was supposed to provide, but it was likely that the chief electrician would give Ron a poor evaluation for this, his first voyage. He did not see a way out of his dilemma.

During the three days that it took to unload the cargo from the ship and take on new goods at its first port of call, Marseille, Ron had an opportunity to see the sights. Although, at first, his French was a bit rusty, it came back to him. After Marseille, the ship headed to Southampton, the largest marine port in the United Kingdom. Ron wanted to visit London, which is about 80 miles from Southampton, but he knew he did not have enough time, so he remained in port.

As the ship set sail for the return trip to the United States, one of the officers informed Ron, to his great delight, that he was being rotated from the chief electrician to the second assistant engineer. When he thought about the change, Ron wondered whether he was being transferred because one of the officers or the chief engineer had gotten wind of how the chief electrician had been treating him. He felt relieved. To add icing to the cake, Ron was delighted to learn that the chief electrician played no part in rating him.

The second assistant engineer was a courteous man who patiently instructed Ron in ship operations, such as how to monitor and log temperature and pressure readings, along with all he had to know about condensers, evaporators, distilling units, and air conditioning equipment. In addition, the man taught him how to stand watch.

When the SS American Producer returned to Brooklyn on April 20, its cargo was unloaded and then it immediately took on new merchandise. The next day it departed on what was to be a seven-day trip, discharging and picking up cargo at several ports along the east coast of the United States. The first port of call was Boston, at which the ship remained docked for two days, giving Ron the opportunity to visit Lucy, who was in her second term at Boston University. Their joyous time together erased any doubts that either of them may have had during the period of their long separation regarding their relationship. In fact, those two days helped to reaffirm and solidify their loving bond to one another. Although they longed to spend some time in a secluded spot, they contented themselves by visiting local pubs with a few of Lucy's friends. In one popular place, they accepted the bartender's recommendation to try a Singapore Sling, a drink they enjoyed ... and enjoyed ... and enjoyed. As they sipped their cocktails, commenting on the lovely sweet taste and ordering yet another round, they felt better and better. They had to lean on each other as Ron walked Lucy back to her dormitory that evening.

On his second night in Boston, Ron visited Eva, Victor, and Sidney. Victor was serving as the rabbi in a Reform synagogue in nearby Brookline, Massachusetts. Eva held Ron's hand as she proudly paraded him through her fine home, after which she served a wonderful dinner, the first home-cooked meal that Ron had eaten since he had been with his parents in Middletown several months before.

On the morning that the American Producer was scheduled to set sail from Boston, Ron and Lucy held each other tightly for a long, sweet time. Then Ron said good-bye and rushed off to the dock. As he made his way to his ship, his sense of utter desolation at leaving Lucy began to be diluted by a powerful, deep-seated sense of exhilaration at the thought of returning to his other love, the sea.

The next ports of call on the coastwise trip were Philadelphia and Baltimore, after which, on April 28, the ship returned to Brooklyn. The following day, the SS American Producer, with new cargo, set sail across the Atlantic once more, stopping again at Marseille and Southampton, along with Cadiz and Barcelona, Spain. Ron was able to spend time in the latter city, where his fluent Spanish enabled him to communicate like a native as he walked along the streets and ordered food and drinks in cafes.

On June 1, 1961, having completed three demanding months at sea on the SS American Producer, during which he had learned, mostly via hands-on lessons, a great deal about marine engineering, Ron was transferred to the SS Santa Isabel. The new ship was a huge refrigeration cargo vessel that was owned and operated by Grace Lines, which, like the United States Lines, was based in Brooklyn. It hauled tons of fresh fruit, mostly grapes and green bananas, from Colombia, Ecuador, Peru, and Chile to the United States. Ron barely had time to report for duty and stow his gear before the Santa Isabel set sail for the Panama Canal.

The Panama Canal, a marvel of engineering, allows ships to easily and quickly travel back and forth between the Atlantic Ocean (via the Caribbean Sea) and the Pacific Ocean. Before the canal was built, a ship sailing from New York to San Francisco had to travel south along the Atlantic coast of the U.S., through the eastern edge of the Caribbean Sea and then the Atlantic coast of South America, round Cape Horn—or the treacherous Strait of Magellan—and then north along the Pacific coasts of

South America, Central America, Mexico, and California to its destination. Traversing the Panama Canal saves approximately 7,800 miles in reference to that voyage.

A canal through the isthmus of Central America had long been the dream of explorers, sailors, and entrepreneurs. Beginning in 1881, a French company attempted to build a sea-level canal through what was then the Colombian province of Panama. The hot, damp climate, deadly tropical diseases, the incredibly difficult terrain, and financial mismanagement brought that effort to a halt in 1894. In November 1903, with support from the United States Navy and President Theodore Roosevelt, rebel groups in Panama declared independence from Colombia. The United States immediately recognized the government of the now independent nation of Panama and signed an agreement to build a canal. Begun in 1904 and completed 10 years later, the canal built by the U.S. relies on a series of locks to bring ships up and down to different levels.

Standing on the scorching, sun-drenched deck of the Santa Isabel, Ron's heart throbbed with excitement and anticipation, almost as if it were matching the rhythmic beat of the big engines as the ship approached the Caribbean gateway to the Panama Canal. Even though Ron and his family had traversed the canal—in the other direction, from the Pacific to the Caribbean—when they traveled by ship from Antofagasta, Chile to the United States, that had been eight years ago—1953—and his memory of that voyage was hazy.

He watched as a pilot came on board and took over from Captain McCormick to guide the ship through the canal to the Pacific exit. He was pleased to learn from one of the other crewmen that many of the canal pilots were United States Merchant Marine graduates. On each of his breaks, he came up on deck to observe, with professional interest, portions of the 50-mile almost 10-hour-long journey. He was particularly impressed by three wonders: the astonishing ability of the water that flowed into and out of the enormous locks to raise and lower the ponderous ship, the incredible mechanical muscle of the electric "mules" that pulled the vessel by means of thick steel cables, and the alarmingly small space—sometimes only inches—on each side of the Santa Isabel as it was tugged through the lock chambers. Ron was ecstatic to be experiencing one of the man-made marvels of the world.

Ron's first split sea year ended on July 17, 1961 when the Santa Isabel returned to Brooklyn. Choosing to accentuate the overwhelming number of positive aspects of the experience, such as the valuable skills he had learned, the exhilarating days at sea he had enjoyed, the sense of satisfaction he had derived from helping to operate the ship, the fascinating ports of call through which he had wandered, and the many friendships that he had developed with hard-working, dedicated crew members, Ron was jubilant. While he made an effort to thrust into a dark, hidden corner of his mind the reprehensible behavior of the anti-Semitic chief electrician, Ron did not forget the lesson that he had learned: that the age-old prejudices and hatreds that had caused his family so much pain and lasting damage in Europe could rear their ugly, dangerous heads at any time and in any place. Of course, he had learned this lesson before, the swastika crudely drawn onto the mirror in his locker being just one example. He would not dwell on that lesson, but he would remember it.

During the three-week break before Ron had to report back to the Academy that summer, he enjoyed being with his parents and the other members of his family and he visited friends from high school who still lived in Middletown. Since Lucy was working as a summer camp counselor at Camp Chipinaw in upstate New York, he managed to get together with her only when she had days off from work. She was eager to hear about his time at sea, what he had done aboard the ships on which he had served, and the places that he had visited. On his last day with Lucy, he repeated what he had said before: he wished they could spend more time together. He was pleased to hear her say that she wanted that too.

NINETEEN

Joy During a Time of Grief

At the beginning of August 1961 Ron began his third year at the U.S. Merchant Marine Academy with eagerness and an enhanced sense of self-confidence, which he attributed, at least in part, to his successful half-year at sea. When he was not at soccer practices or engaged in competitions against other teams, he focused on his schoolwork with laser-like intensity, finding that his ability to concentrate and retain information, even in regard to his most difficult subjects, had improved considerably. In addition, since Ron now shared his room with a new cadet and did not have to come into contact with the former, disagreeable roommate, he was able to relax and sleep well at night. The term moved along smoothly and concluded without incident.

On March 2, 1962, Ron reported to Captain E. Kruger of the SS Export Bay to begin his second half-year aboard ship. He was assigned to four-hour watch periods in the engine compartment, which were followed by eight-hour maintenance work shifts, after which he was off duty until the next day.

After an east coast trip which lasted from March 2 to March 11, the SS Export Bay crossed the Atlantic, stopping at Rotterdam, Netherlands, several ports in Spain and the UK, and then Rijeka, Yugoslavia.[33] Unlike the people who Ron met in the other ports, the ones he saw and attempted to communicate with in Rijeka did not seem to like Americans. That was probably due to how the government, which was Communist, had depicted the United States and Americans in general since the beginning of the Cold War.

The ship returned to Brooklyn on May 3, 1962.

---

[33] The city is in present-day Croatia.

After a restful three-week layover, Ron was delighted to learn that he, along with three other engine cadets and four deck cadets from his split year, had been assigned to serve on the SS United States, America's flagship luxury passenger liner. Built in 1952 for the then-astounding sum of 78 million dollars,[34] partially paid for by the United States government because the ship had been designed to be a troop transport—if the need should arise—the SS United States was a technological marvel. At the time, it was the fastest passenger liner afloat, having sailed from New York City to just off the coast of Cornwall, England on her maiden voyage on July 3, 1952 in an amazing three days and 10 hours at an average speed of 39.59 knots. The ship was equipped with eight high-pressure steam boilers, four steam propulsion systems, and quadruple screws with propellers that were 18 feet in diameter. The "Big U," as the ship was called, could travel for 10,000 miles before needing to refuel. The huge vessel had been designed to carry 1,044 crew members and 1,972 passengers (or 15,000 service members, if the need arose). During its lifetime, which ended in 1969, the SS United States made 400 voyages, covering 2,772,840 miles. That is equivalent to more than 111 equatorial circumnavigations of the globe.

With Ron as a member of the crew, the great ship made three round trips between New York City, Southampton, UK, and Bordeaux, France. Ron's tour of duty ended on July 10, 1962. During his time off before he had to return to the Academy he visited his parents. He also spent as much time as possible with Lucy, who had transferred from Boston University to Adelphi University, in Hempstead, Long Island so as to be able to see Ron on a more regular basis, a development that he greeted with a great deal of satisfaction.

As Ron began to contemplate life after graduation from the Merchant Marine Academy, he knew that he wanted to marry Lucy. As

---

[34] By way of comparison, the cost of constructing a modern cruise ship is generally a billion dollars or more.

American as he felt, he was still guided by old world ways, and so, before formally proposing to her—something at which he had hinted on more than one occasion—Ron discussed his plans with her parents. By this point, they had grown to like him very much, and so they were pleased by this not unexpected revelation. After giving him their blessing, they told Ron to go to the jewelry store owned by an acquaintance of theirs, assuring him that the man would be very helpful. Ron did not find out until years later that Lucy's parents, knowing that he did not have much money in savings, had arranged with the owner of the store to sell to Ron whatever ring he wanted for the few dollars that he had, assuring the man that they would make up the difference.

In October of 1962, Ron presented Lucy with the ring and asked her to marry him. Of course, she said yes. They planned to marry on December 22, 1963.

Ron allocated a great deal of time during the next year to preparing for the challenging examination that he would have to pass in order to graduate from the Merchant Marine Academy and obtain a United States Coast Guard license. Acquiring that certification would allow him to sail on American vessels as a third assistant engineer.

When Ron passed the examination in June of 1963, he reflected on how much he and the other members of his family had achieved during their less than a decade in America.

On July 29, 1963, under a tranquil blue sky, with his family and Lucy in attendance, Ron Isaacson, born René Rudolf Isaacson in Antwerp, Belgium, the country to which his parents had fled to escape persecution, graduated from the United States Merchant Marine Academy. As Ron marched to the podium in his dress whites to receive his official documents—a Bachelor of Science in Marine Engineering, a U.S. Coast Guard license, and a commission in the United States Navy as an ensign— once again, he marveled at the unparalleled opportunities provided by his glorious country.

Ron's time in the Naval Reserve, beginning in his junior year of high school, and his four years at the Academy counted toward six years of credit in the United States Navy. Because of that credit, Ron's pay grade—which would go into effect when he would begin serving as an active duty member of the Navy—would be higher than that of any of the other Merchant Marine Academy graduates who were also newly commissioned naval officers.

As a member of the Naval Reserve, he was obligated to serve two years of active duty. However, knowing that he did not have enough in savings to pay for any portion of a wedding and even a modest honeymoon, Ron asked permission from the Navy to serve aboard a merchant marine vessel—where the pay would be considerably higher—for three months first.

The Navy granted Ron's request for a deferment from active duty for a period of four months. He applied for a position with the Military Sea Lift Command, a civilian/military company that operates ships manned by United States Coast Guard-licensed personnel. On August 8, 1963, he was assigned to the position of junior third assistant engineer on the USNS Upshur T-AP198, a troop carrier that sailed between the Guantanamo Bay Naval Base and the east coast of the United States. With Ron on board, the ship made four round trips between August 8 and November 4, 1963.

During a leisurely lunch one day, a marine engineer who had retired from the Navy took Ron aside and informed him that despite the fact that he had been promised a four-month deferment, he could be called up to active duty at any time and sent anywhere in the world. After thinking for a moment, Ron decided to send a telegram to Lucy, telling her what he had just heard and asking whether she would be willing to move up the date of their wedding. When Lucy got back to Ron later that day, she replied that, under the circumstances, that seemed to be the prudent thing to do.

A few days later, when Ron spoke to Lucy's mother, he told her that he hoped people would not jump to conclusions about why they were moving up the wedding date. Laughing quietly, she told him not to worry, and then added, "Just don't get her pregnant right away."

Lucy's father, who insisted, over Ron's objections, that he and Lucy's mother would pay for the wedding, gave the young couple the choice of a lavish reception or a less expensive one and a new car. After a bit of thought, Lucy and Ron chose the latter, and picked out a dark-gray Plymouth Valiant.

The new date that Ron and Lucy chose for their wedding was November 24, 1963, a Sunday. Of course, they had no way of knowing at the time that it would be two days after the assassination of President John F. Kennedy.

Ron and Lucy's wedding day was one of dramatic contrasts: a festive atmosphere of warm, bright hope in the midst of shared feelings of dark, cold despair, a time of great happiness and celebration during a period of sadness and reflection. Rabbi Mordecai Waxman of Temple Israel in Great Neck officiated and, by virtue of his warmhearted humor and abundant benevolence, helped those in attendance on that bittersweet day to focus on the joy of the occasion. Despite the fact that the wedding guests, like most Americans, had been caught up in the great national mourning, they acted cheery and light-hearted and managed to push thoughts of the enormous tragedy out of their minds. They danced and sang along with the happy couple and their parents, ate the wonderful food, and wished Ron and Lucy well.

It was not until later in the day that the newlyweds learned—to their horror—that Lee Harvey Oswald, the man who had been arrested for the murder of Dallas police officer J. D. Tippit and was the suspected assassin of President Kennedy, had been shot to death in the basement of Dallas police headquarters by nightclub owner Jack Ruby. That shocking moment, which had been broadcast on live television and played over and over again, added another layer of incongruence and unreality to Lucy and Ron's wedding day.

During the five lovely days that the couple spent at the Carillon Hotel in Miami Beach for the first part of their honeymoon, the lingering gloom of the assassination intruded from time to time. At one point or another, Lucy and Ron's conversations with other guests and with employees of the hotel inevitably turned melancholy and eyes became watery as they and the others talked about the national tragedy and the images they had seen on television: the president's body lying in state in the majestic rotunda of the Capitol Building; the solemn funeral cortege with the steady, mournful drumbeat; Black Jack, the lively caparisoned[35] riderless horse with a pair of boots reversed in the stirrups; the funeral Mass; John-John (John F. Kennedy Jr.), who had turned three that day, poignantly saluting the casket holding his father as it passed; the burial at Arlington National Cemetery; the eternal flame at the grave.

Although Ron and Lucy experienced some of that heavy grief, they could not help but be blissfully excited that they were finally a married couple. They smiled as they talked about what they knew would be their wonderful lifetime together. But then, every so often, in the midst of their delightful reveries, they returned to thoughts of the now-dead president and his widow and his children.

After their stay at the Carillon Hotel, they took a taxi to the airport so that they could fly—via a small two-prop airplane—to Nassau Beach, Bahamas. Since Lucy was frozen with fear each time she had to fly and since she was more nervous about this flight than the one from New York to Miami because now they would be in a small aircraft, Ron made sure she had a drink or two. He chose Singapore Slings, their favorite cocktail. Those soothing beverages helped to put Lucy into a serene state of mind, which, due to the fact that the plane encountered a great deal of turbulence during the short flight, she ended up needing. The entire time

---

[35] A reference to a decorative covering or blanket placed on a horse.

they were in the air, Lucy held Ron's hand tightly, digging her fingernails into his skin each time the plane traversed a particularly bumpy patch of sky. Ron ignored the pain and held Lucy's hand in a firm grip.

Their stay at the Nassau Beach Hotel was quiet, but not *too* quiet, for they were new lovers and they delighted in their sweet time together. They slept late each morning and snuggled, ignoring the slivers of tropical daylight and the muted sounds of happy people that slipped into their cozy room. When they finally decided, at around noon, that they were hungry and they managed to tear themselves out of their hotel suite, they ate, lounged on the beach, swam, indulged in beginner water skiing, and enjoyed the sights. At night, they danced to the music of a reggae band and sipped their favorite cocktails.

It was a magical moment in time.

Ron and Lucy returned to New York in the middle of December 1963 and immediately moved into a rented apartment with a month-to-month lease in Jamaica, Queens. They smiled with excitement and contentment as they thought about their new life: they would be living together and going to bed together and waking up together for many years, for many decades to come. By the time they had gone grocery shopping and settled into their first home as a married couple, they were exhausted, but happy and filled with anticipation.

The next day, Ron went to the post office to retrieve their mail. When he returned to the apartment and opened an official-looking letter, his face fell as he read his Navy orders: he was to report for duty on January 31, 1964.

TWENTY

From Norfolk to the Mediterranean

Ron's orders stated that he was to report to Naval Station Norfolk (Virginia) no later than the last day of January 1964. During that first month of the new year, Lucy worked hard and put in many hours of study to make up for the class work she had missed during their honeymoon so that she would be able to graduate from Adelphi with a bachelor of arts degree. Then, although they had just moved in, she and Ron gave notice to the landlord, packed up their belongings, and drove their new Valiant the roughly 450 miles to Norfolk. After a couple of nights in a motel, they found an appealing furnished apartment near the base and signed a two-year lease that was subject to cancellation if Ron were to receive orders to move to a different location. Since Norfolk is a town with strong ties to the naval base, rental policies are generally geared to the needs of military personnel. Ron's allowance for quarters as an ensign was $110.00 per month, which was enough to cover the rent.

Despite the fact that the apartment was furnished, Ron and Lucy decided they wanted some of their own pieces, so they went to Haynes Furniture, an establishment that one of their new neighbors had recommended. They purchased a bedroom set and some living room furniture. When everything was in place, they felt that the apartment was actually their home.

During the next two months, while Ron took classes at the base on damage control aboard combat vessels, Lucy obtained a position as a substitute teacher of French in Norfolk. When Ron had completed his training, he was assigned to the SS Cambria, APA 36, a converted World War II Liberty Class steam vessel with a single screw (propeller). The ship served as a military troop carrier. American shipyards had produced almost 3,000 of this kind of vessel during World War II. Both the United States and the United Kingdom had used them extensively from 1941 through 1945. The two high-pressure steam boilers used very heavy bunker C or #6 fuel, which had to be heated so that it would flow. It then was ignited in a combustion chamber to bring water to the boiling point to produce steam; the steam was delivered to two triple expansion engines.

Ron was delighted with his assignment as the engineer division officer in charge of the two divisions that ran the engine room—the boiler division and the main propulsion division, each composed of 10 men and each under the command of a chief petty officer. All of the men, including Ron, were under the supervision of the chief engineer with the rank of commander. Ron was pleased to be in such an important position involving so much responsibility. Since he had learned about the type of propulsion system that the Cambria used while he had attended the Merchant Marine Academy he felt confident in his ability to perform the job competently.

The APA Cambria was part of the Sixth Fleet's amphibious squadron, which consisted of LSDs (landing ship dock), destroyers, submarines, and the Saratoga, an aircraft carrier. The fleet was scheduled to sail from Norfolk in August 1964 to participate in Marine amphibious landing exercises (with NATO allies) at a number of ports along the Mediterranean during the course of the following six months. A fleet commodore onboard the Saratoga was in charge of the planning, coordination, and execution of the exercises. Despite the strict regimen and discipline aboard all of the ships, time-honored rivalry between sailors and Marines led to occasional fistfights.

Since Ron was so busy fulfilling his engine room duties, he did not pay much attention to what was going on in the rest of the ship, including the juvenile behavior that led to the brawls. His main concern was the condition of the Cambria's engines and propulsion system, which utilized outdated technology. On several occasions during the cross-ocean voyage the ship lost all of its power and blacked out because of a problem with some of the thick, heavy bunker fuel. Two emergency electric generators were used to provide power for the navigation equipment during those blackout periods. On each of those occasions, Ron ordered the men in the engine room to flush out the bad fuel and switch to a standby fuel tank to restart the engines. Once he had conducted a thorough investigation of the recurring problem, Ron determined that some of the bunker fuel that the ship had taken on in Norfolk had been contaminated with water. He instructed the men to re-circulate that batch of fuel so as to remove the water. That kind of problem is rare nowadays because third-party inspectors with specialized sampling and measuring equipment generally test fuel before it is taken on by ships.

Before Ron shipped out, he and Lucy decided that they would vacate the apartment, put their belongings into storage, and she would move in with her parents. They also agreed that she would meet him at some port in the Mediterranean during the six months that he would be away. After Lucy had driven to her parents' home in Great Neck and settled in, she made some inquires and then decided that rather than flying to a single port in the Mediterranean and then returning home after she and Ron had spent some time together, she would live for the next few months in Provence and take classes at Aix-Marseille University. The location of the college—on the Mediterranean—would allow Lucy to travel to several ports of call so as to spend time with Ron. Her mother contacted a family in Aix-en-Provence who rented rooms to students. They said that they would be happy to allow Lucy to board with them for as long as she liked.

A few days before Lucy was scheduled to travel to France she panicked (again) at the thought of flying, so she cashed in her ticket. Then, thinking quickly, she booked passage on the only ship that would arrive in France in time for her to begin her college classes: the SS United States, the same ship on which Ron had trained as a cadet two years before while he had attended the Merchant Marine Academy.

Once Lucy disembarked in Marseille, she purchased a Eurail pass which she used to travel to many of the ports at which the Cambria docked. This worked out beautifully for the couple. Lucy was able to spend many days and evenings with Ron in lovely cities all along the Mediterranean when he had shore leave. When they had enough time they traveled inland. They visited some of the most stunning places in Europe: Madrid, Valencia, Toledo, Rome, Naples, Genoa, and Athens, among others. Their favorite destination was Barcelona. While they were there they stayed at a lovely old hotel with a canopy bed in their room; large windows and sliding doors leading to a balcony provided a dazzling view of the Mediterranean Sea. The room cost $3.00 per night.

At another time, while traveling by train to meet Ron, Lucy became acquainted with a young Navy wife whose husband was assigned to one of the ships in the squadron. Once they had become friends the two women traveled together to meet their husbands.

When Lucy, who was fluent in French, was not with Ron she concentrated on her courses in Marseille and lived with the French family. She enjoyed both aspects of her life: her occasional days and nights with Ron and her time living in Provence.

One day, when the Cambria was anchored off the French coast facing Golfe-Juan, which is a city on the Côte d'Azur not far from Cannes, Ron received the permission of the executive officer (XO) for Lucy to come aboard for a few hours. As Ron traveled on a landing craft to pick her up at the pier, she was already on her way to the ship aboard a returning LCD; they passed each other without realizing it. By the time Ron returned to the Cambria, without Lucy, he was distressed to learn that due to the rocking of the ship caused by choppy seas she had not been allowed to board and had been sent back to shore. He stared in that direction, hoping that he might catch a glimpse of her.

The next day, all of the sailors in the fleet who were aboard their ships were ordered to remain in place because the police in Golfe-Juan were conducting an investigation into the rape of a woman in town by an American. Since Ron was not able to go ashore he again asked the executive officer for permission for Lucy to come aboard. After a moment's hesitation, the officer told Ron to go ahead and telephone her. Shortly after Lucy boarded the ship the barometric pressure dropped precipitously and the wind speed increased dramatically. Once the executive officer was certain that this serious turn for the worst was not likely to improve any time soon, he gave the order for all crew members to man their stations and for the anchor to be lifted so that the ship could sail to calmer waters. The Cambria moved in slow, wide circles in the bay. Only about half of the crew was aboard; the others, along with Captain Snyder, had gone ashore earlier that day. Ron, who had been in the engine room doing the work of three men because so many of his people were onshore, managed to spend only a bit of time with Lucy that day. When he realized how late it was he approached the executive officer to say that his wife was still aboard. The XO said that no one would be allowed to leave the Cambria that night, and that Lucy would have to remain on the ship. He told Ron to set her up in the stateroom that the fleet commodore used on the occasions when he was aboard. As Ron was about to turn and walk away to find Lucy, he had a thought; after quickly weighing the possible consequences, he decided to throw caution to the wind and ask his question: "Would I be allowed to sleep with my wife in the stateroom tonight?" The XO, displaying his most rigidly military facial expression, replied, "I do not believe I heard that request."

Ron decided to interpret that response positively.

Early the next morning, as Ron left Lucy so that he could return to his own quarters, he smiled and thought that he was probably the only ensign to have ever slept in the commodore's stateroom.

*****

On July 19, 1964, while Ron was at sea, his sister Eva gave birth to her second child, a girl whom she and Victor named Ilana. During the previous three years, the Mallenbaums had moved from Brookline, Massachusetts to Milford, Connecticut. Then they relocated to Newington, a suburb of Hartford, so that Victor could serve as the rabbi in a synagogue in that town. Within a few months of the birth of Ilana, Victor was offered a rabbinate in a Reform temple in Rocky Mount, North Carolina. After a great deal of discussion and much hand wringing because accepting this new offer would mean that the Mallenbaums would be living 500, as opposed to 100 miles from their parents, they agreed that it would be a good opportunity for Victor.

Victor and Eva quickly adjusted to the mild climate and the genteel lifestyle of the quiet southern hamlet. Victor threw himself into the responsibilities of his new position and still managed to devote a great deal of time to working toward a doctoral degree in psychology. Eva balanced motherhood, household duties, and a Sunday School teaching position at the synagogue. At the same time, she took classes at North Carolina Wesleyan College, where she majored in Spanish. Since she had lived in and gone to school in La Paz for six years and was fluent in Spanish she found her classes very easy.

*****

By mid-February 1965, the fleet had left its last port of call and sailed westward across the Mediterranean on its way back to the United States. Lucy had sailed from Marseille the month before on the SS Julio Cesare, bound for New York. She stayed at her parents' home in Great Neck for a week. Then she drove back to Norfolk to meet Ron upon his arrival. They found a lovely apartment in Little Creek, Virginia, not far from the Amphibious Naval Base, where the Cambria was docked. Knowing that Ron would probably be sent to other places within the year, they signed a month-to-month lease.

In August 1965, after six agreeable but uneventful months in Virginia, Ron was sent to Philadelphia for a four-week training course. Since they did not want to be apart and since it did not make sense for Ron and Lucy to rent an apartment or stay in a motel in the Philadelphia area, they rented an RV in a trailer park in a down-and-out section of nearby Camden, New Jersey. Because they did not feel safe in that seedy locale, with its many unsavory characters, and since the RV did not have air conditioning, they spent much of their time in stores, movie theaters, and other nicer, more comfortable places.

In September, the Cambria steamed into the Philadelphia Naval Shipyard for a long-overdue overhaul which was estimated to require several months. Ron and Lucy signed a one-year lease, with a military clause, for a fully furnished apartment in Glenolden, Pennsylvania. They liked the area and were especially pleased to see that many other young, newly married couples lived in the same apartment complex. Then they heard whispers about the parties that some of their neighbors hosted: allegedly, the gatherings involved the consumption of huge amounts of alcohol, which was often followed by games in which couples switched partners for the evening. Needless to say, Ron and Lucy were shocked. They made sure to come up with excuses when they were invited. After a while, to their great relief, the invitations stopped coming.

The repairs on the Cambria were finished by the end of 1965, and it sailed to Little Creek Naval Base in Norfolk, Virginia about a month before Ron was due to complete his two years of active duty. He had enjoyed his time in the service, and now that he had been promoted to LTJG (lieutenant, junior grade) he was considering remaining in the Navy, so he investigated the possibilities. He was disappointed to learn that his request to be posted to a stateside naval shipyard—he did not care which one—could not be granted because there were no openings. Then he learned that the Navy was looking for volunteers to serve in patrol boats in the waters of and around Vietnam. This was at the very beginning of American involvement in what would soon be known as the Vietnam War. Even though serving on a patrol boat in Vietnam sounded interesting and would have entitled Ron to combat pay, something that he found very appealing, he and Lucy were determined that they not be separated again, especially since this deployment would be for a long period of time and in a war zone. Ron had fragmentary, sad memories of his father being away from the family during the time that he had been interned in Gurs—or perhaps they were not first-hand memories, but recollections of what his parents had told him. In any case, the thought of being away from Lucy was unbearable to Ron. Besides that, they wanted to start a family, so he decided not to extend his active duty status, but to remain in the Naval Reserve.[36] He also told Lucy that as much as he had enjoyed going to sea, he would not look for a position on a merchant marine vessel.

As 1965 came to a close, Ron began making plans for a future on dry land.

---

[36] Which he did until 1972, retiring with the rank of lieutenant commander.

TWENTY-ONE

To the Moon and Back

At the beginning of 1966, Ron, a civilian once again, decided that he wanted a job that would allow him to use the knowledge and skills that he had acquired at the Academy and during his time at sea, preferably in the field of marine engineering. After consulting a job-listing pamphlet that the United States Merchant Marine Academy published and distributed on a monthly basis, he decided to send his résumé to several corporations on the east coast that specialized in ship building, general engineering, and/or aircraft construction. He was pleased to receive invitations for interviews from Pratt and Whitney/United Technologies, which was headquartered in Bridgeport, Connecticut, and Grumman Aerospace Company, which was in Bethpage, Long Island. He set up and attended interviews with both companies, hoping that Grumman would hire him. Ron had heard good things about the aircraft manufacturer. In addition, he liked the fact that Grumman was located only a short distance from Great Neck, where Lucy's parents lived. He and Lucy decided that if Grumman hired him they would live on Long Island.

Both companies offered entry-level engineering positions to Ron. He chose Grumman. They found an apartment in West Hempstead, which was 10 miles from where Ron would be working. Lucy was hired as a substitute French teacher in the Hempstead School District.

Ron was employed as a test engineer on a team that was playing a major role in the groundbreaking Apollo moon landing project. The main responsibility of the team was to test and refine the propulsion system of the lunar excursion module, known as the LEM or LM. The LEM was the portion of the Apollo spacecraft that would eventually land on the moon with astronauts on board.

Although it was a far cry from a marine engineering position, Ron was enthusiastic about his job. He was part of a 24-hour, seven-day-a-week operation that involved hundreds of people. He alternated between day and evening shifts, both of which were long and grueling. Even though he wished he had a more regular schedule that would allow him to go home for dinner with Lucy each evening, Ron was delighted that he was able to use the engineering expertise that he had learned at the U.S. Merchant Marine Academy and had refined during his time in the Navy.

The massive Project Apollo, which had been in operation since 1961 and would conclude in 1972, had first been discussed and outlined during the administration of President Dwight D. Eisenhower. It had been envisaged as a series of three-man missions to the moon to follow on the heels of the Mercury program, which would be the first to put a human in space, and Project Gemini, which would send two-man crews into orbit. After the untimely, tragic death of President Kennedy, the administrators at NASA decided to dedicate the Apollo project to him. Kennedy, who had been an enthusiastic and inspiring voice in favor of manned space flight, on May 21, 1961, told a joint session of the United States Congress, "I believe that this nation should commit itself to achieving the goal, before this decade is out, of landing a man on the moon and returning him safely to the earth."

After many years of testing, adjusting, retesting, refining, failures, frustrations, disappointments, and, finally, successes, the first Apollo spacecraft, consisting of a command module (CM), a service module (SM), and a lunar excursion module (LEM), was attached to the top of a powerful Saturn rocket. Following a number of successful unmanned test flights, Apollo One, with three astronauts on board, was scheduled for launch into a low Earth orbit on February 21, 1967. Everyone who had worked on the project, including Ron, waited impatiently, knowing that if all went as planned, future Apollo missions would head for the moon.

Communication problems between the crew and Ground Control led to a hold in the countdown. Then, as the spacecraft sat atop the Saturn rocket on its launch pad at Cape Canaveral, disaster struck: an electrical fire erupted, quickly spreading and blossoming out of control in the 100% oxygen atmosphere of the command module, asphyxiating Command Pilot Virgil I. "Gus" Grissom, Senior Pilot Edward H. White II, and Pilot Roger B. Chaffee. The fire also destroyed the CM.

That fiery tragedy struck Americans hard, especially those who had worked on the Apollo project, but after a short period of mourning, the engineers and scientists at Grumman and at the other commercial contractors went back to work. Their first goal was to discover what had caused the inferno that had taken the lives of the astronauts and determine how to make sure nothing like that would ever happen again. As a result of the investigation, many changes were made to the design of the command module and new escape protocols were put in place.

More than a year and a half later, after many tests and six unmanned test flights, on October 11, 1968, Apollo 7, with its three-man crew, was successfully launched into space. It remained in Earth orbit until October 22, at which point the spacecraft dove through the atmosphere and splashed down in the North Atlantic. That was followed by Apollo 8, launched on December 21, 1968, which was the first manned flight to the moon. After completing 10 orbits of the moon, the capsule returned to Earth and safely parachuted to a spot in the northern Pacific Ocean on December 27. Those flights were followed by Apollo 9 and Apollo 10, both of which were complete successes. Everyone involved in the project looked forward to Apollo 11, which was scheduled to do what had never been done before: land people on the moon, allow them to walk on its surface, and then bring them back to Earth.

At 9:32 a.m. EDT on July 16, 1969, Launch Pad 39 A at the Kennedy Space Center erupted in blossoms of red-orange flames and an ear-splitting wave of man-made thunder radiated from the site as a powerful Saturn V rocket with Apollo 11 fastened to its nose lifted off. The launch pad was quickly obscured by immense clouds of billowing white smoke as the spacecraft blasted into the sky and speedily thrust itself beyond Earth's atmosphere. Four days later, July 20, 1969, the lunar excursion module, with Neil Armstrong and Buzz Aldrin aboard, landed on the moon's Sea of Tranquility. The third astronaut, Michael Collins, remained in the command module, the only part of the spacecraft that would return to Earth at the end of the mission; Collins orbited the moon and remained in communication with the two men on the surface. People throughout the world watched a live television broadcast of Neil Armstrong stepping onto the surface of the moon and saying, "one small step for [a] man, one giant leap for mankind." The two astronauts remained on the moon for $21^1/_2$ hours, after which they blasted off and docked the LEM with the CM. They returned to Earth, splashing down in the Pacific Ocean on July 24, 1969.

That astounding mission was followed by six others, all of which, with the exception of Apollo 13, which was forced to return to Earth early because of mechanical failures, landed on the moon. The final mission was conducted by Apollo 17, which was launched on December 7, 1972 and returned to Earth 12 days later.

During the three years that Ron worked on the Apollo project, he often put in 13-hour days, working through the night and getting home after Lucy had left for work. To help her deal with bouts of loneliness they bought a white female miniature poodle puppy that they named Bijou. The dog was a bouncy bundle of fluff and fun that very quickly filled an empty spot in their lives. At that same time, they decided that since they both had secure jobs they would like to purchase a house. After a short search, they found a three-bedroom ranch at 207 Southwood Circle in Syosset, Long Island. The good news was that they paid only $19,000 for it; however, it required a great deal of painting and modernizing, along with new plumbing. Ron and Lucy did most of the work themselves.

During that same period of time, they had been trying, unsuccessfully, to start a family. One day, Lucy expressed her concern to her gynecologist, Dr. Levitan. After the physician had conducted a thorough examination, he assured her that there was no reason to believe that she would not, in time, be able to conceive. Ron submitted a semen sample to a lab, and was told that he had a low sperm count, but not low enough to prevent conception. Deciding that they were ready for a child and did not want to wait, the Isaacsons contacted Louise Wise Services, which arranged adoptions.

During a regular office visit, Dr. Levitan informed Lucy that he might be able to be of some assistance in terms of their desire to adopt; he knew of a pregnant college student who wanted to give up her baby immediately after birth. Even though another couple had signed the necessary adoption papers for it, when they abruptly moved from New York to Connecticut they invalidated their rights to the child. Dr. Levitan told Lucy and Ron that the young woman was in her sixth month, so if they were to fill out and sign the necessary papers and agree to an interview with a social worker, within three months, they could be parents.

After they completed the interview and paperwork and had been approved for adoption, Ron and Lucy prepared a nursery in their home. Then they awaited, with much anticipation, the birth of the baby. On May 24, 1968, while Ron was at work, he received a phone call from Dr Levitan, who informed him that their baby girl had been born. Ron immediately called Lucy, who was at her school, to tell her the good news. She jumped up and down, shouting, "It's a girl. It's a girl!!" She told the students in one of her classes that the baby that she and her husband were going to adopt had been born.

Since Syosset Hospital had a longstanding policy requiring the biological mother to hand her baby directly to the adoptive parents, Lucy's mother, knowing that her daughter would be uncomfortable with that procedure, said that she would pick up the infant. Four days after her birth, a beautiful pink-skinned blue-eyed baby girl with golden blonde hair was brought home to Lucy and Ron. After everyone had held, kissed, and admired the little beauty, Lucy's mother, in an attempt to relieve some of her daughter's anxiety, said that the hospital had allowed her to retrieve the baby without having to meet the biological mother. It was not until many years later that that she admitted to Lucy and Ron that, in truth, the birth mother had handed the baby to her.

They named the little girl Kim Jennifer. When Lucy returned to school, the French class to whom she had told the good news surprised her with a party and gifts for the baby. Lucy was so touched by this that she cried and said that she loved them for their thoughtfulness.

Two weeks later, Lucy and Ron brought their lovely daughter to Temple Israel during a Friday night Sabbath service, where she was given her Hebrew name, Tzviyah Yoninah (which means Doe Dove), and introduced to the congregation.

TWENTY-TWO

"No Trees Grow So Tall That They Reach the Sky"

In the spring of 1969, Eva graduated Cum Laude from North Carolina Wesleyan. That fall, she obtained a position teaching Spanish at Rocky Mount High School. She and Victor believed that other than the fact that they lived so far from their parents, their life was perfect. Margot and Walter did not feel comfortable driving the 500 miles from Middletown to Rocky Mount, so, when they visited they traveled by bus. Victor and Eva, who had grown up driving, thought nothing of packing a bag, securing Ilana and Sidney in their car, and making the road trip to New York to see both sets of parents as often as they were able to take time from their work responsibilities.

A couple of years earlier, in 1967, Margot had sent Susan by bus to spend the summer with Eva and Victor and their children. Even though Susan and Eva were sisters, and quite naturally loved each other, there was an almost 18-year difference between them. Susan had been only 14 months old when her sister had gotten married. Because the Mallenbaums had moved, first to Brooklyn, then Israel, then Massachusetts, then Connecticut, and now to North Carolina, Eva and Susan had never had an opportunity to bond as sisters. That summer, Susan, who was almost 12, spent the bulk of her time playing with and helping to care for her nephew and niece and growing close to 29-year-old Eva. By the time they parted in September, the sisters knew that they would miss each other very much.

Susan returned to Middletown bubbling with exhilaration as she exclaimed how wonderful it had been to spend the summer with Eva and her family. As Margot listened, glowing with pleasure, she attempted to convince herself that it was not so awful that Eva and her family lived far from her and Walter. In the middle of that thought, she suddenly pictured her long-dead parents. Even though she always attempted to push those painful, jagged memories to the back of her mind, she could not help but visualize what she knew had been their anguished, lonely deaths. She did not want to fall into a state of hopeless depression, so she reminded herself that despite all of the misery and loss, she and Walter had much to be grateful for and had experienced much good fortune in their lives: they had each other and they were blessed with three healthy, successful children—two of whom were happily married—and three beautiful grandchildren. Then she smiled, thinking, *Of course, life is all about family and joy and always striving to succeed.*

Margot never stopped striving. From the time she had begun working as a secretary at Memorial School in Middletown in 1961, she had taken classes at the State University of New York at New Paltz, majoring in elementary education. The principal of Memorial School had allowed Margot to leave her post at noon three days a week to attend her classes. In the fall of 1970, she took a leave of absence so that she would be able to enroll in the Professional Core, a program that consisted of Methods of Teaching, three weeks of observation in an elementary school, and a semester of student teaching. She was pleased to learn that the school to which she had been assigned was located almost next door to where she lived. She felt that she was on top of the world, and told herself that she was the luckiest person alive. Suddenly, she had an ominous thought, and then she remembered the old German proverb "Keine Bäume wachsen so hoch, daß sie den Himmel erreichen," which, loosely translated, means "No trees grow so tall that they reach the sky."

Right after Thanksgiving 1970, when Margot was preparing to begin her classroom observation period, Victor called from Atlanta, Georgia to inform her and Walter that Eva had to undergo surgery. A year before that, Victor had resigned from his position as rabbi in Rocky Mount and he and the family had moved to Atlanta so that he could pursue graduate studies there on a full-time basis. Eva obtained a teaching position in town. During this period of time, during phone calls, although Eva had never complained of feeling ill, Margot had sensed that something was wrong with her daughter. Eva eventually revealed that her abdomen had been uncomfortably distended and painful for weeks and that her primary care physician had diagnosed the problem as being caused by "nerves."

Victor explained to his in-laws that on the previous morning, as Eva drove to her teaching job, the brakes on her car failed and it rolled down a hill, landing on its side. Eva had managed to crawl out just as an ambulance arrived at the scene. She was brought to the local hospital for observation, at which point a doctor said that her distended abdomen was a symptom of what could be a more serious condition than simply "nerves." He recommended immediate exploratory surgery. When Margot heard her son-in-law say this, she caught her breath and then she said that she would be on the next flight to Atlanta.

When Margot arrived at the hospital, Victor told her that the surgeons had discovered that Eva's abdomen was filled with—had been completely engulfed by—cancerous tumors that had spread from her ovaries. During a somber conference with Victor and Margot later that day, an oncologist said of Eva, "If she is lucky, she'll live six more months. All you can do is pray."

Margot was stunned. She doubled over in pain as if she had been kicked in the stomach. Later that day, she looked at her eldest child, shrunken, weak, and frightened as she lay in her hospital bed. Margot remembered—actually *felt*—the anguish that had run through her each of those days that she and Walter had spent without their children during the time that they had lived in the convent. And now? Were they to lose Eva? She thought of Susan's bat mitzvah. It had been two years before, December 1968. It had been a wonderful day, a festive occasion, and everyone had been proud of Susan. Of course, no one knew it then—and, now, Margot tried to convince herself it was not true—but that day would be the last time that all of her children would be together to celebrate a joyous event.

Margot stayed in Atlanta for three weeks, accompanying her gravely ill daughter to the hospital for cobalt treatments and taking care of Sidney and Ilana; she maintained a brave face and hoped that the doctors were wrong. Once Eva had recovered from those first few weeks of treatments and appeared to regain a semblance of her old strength, Margot flew back to New York, promising her daughter that she and her father would return soon.

In early spring of 1971, Eva insisted that she felt almost back to normal. Saying that she had to take care of her husband and children, she declared that she was determined to stay alive for as long as possible. In late May of that year, she and Victor traveled to Rocky Mount to see old friends, after which they visited Victor's parents, who had recently relocated to Florida. Eva seemed to know that despite her plucky assertions, she was at the end of her life, and she wanted to say good-bye to people she loved.

When Eva and Victor returned to Atlanta, Walter and Margot flew back down and spent several days with their daughter. Later, on the flight back to New York, they sobbed because they suspected that they would never see her again.

On June 13, 1971, two short weeks after Margot had graduated from SUNY at New Paltz, Eva died. The dark cloud that had hung over the family for so many months seemed to descend and swallow them up in a cold, dank blanket of grief. Although they all had known that her end was near, they could not help but think that Eva, at 33, should have had many more years to live and to love and to be loved. Victor, overcome with choking, claustrophobic grief, managed to hold himself together so that he could make the arrangements for the funeral service and burial. Walter, Margot, Susan, Ron, Lucy, and Victor's parents leaned on each other for support and did their best to comfort Sidney and Ilana.

After the graveside service, those who loved Eva found it gut-wrenchingly difficult to leave; they lingered, looking around sadly, as if they hoped to see her standing nearby.

Margot, feeling as if her heart had been torn from her breast, was not able to visit Eva's grave for ten years.

A few months after Eva's death, Victor completed his graduate studies and was awarded a PhD in psychology. Very soon after that, he and his children moved to Greenville, North Carolina, where he had been offered a teaching position at East Carolina University. Two years later, Sidney celebrated his bar mitzvah. All of the Isaacsons attended and were immensely proud of the young man, but their pleasure and sense of gratification were tempered by the pain of the still-open wound that was Eva's death.

Not too long after that wonderful event, Victor informed Margot and Walter that he had remarried. At the bar mitzvah, the Isaacsons had met the young woman who Victor had introduced as his friend Ella. They had liked her and had suspected that Victor had been contemplating marrying her. Born Christian, Ella, and her daughter Scarlet, who was the same age as Ilana, had converted to Judaism shortly before the wedding. On the too few occasions when Walter and Margot were able to see Sidney and Ilana during the next few years, they could not help but feel pleasure, mixed with a degree of discomfort and grief, at the thought that their grandchildren had a new mother.

One of the times that they saw their grandchildren was when Ilana and Scarlet celebrated a joint bat mitzvah. At one point during the service, at which both girls fluently recited their Hebrew blessings, Ilana momentarily broke down in tears. Later, when her loved ones congratulated her, Ilana smiled and thanked them. No one asked and she did not say why she had cried, although it was clear that she missed her mother. Perhaps thoughts of how proud her mother would have been to have seen her on the *bimah* had been the cause of Ilana's tears.

TWENTY-THREE

On His Own

In early 1969 Ron had realized that Grumman's role in the Apollo program was due to end soon, so before he found himself out of work he began to search for a new job. By the middle of the year, he had accepted a position with Sperry, which was located in Lake Success, New York, where he was trained in computer software language. Within a few months, recognizing the fact that the new job was not right for him, Ron utilized the United States Merchant Marine Academy employment listing service once again to find a new position. After he had sent copies of his résumé to a number of companies, Ron was interviewed via telephone by James Anderson, senior vice president at Combustion Equipment Corp. (CEA), a New York City firm that manufactured combustion automation systems for cargo ships. The company's burner automation system was much more efficient than the old manual system, reducing the amount of fuel consumed, resulting in savings for the owners of vessels. Anderson, who was a U.S.M.M.A. graduate (class of 1961), hired Ron as a salesperson for the New York City-based company on the strength of his Merchant Marine Academy education and his work experience. Ron was pleased to be starting a new job and was thrilled that he would receive a substantial increase in salary over what he had earned at Grumman.

During the following three years with CEA, Ron proved to be a successful technical salesman. His greatest accomplishment involved the sale of inert gas systems (IGS) for three tankers that were being built at Avondale Shipyard in New Orleans. Inert gas systems are used to dilute the amount of free oxygen present in the area around volatile liquids, such as crude oil or gases, being transported, thus reducing the likelihood of combustion due to static electricity. The million dollar cost of the systems was quite a lot of money in the early 1970s and the largest sale in the history of the company.

Since the engineers at CEA had no working experience in terms of actually manufacturing inert gas systems, the company developed a joint venture with an entity located in Bremerhaven, West Germany which was knowledgeable in reference to this technology. Ron, as the project manager, made frequent trips to the Avondale Shipyard in New Orleans, CEA's plant in Stamford, Connecticut, and to Bremerhaven during the course of this business endeavor. At first, he had been uncomfortable at the thought of traveling to Germany because he could not help but associate that country with the racist policies that had been the cause of so much misery to his family and the other Jews of Europe. However, after his first trip, he began to believe that this might be a New Germany, a nation whose people deeply regretted what its leaders and its military had done during those 12 dreadful years and would never repeat the tragic mistakes of the past. That is what Ron thought, or hoped was true. Even though the people with whom he spoke were cordial and helpful, Ron always felt like an outsider; in addition, when he made a point of saying that he was Jewish, he had the feeling that people perceived him as an unwelcome reminder of their past.

Perhaps because the Isaacsons no longer felt under pressure to conceive, or maybe it was just finally the right time, but much to their surprise and delight, when Kim was two years old, Lucy discovered that she was pregnant. On October 15, 1970, she gave birth to a boy; they named him Kenneth Scott. Each time Lucy and Ron looked at their beautiful children they were filled with joy. Their pleasure was multiplied each time they saw the glowing faces of their parents.

At the conclusion of the IGS project, CEA increased Ron's salary and awarded him 100 shares of the company's stock option. Then they sent him to the United Kingdom to promote the inert gas system that he had just helped to develop.

In 1975, during one of the monthly cocktail parties in New York hosted by the Society of Naval Architects and Marine Engineers, Ron met a man by the name of Charles Schmukler, the founder and president of Marine Moisture Control Corp. (MMC). His company, which was located in Inwood, Long Island, manufactured unique portable measuring instruments designed for the marine and petroleum industries. The instruments were used throughout the world during custody transfers and the monthly inventories taken in refineries and tank farms and for marine petroleum tankers and barges. During the course of the evening, Schmukler asked Ron whether he would be interested in working for his company. The next morning, Ron appeared at the company offices, where he was interviewed by Mr. Schmukler, who hired him to fill the position of marine engineer technical salesperson. Ron was told that he would receive a company car and a 20% increase in salary over what he had been earning at CEA, plus an end-of-the-year performance bonus.

During the next few years at MMC, besides earning a first-rate income, Ron learned a great deal about the operation of refineries, tank farms, marine tankers, and fuel pipelines. As he became proficient at his job and confident in his understanding of the products that he was selling and as he made contact with hundreds of customers, Ron began to learn about other devices and applications that would be useful in this unique commercial niche. At the same time, he began to experience a driving need to develop his own business, and so he started to hesitantly ask his customers whether they would support him if he were to become an independent supplier. Not only did they encourage Ron, they made suggestions in terms of what additional products to sell that were exclusive to the industry and not easily available.

Then Ron made one of those careless errors that can have far-reaching consequences. This one changed his life. As Ron was still in the midst of planning his break from MMC but still visiting their customers, he inadvertently left a folder filled with sales brochures from other companies on his desk overnight. The next morning, he was confronted by Mr. Schmukler who angrily asked Ron why he had the pamphlets. In the midst of the highly upsetting conversation that followed, Ron nervously said what he had only begun to formulate: that he continue his association with MMC, but as an independent sales representative, and not as an employee. He explained that in this position he would still represent products made by the company, but would also be free to market devices produced by other companies that did not compete with those offered by MMC. Ron went on to say that this arrangement would mean that MMC would no longer have to provide him with a salary, an automobile, or traveling expenses; in return, he would be a free agent. As Mr. Schmukler, who was still angry, considered this proposal, Ron knew that he had spoken too soon because he did not have enough in savings to sustain him and his family during the initial period of time it would take to develop a sales following and begin to earn even a marginal income. After Schmukler had cooled down a bit, he said that he would be willing to take a chance on the new arrangement. Ron then said that he would need a six-month draw against whatever commissions he earned at MMC. Much to his relief, Mr. Schmukler agreed, saying that he would have the papers for the agreement drawn up by the end of the day.

Once Ron had caught his breath and allowed himself a moment to unclench his fists and relax his tense, aching back, he thought with satisfaction and a great deal of excitement that he had just opened up an exciting career pathway for himself, one that would surely be good for Lucy and the children. However, as he elatedly drove home that night, his bubbling exhilaration and optimistic vision of the future suddenly became clouded with uneasiness and concern. He worried about how he would tell Lucy that, for the first time in his working life, he would no longer be drawing a regular paycheck.

Now he was on his own.

TWENTY-FOUR

Land of Youthful Dreams and Hellish Nightmares

During the next few years, although Walter and Margot felt a natural and profound attachment to and love for Sidney and Ilana, they managed to see their grandchildren only on rare occasions, a painful fact that they found distressingly difficult to accept. The physical distance between Middletown, New York and Greenville, North Carolina, along with the inevitable emotional remoteness between the Isaacsons and Victor's new wife acted as deterrents to frequent visits. However, during the four years that Sidney attended McGill University in Montreal, he visited his grandparents several times, generally staying with them overnight when he drove home to Greenville and back to school during vacations. Besides the fact that they enjoyed seeing their grandson, his visits allowed Margot and Walter, in a small way, to feel connected to Eva once again.

During this period of time, Margot, who had been awarded her Bachelor of Science in Elementary Education one week before Eva had died, obtained a position as a special education teacher in a new school in Middletown. She taught during the day and attended graduate classes in the evenings. In 1973, she earned a Master of Science in Special Education and was granted tenure in her teaching position. She enjoyed every aspect of her job and derived great pleasure from helping students who needed specialized kinds of instruction.

During the same year that Margot earned her master's degree Susan graduated from high school and announced that she wanted to be a dentist. Margot and Walter, who were both earning decent but not sizeable salaries, did not know how they would be able to cover the cost of dental school. Susan, a decisive, determined young woman, told them not to be concerned. Over the course of the next four years, as a college undergraduate, while maintaining a high grade point average, Susan worked at a series of part-time jobs and made sure to work during all of her vacations. One summer, she participated in a University of Colorado research program; during another one she worked in a Washington, D.C. school for children with emotional issues.

Upon graduation, Susan enrolled in a six-year dental education program at Case Western Reserve University in Cleveland, Ohio. In 1979, she graduated with a degree and obtained certification as a dentist in 18 states. Walter and Margot, along with Ronald and his family, attended the graduation. They beamed with pride at her accomplishment.

Susan moved to Seattle, Washington to practice medicine. Once again, Margot and Walter were separated by a great distance from one of their children, this time by more than 2,800 miles. Even as they reveled in Susan's brilliant achievements and experienced a sense of deep satisfaction, they missed her terribly.[37]

Walter retired in 1975, when the factory at which he had been working closed; he was 68 years old. Margot retired in 1981, after ten years of teaching; she was 65. Although they took pleasure in their leisurely, uneventful days, the Isaacsons decided that they would like to travel. They toured the Caribbean and Mexico, traveled to Hawaii and then to Spain, and in 1980 they visited Margot's sister Ruth and her family, who were living in Melbourne, Australia.

In 1982, Margot and Walter moved from Middletown to Century Village, an adult condominium community in Deerfield Beach, Florida. Despite the aches and pains of the passing years, they enjoyed being retired. They loved their new home and their new life. They made friends with many people their age and took pleasure in the year-round warm weather and sunshine. More and more often now, Margot reflected with a

---

[37] In the years that followed, Susan would meet Robert Jaffe, a primary care physician. They would marry in 1990 and have two children, Miriam and Ben.

combination of surprise and dismay on how she and Walter had suddenly become "senior citizens," a term she disliked. Then she mulled over for the thousandth time the joys and good fortune that she and Walter had shared in America and how dreadful their lives had been during their last years in Germany and during the time they had lived in Belgium. For that reason, she was surprised when, upon hearing that the West German government had issued a general invitation to those who had fled during the era of the Third Reich, she experienced a momentary sense of longing for her place of birth. She asked herself, *Would it be so bad if we were to visit Duisburg?* The war had been over for 37 years. The Nazi monsters were gone; hopefully, they were all dead. As American as she and Walter felt and as grateful as they were for all of the blessings that had come their way in their wonderful country, Margot could not deny that she still felt German too. Despite the fact that she had never wanted her children to learn German, she loved to hear and speak the language, read the literature, become enveloped by the music, and learn the history—except, of course, for the ghastly, dark 12 years of the Third Reich.

When Walter said that he too would like to visit West Germany, Margot obtained the necessary contact information and wrote to the municipal government of Duisburg, the town of her birth and childhood and where she and Walter had lived right after they married. A letter from the city council in Duisburg arrived in the mail at the beginning of 1983, but upon reading the enclosed invitation, both Margot and Walter were suddenly overcome with alarm and a sense of unease. Their desire to visit the land of their youthful dreams dimmed and turned cold because they could not help but perceive it also as the land of hellish nightmares. They put the invitation aside and did not reply. When a second invitation arrived at the start of the next year, Walter was scheduled to undergo surgery, so they had a convenient excuse to decline once again.

In November 1984, a letter arrived from Eva Frank, the eldest daughter of Rabbi Neumark of Duisburg; she was the sister of Ruth

Neumark, Margot's childhood friend. In it, Eva said that she and Ruth, along with their two brothers, all of whom lived in Israel, had decided to accept the invitation of the city of Duisburg to attend a ceremony in 1986 at which a street was to be renamed in honor of their father. He had been the only rabbi in the town from 1905 until 1942, at which point he and his congregation had all been deported to Theresienstadt. Eva explained that the city was attempting, in a small way, to rectify the wrongs that had been done by honoring the victims of Nazi persecution who had lived in Duisburg. Walter and Margot decided that when the next invitation arrived in the mail they would accept.

In the spring of 1986, Margot and Walter attended Sidney's graduation from the medical school at the University of North Carolina. At the conclusion of the ceremony, Sidney told his grandparents that he was going to specialize in neurology ... and that he was getting married. Then he introduced them to his future wife, Rita, and to Joshua, their child, who was eight months old. Walter and Margot, despite their initial shock, smiled as they marveled at how their family was growing.

On September 8, 1986, the Isaacsons flew across the ocean, landing at Düsseldorf-Lohausen Airport, a short distance from Duisburg. Three months earlier, in America, they had celebrated their 50th wedding anniversary, and now they were in the country of their birth, the land in which they had been persecuted and with which they hoped they would be able to reconcile. An official from Duisburg met them at the airport and drove them to the city in the mayor's car.

As Margot and Walter looked out of the windows at the passing countryside, they recognized very little of what they saw. When the car approached and then entered the city of Duisburg, they wondered whether the driver had made a wrong turn because nothing looked familiar. The man explained that most of the city had been destroyed during the war; allied bombers had been sent again and again to obliterate the iron and steel factories operated by Krupp, Thyssen, and Mannesmann. In the years following the war all of the buildings in those devastated areas had been replaced with new structures. Margot felt cold, as if she was being taken to a strange place that held no meaning for her. However, as the car in which they were riding entered the town center, a large group of smiling people greeted them with a hearty welcome. They were members of a Christian-Jewish *arbeitsgemeinschaft*, which means "working group" or "joint venture." Among those in the group, which had been organized in 1965, were some of Walter's old classmates and a few who had gone to school with Margot's sister Ruth. Walter and Margot were invited to a lovely *kafeeklatsch*, where, besides sipping coffee and eating delicious pastries, they talked about their life in America and their old, innocent, delightful lives in Germany before the rise of Nazism. As they brought up charming recollections of that era, Walter and Margot, along with many of the others, became teary-eyed.

Ilse Van Ackeren, the president of the *arbeitsgemeinschaft*, and another member, Luise Terlinden, treating the Isaacsons like long-lost friends, guided them through the town. Then Margot and Walter were escorted to city hall, where they met the lord mayor. When they said that they would like to visit the synagogue, Ilse regretfully explained that it had been destroyed during the war and had not rebuilt because very few Jews lived in Duisburg now. That news left Margot feeling empty, as if someone close to her had died. Of course, many people who had been close to her *had* died. *No*, she thought. *They had not died. They had been dragged from their homes and murdered, perhaps by some of the same people who are walking with us through Duisburg right now.* She pushed those painful thoughts from her mind.

They were driven to a synagogue in neighboring Muhlheim, the only Jewish house of worship in the area. The Isaacsons were told that it was home to a small but growing congregation; the children of the congregation traveled by bus to a larger synagogue in Dusseldorf for Hebrew lessons. A few thousand Jews had settled there since the end of the war. *Those people*, thought Margot, *are true optimists.*

For the final part of their visit to Duisburg, which brought to the surface a tangle of conflicting emotions, Margot and Walter attended the ceremony honoring Rabbi Neumark. Afterwards, they spent some time talking with the daughters and sons of that highly principled man, all of whom had flown to Germany from their homes in Israel.

A few weeks after she and Walter returned home, Margot, who had not yet decided how she felt about the trip to Germany, opened an old, storage chest to look for what she remembered as a section of crochet work that her mother had started but never completed. She was dismayed to see that the cloth had, over the years, become thread-like and had all but disintegrated. As she tenderly ran her fingers over the aged fabric, she saw that there was another remnant, a small piece of musty, timeworn material underneath. Gently moving the crochet work aside, Margot looked down at the other piece of cloth. She remembered it, and it warmed her thrumming heart while, at the same time, it distressed her.

Blinking away tears, she read the inscription on the cloth:

Oskar Landau, Duisburg, Casino Strasse 16
Das Haus Der Guten Qualitäten

She smiled as she thought about the meaning of the second line: "Household of good quality" or "Fine household." *Yes, it had been a fine household, a loving family composed of parents and children who had been loyal Germans and proud, if not very devout Jews.* Once more, Margot felt that emptiness in her core, in her soul, the place ripped open by the violent, senseless deaths of her parents and of Walter's father and of so many others. Of course, she also still ached—would always ache—for Eva. That scalding pain, that scar on her soul would never disappear; that void would never be filled.

At that point, Margot knew what she had to do. Going to a closet and standing on a wooden stool, she pulled out boxes and packages until she found the object of her search: the Smith-Corona typewriter that she had bought so many years before, the one on which she had practiced because she had wanted to apply for an office job.

Once she had purchased a ribbon and typing paper, she would sit at the keyboard and think for a long time—there was no need to rush—after which she would briefly tell the story of her parents and her extended family and all of their friends. In her short memoir, which she planned on calling *Story of My Life*, Margot would write about the love and the laughter that had marked her idyllic life in Germany. She would recollect her childhood and her school days and her first job and how hard her mother and father had worked to provide for her and Ruth. Of course, she would tell how she met Walter and how they fell in love and married. She would write about Eva, their beautiful first born, and how she grew and married and had children of her own ... and how she had died, but that would come later in the story. She would write about Ron and Lucy and their children and about Susan, but that would come later too. Before that, she would write about how life in Germany had turned into a hellish nightmare. She would have to find the words to describe how the lovely brightness and the warm, reassuring essence of Duisburg changed—first in minor but evil ways, and then in a gut-wrenching manner—into a hideous atmosphere of perpetual darkness and hate-filled deadly despair. She would have to write about the dark, cold fear she and her family had lived with and the loathing with which they were perceived by others—even by those who had been friends and neighbors—and the routine mistreatment and random acts of violence they had endured. She would put down on paper the stories of those who were taken away, never to be seen again.

She would struggle to find the words to describe all of that horror because her children and her grandchildren and others she would never meet had to know.

Then she would write about America.

212

TWENTY-FIVE

Petro-Marine

Near the end of 1977,[38] in the weeks after his tense conversation with the manager at MMC, Ron established his own business, which he and Lucy named Petro-Marine Company, Inc. After almost three years at MMC as a salaried salesperson, Ron set out on what he hoped would be a successful career as an entrepreneur.

Two years earlier, they had moved from Syosset to a house in Woodbury, also on Long Island. That is where they set up the company's headquarters. When Ron first asked Lucy to help him operate Petro-Marine she hesitated because she enjoyed her position as a substitute teacher of French in the Plainview School District and did not want to relinquish it. However, at about the same time, as student enrollment fell, the district had begun to "excess" teachers, so Lucy agreed to assist in the new business, but only on a part-time, temporary basis. Even during Petro-Marine's early days, Lucy's tasks, which included office administration, invoicing, customer service, inside sales, and the creation of purchase orders, quickly turned into a full-time job. Her "temporary" position evolved into one that she would keep for the next 28 years.

Although MMC, as agreed, allowed Ron to draw against his commissions for six months, he knew that was not much time in which to establish the business. Therefore, he and Lucy were relieved and felt blessed when they saw that during that initial period Petro-Marine's customer base steadily grew. By the end of that six-month time span, they had sold a large number of products and brought in more income than Ron had earned during a comparable period of time at MMC. The downside to their early success was that since most of their clients were in New Jersey,

---

[38] Almost a decade before his parents' bittersweet return to Germany.

Pennsylvania, and Maryland, and not Long Island, Ron was often on the road, sometimes for two or three days at a time.

One of the most useful devices that Ron had come across during his years working as a salesperson for MMC was *Little Joe Wiper*, which is used for oil gauge line control and tape wiping. As Ron introduced it to his customers, it became one of Petro-Marine's best sellers and one of its most reliable sources of income.

In June of 1978, so as to be closer to their customer base, Ron and Lucy moved from Long Island to an expanded ranch with a huge finished basement in Marlboro, New Jersey, a town with a highly rated school system. The new location was halfway between New York City and Philadelphia, where most of their customers were located.

In 1979, partly as a result of the revolution in Iran, the worldwide price of petroleum quadrupled and the supply decreased. Because of that economic cataclysm, the American Petroleum Institute (API) raised its standards, especially in reference to temperature measurement accuracy, which has an enormous impact on the volume of oil in containers and tanks as calculated by third party inspection companies during custody transfers and monthly inventories. The continuing global energy crisis encouraged Ron to develop tools to more accurately gauge the temperature of petroleum products. His first device was the *AvTemp20*, a portable digital electronic thermometer with the ability to measure the average temperature of up to 20 levels of petroleum products inside storage tanks to within 0.03^0 F. No other product on the market at the time was capable of conducting measurements of fuel temperatures as accurately as the *AvTemp20*. Ron had to wait for over a year to obtain safety approval from FM Global, which is a Rhode Island-based mutual insurance company that specializes in loss prevention services for large businesses. Once he received the needed approval, he authorized the first 50 units of *AvTemp20* to be manufactured by John Croddick, the former mayor of Marlboro, who owned and operated an electronics shop in town. Ron, along with Tom

Campbell, an electrical technician, and Larry Fickett, an electronic genius, formed Precision Gauging Inc. (PGI) solely for the production of the *AvTemp20*. Petro-Marine was designated to market the product and establish reliable distributors in the U.S. and worldwide.

The product sold well because it was so accurate and dependable. Each time Ron and his partners discovered or were made aware of problems in reference to the functioning or reliability of the *AvTemp20* they immediately took steps to correct the defect. Because the *AvTemp20* had developed a reputation as a trustworthy device, sales to inspection companies, refineries, tank terminals, pipeline operators, and the owners of marine tankers and barges were brisk. Those businesses became steady customers of Petro-Marine.

After attending many American Petroleum Institute meetings and seminars in Houston, Texas and New Orleans, Louisiana, where Ron talked about the virtues of the *AvTemp20*, it was approved by the API Temperature Committee. Three years later, Ron's partners wanted to be released from their obligations, so he bought them out. Lucy and Ron continued to produce and market the *AvTemp20*, eventually selling it to clients in Canada, the Netherlands, Belgium, the UK, Mexico, Brazil, and Singapore. They made many trips to those countries during the next few years. Ron also initiated the process of having a patent approved, but was unable to pursue it because of the high cost involved.

In 1983, the Isaacsons moved their business ventures from their home to a building in a commercially zoned section of Marlboro. By that time, they employed 10 people, including three technicians, led by Tim Malavasi, who had just been discharged from the Navy; the technicians were trained to repair *AvTemp20* units. Lucy continued to be in charge of the office, and Ron, along with another man, traveled and conducted outside sales. Despite the company's success, when the Isaacsons examined the bottom line, they sadly concluded that they had been too generous in terms of providing full health coverage, life insurance, and pension plans to all of their employees, as well as an automobile for the outside salesman. As the costs of those benefits increased dramatically each year, Ron and Lucy, much to their chagrin, had to ask their workers to make contributions (which also increased each year) to them.

In 1985, after a great deal of discussion with Lucy, Ron decided that he was finally ready to do what he had thought about for a long time: travel to the convent at Miséricorde. He believed that he would never be able to fully come to terms with his past and feel at ease with his future until he returned to the place where he and Eva had been hidden during the war. They planned their visit for the summer of that year, 1985, because they had business meetings to attend in the United Kingdom, the Netherlands, Switzerland, and Belgium during that period of time.

Ron and Lucy flew to London, where they had meetings with representatives of British Petroleum, Texaco, and Shell in reference to the *AvTemp*. When they had concluded their business obligations they traveled by taxi to the home of Ron's Uncle Heinz, his father's brother. They ate dinner together and exchanged news about their families.

From London they traveled to Switzerland and then to Rotterdam, Netherlands, where they met with their European distributor of the *AvTemp*, Chris Zeger, who owned Zematra, a testing supply company. Then they visited several inspection companies based in the city. When they had completed their last meeting, they traveled by train to Brussels, where they rented a car. During the 30-minute drive to the convent, Ron alternated between feelings of cheery anticipation and dark dread.

When they reached Miséricorde, Ron parked the car in the courtyard and, after staring at the building for a moment, he and Lucy walked to the front door and knocked. An elderly nun greeted them. Once they had explained the reason for their visit, she took them on a tour of the convent and then invited them to have lunch with her. As they ate, they conversed easily in French. The nun, who was in her 80s, said that while she did not remember Ron, she had a crystal clear memory of that sad time and of the Jewish children who had been sheltered there. Ron said that while he had no clear recollection of specific events that occurred during the time that he and Eva had spent in the convent, he did sense a sad familiarity with the place. He told the elderly nun that Eva, who had died 14 years earlier, had always spoken fondly and with great appreciation of the women who had sheltered and cared for her and her little brother. He added that he and his parents owed the nuns of Miséricorde a lifetime debt of gratitude for all they had risked to protect him and his sister from the Nazi beasts who prowled the countryside in search of Jews.

After lunch, Lucy, Ron, and the nun went outside, where they silently admired the lovely grounds. Then, remembering the faded group photographs, one of girls, including Eva, and one of boys, including him, posed in the courtyard that had been among his mother's belongings, he asked Lucy to take a picture of him and the nun. After Lucy had done that, Ron handed a donation for the upkeep of the convent to the nun; then he and Lucy embraced the elderly woman and said good-bye.

As they drove back to Brussels, Ron was overwhelmed with a complex set of feelings that ranged from tranquility and fulfillment to sadness and loss, finally deciding that he was pleased that he had made the trip. He thought about how, at the age of 45, he had fulfilled a long-deferred obligation, a kind of bittersweet rite of passage.

He was ready to go home and get back to business.

On March 24, 1989, the Exxon Valdez, an oil tanker bound for Long Beach, California, went aground on a reef just off the southern coast of Alaska, eventually spilling between 11,000,000 and 38,000,000 gallons of crude oil[39] into Prince William Sound and onto the rocky shore. That remained the worst oil spill disaster in United States waters until the 2010 blowout of the Deepwater Horizon in the Gulf of Mexico. In the wake of the Exxon Valdez calamity, the United States Coast Guard began informing governmental agencies in coastal states, along with those that

---

[39] The exact figure is in dispute.

border navigable bodies of water, of new environmental safety measures. Those states were required to ensure that all marine terminals and refineries have permanent booms in place under their docks—as well as deployable booms that could be placed around vessels loading or discharging oil—for the purpose of containing fuel spills. The only exception to the rule involved the movement of light hydrocarbons, such as gasoline, because it is safer to allow those fuels to evaporate than to contain them through the use of booms.

Years earlier, Ron had developed a business and, later, a social relationship with Randy O'Brien, the founder and owner of American Boom and Barrier Company (ABBCO), a manufacturer of oil spill containment products; Petro-Marine had become a major distributor of ABBCO's spill booms. In the wake of the Exxon Valdez disaster and because of the new Coast Guard regulations, Petro-Marine found itself in the enviable position of selling large numbers of booms to petroleum-related businesses and winning contracts to install permanent boom systems under docks all over the country, particularly in the northeast region. At one point, Ron and Lucy were invited by management to visit a Sunoco refinery in Yabucoa, Puerto Rico and submit a bid for the installation of a boom system. Petro-Marine was awarded the bid. As word of the company's expertise in this field spread, Petro-Marine began to receive orders for other pollution control products, such as sorbents (materials used to absorb fuel spills) and skimmers.

During that period of time, fuel tank inspection companies began claiming that they needed a device that would allow them to sample oil under inert gas pressure in tankers carrying volatile products such as crude oil with more accuracy than what was currently available. Inert gases, which contain less than 5% oxygen, are fed under slight positive pressure into fuel tanks so as to eliminate the possibility of explosions once the tanks are filled with volatile fuels. In response to this pressing need, Ron invented the *Petro-View Multi-Function Sampling System*. Once he had received the approval of the American Petroleum Institute for this device, he began marketing it. Almost immediately, *Petro-View* units began to sell, and continue to do so.

Despite the strong sales of the *Petro-View* and the *AvTemp20*, Petro-Marine was experiencing a cash flow problem, mostly due to increased competition. In order to maintain their sales numbers, Ron and Lucy had to dramatically reduce the markups on the devices that they sold.

In 1995, they decided to move their business from the building in Marlboro to an office in an industrial park in nearby Morganville, New Jersey. A short while later, as a result of an unexpected further decrease in sales, they had to reduce the number of people working for them. Even after they had taken that drastic, heartbreaking step, their business was still not bringing in enough money to cover their payroll and rent for the office, so, in 2000 the Isaacsons moved Petro-Marine back to the basement of their home and reluctantly pared down the number of employees to three, plus Lucy and Ron.

Ron scratched his head and thought long and hard about how to maintain Petro-Marine and, hopefully, help it to grow. He finally decided that he had to find a new, unique product that was not dependent on the unpredictable petroleum or marine industries or on fuel inspection companies. After a long search, Ron found just such a device at an oil spill conference in Seattle, Washington that he and Lucy attended. The apparatus, known as *Drain Diaper* or *Catch Basin Insert* or *Catch Basin Filter*, is a durable cloth filter that is used to collect oil, coarse sediments, grease, and debris in storm water runoff. It is inserted in the street-level entrances of catch basins.

At the conclusion of the Seattle conference, Lucy and Ron made a short visit to the nearby home of Ron's sister Susan and her family. Then they returned to New Jersey. After some negotiations, Petro-Marine was designated the exclusive east coast distributor for MetroChem, which manufactured the *Drain Diaper*. Petro-Marine sold the device to manufacturing facilities with large parking lots, municipal maintenance shops, repair businesses, bus garages, and other entities with catch basin systems. Two years later, Ron learned that MetroChem's *Drain Diaper* was infringing on a *Drain Guard* patent held by Ultratech International. He immediately ended Petro-Marine's association with MetroChem and began selling *Drain Guard* and other products manufactured by Ultratech.

Six months later, Ron discovered that there was a design problem in terms of how the *Drain Guard* was held in place. It is normally flush-mounted under catch basins and secured on all four sides by the weight of the heavy iron storm grate. This works very well in parking lots and other wide-open spaces, but not along streets because in those locations catch basins are usually put in place against a curb, leaving that side open and, thus, that edge of the *Drain Guard* unsecured. To solve the problem, Ron invented and produced a spring-loaded adjustable support rod to hold the fourth side of the *Drain Guard* in place. He applied for and, on October 4, 1999, was granted a patent (US6214216) for what he called the *Drain Filter Support*. The description reads as follows:

A catch basin insert or filter is supported in an open type curb inlet storm drain found on streets and in parking lots. Catch basin filters and inserts are designed to collect coarse sediments, oil, grease and debris from storm water runoff. Such filters normally require support on all four sides by a grate using the weight of the grate. A loop and rod attaches one or more sides of a filter or insert inside a curb inlet storm sewer vault instead of using the weight of the grate.

The *Drain Filter Support,* which was not dependent on the petroleum industry, became a reliable seller for Petro-Marine, thus helping the company to prosper for years to come.

TWENTY-SIX

Loss and More Loss

It was not obvious at first, but after a while it seemed that something was a bit different. Some of those who loved her began to perceive a slight alteration in her appearance and in her demeanor, as if the years had suddenly caught up with her and pulled her down. However, in the same way that in early autumn, as the weather begins to cool and the days grow shorter, the leaves on trees appear to be only slightly different from how they had been during the summer, Margot appeared to be only marginally changed from how she had been for years. Of course, as she advanced from her sixties to her seventies, her hair had turned finer and whiter and her skin had grown progressively more wrinkled, but that was to be expected. She was still a resilient and attractive woman, although she stood a bit less erect and, from time to time, she was somewhat unsteady on her feet. Everyone who saw her assumed those modifications were simply the natural, inevitable results of the aging process.

But that was not the critical change that was taking place in slow, insidious steps.

Walter, who was eight years older than his wife, had aged too. Ron, Lucy, and others in the family had seen, without surprise or alarm, evidence of Margot's and Walter's slow evolution from middle age to mature adult to senior citizen.

It was Lucy and Susan who made Ron aware of what they were beginning to believe: Margot was, more and more often, displaying symptoms of depression or some other serious condition. Whenever Lucy and Ron visited his parents in Deerfield Beach, they made every attempt to show their love and envelop the older couple in joy. Margot and Walter had always been happy to see Ron, Lucy, Kim, and Kenny and all of the other members of their family, but, now, Margot seemed to be unable to emerge from what Lucy and Susan feared was an abyss of chronic unhappiness. In addition, she slept very little and never seemed to have much of an appetite.

Then there were the episodes of confusion and mental fog, along with occasional alarming occurrences of slurred speech, a condition which made it progressively more difficult for others to understand what Margot was saying. From time to time, she was unable to complete her sentences. The physicians who examined her said that she had developed a form of dementia. To this woman who had vigorously employed her intelligence and her inner reserves of courage to protect her family through so many years of misery and heartache and who had achieved so much in America, this diagnosis was almost too much to bear.

As Walter sat stiffly, looking stricken and exceedingly worried, a different doctor told Margot that she also had developed multiple myeloma, a form of cancer that causes plasma cells to accumulate in the bone marrow, where they interfere with the production of normal blood cells. That illness results in a critically compromised immune system. This terrifying diagnosis brought Margot and Walter to their knees.

As Margot began to receive chemotherapy, her depression evolved into a deep, dark, pervasive condition. She ate even less than she had during the previous few months. Also, despite the fact that at this point her dementia had completely robbed her of the ability to speak, it was obvious to all who saw her that she was often in pain. Since Walter was unable to attend to all of his wife's needs, he hired a full-time aide to live with them and help him to transport her to and from the hospital for treatments. A few short months later, Margot had become so ill, fragile, and weak that Walter, after much discussion with Ron, had her transferred to the Horizon Club, a senior living facility in Deerfield Beach. Once he had sold their condominium and disposed of most of their furniture and a lifetime of other possessions, he moved into the room with her.

On November 6, 1993, Margot Isaacson, born Else Margot Landau, but registered as Else Margarette Landau at town hall in Duisburg, Germany, died. She was 77 years old.

Walter, Ron, Susan, and the others in the family were overcome with grief. Margot had been the rock on which the Isaacsons had always depended. For as long as they could remember, she had served as a tenacious, unyielding source of unconditional love, guidance, and strength. Now she was gone.

In addition to his sorrow, Ron was assailed by intense feelings of cold, dark guilt because he believed that he had never fully appreciated all that his mother had suffered and the great risks that she—along with his father—had taken to keep him and Eva alive during their years in Belgium. He wished he had expressed to her how much he appreciated the great gift that she had granted to him: life. Lucy, Walter, and Susan told Ron that what he was experiencing was a sense of profound loss, which was natural, and that he had no reason to feel guilty. They assured him that he had been a good son and that his mother had known that he loved and appreciated her. She had been proud of all of his accomplishments; in fact, she had thought of the achievements of all of her children as rewards for what she and their father had sacrificed during those awful years.

Once Walter, who was 86 years old, had come to terms with the death of the only woman he had ever loved, he attempted to create a new life of sorts for himself at the Horizon Club.

A few months later, during one of their regular visits to him, Ron and Lucy took Walter to a cardiologist, who told Ron that his father had a partial heart blockage and had to undergo bypass surgery. Two days later, they took Walter to North Broward Medical Center in Pompano Beach, Florida, where they were assured that the surgery was routine and that Walter would be fine. Even though they desperately wanted to stay, Ron and Lucy had to fly back to New Jersey to take care of pressing business obligations, so, telling Walter that they would return as soon as possible, they kissed him goodbye and rushed to the airport.

Two days later, February 10, 1994, when Ron answered the telephone, he was stunned and very upset to hear his father howling, "Get me out of here! They are killing me!" Ron called Hazel, the woman who had served as a caretaker for his mother, but was unable to reach her. Early the next morning, Lucy and Ron flew back to Florida, rented a car, and drove directly to the hospital, where they asked for Walter Isaacson's room. A nurse pointed to a door a short distance down the hall. As Ron and Lucy entered and approached the bed, they knew what they saw, but it did not make sense to them; it did not seem real. Ron stood there and called to his father. After a few seconds, Lucy and Ron did what they had, at first, feared doing: they tentatively placed their fingers on the ash-colored, cool skin of Walter's shrunken face, and then they looked at each other in sorrow and dismay.

The nurse who had directed Ron and Lucy to the room appeared in the doorway. They looked at her with stunned, grief-stricken expressions. After a few seconds, Ron asked when his father had died. The nurse replied that it had been shortly before they had arrived; then she apologized, saying she thought that someone had told them.

Ron was too bewildered to say anything else or to fully express his sorrow. Only three months after the death of his mother, he had now lost his father. He was overwhelmed by a tidal surge of powerful emotions. There was so much he wanted to say, but, for now, his words would have to wait.

TWENTY-SEVEN

Watchful Waiting

In January of 2000, during a routine annual examination, Dr. Frank Alario expressed concern regarding Ron's abnormally high white blood cell count and his lower than normal red blood cell and platelet counts. Ron's longtime physician recommended that he consult with Dr. Kenneth Nahum, a highly respected hematologist/oncologist with an office/clinic in nearby Howell, New Jersey. A few days later, after a full examination and analysis of the blood test results, Dr. Nahum conducted a bone marrow biopsy. In early February, just around the time of Ron's 60th birthday, someone from Dr. Nahum's office called Ron and asked him to schedule a follow-up appointment. The person on the phone suggested that Lucy accompany him.

When Ron and Lucy arrived at the physician's office, Ann Nahum, the chief nurse, who is Dr. Nahum's wife, escorted them to a private conference room. She settled Ron and Lucy in and then said that she and the doctor would return shortly to discuss the biopsy results with them. Even though they waited for only a few minutes, with each passing second, Ron became increasingly anxious and ever more convinced that something was seriously wrong with him. Lucy, who was, of course, also very concerned, held Ron's hand in an attempt to reassure him.

Dr. Nahum and Ann entered the room, both with fixed smiles plastered on their faces. After a few pleasantries, Dr. Nahum got right to the devastating point: Ron had leukemia. Even before the doctor had finished pronouncing the word, in fact, as the first syllable left his mouth, Ron felt weak and dizzy and enveloped in a chilly haze; he thought that what he was hearing was not real. During those next few unnatural seconds, Ron thought he understood what Dr. Nahum was saying, but he thought that those words did not apply to him. Surely, there was a mistake; perhaps the doctor was talking about someone else ... or, perhaps, even though he remembered waking up and eating and doing a dozen other mundane things, he actually was still asleep and dreaming, which meant that he did not have a fatal disease.

When Ron was able to focus again, he listened as Dr. Nahum told him that he was quite fortunate because he was at the beginning stages of a very treatable, slow-moving form of the disease known as chronic lymphocytic leukemia (CLL). The doctor assured Ron that the standard protocol for treating CLL, chemotherapy combined with a monoclonal antibody, was very effective. He then added that, even as they spoke, new medications were being developed to treat CLL.[40]

Then Dr. Nahum explained that he could not begin Ron's treatment until his white blood cell count reached a specific higher level. Ron would have blood drawn monthly and Dr. Nahum would monitor the results. Ron, feeling somewhat reassured, but still unable to believe that what he had just heard was true, willed himself to relax.

However, during the next few days, as the news sank in that, yes, he had developed a very serious disease—a form of cancer—although Ron understood that it was treatable and that, according to his doctor, he would most likely die *with it*, and not *as a result of it*, he fell into a state of sadness and utter hopelessness. With time, Ron developed an additional disease: chronic depression. Perhaps as a result of his gloomy mental state, he often felt nauseous; because he had lost his appetite and ate very little, he lost 15 pounds. Lucy, understanding her husband's condition, provided him with unwavering love and support and always attempted to bolster his emotional state. To make certain that he was being properly nourished, she insisted that he drink nutritional supplements.

Ron's mind sometimes wandered, and because he was often

---

[40] Late in 2014, the Food and Drug Administration approved the use of a new, game-changing medication, Imbruvica, for patients with CLL.

consumed with dire thoughts regarding his compromised health, he had great difficulty falling asleep and remaining in that state. He felt weighed down by life and chronically fatigued. He could not help but think of the depression that had seized his mother shortly before she had died.

During this dark, difficult period of time, Petro-Marine began to lose business, a shocking development that gave rise to new, very burdensome thoughts.

During the following two years, Ron had blood drawn each and every month and Dr. Nahum monitored the test results. He kept Ron informed and urged him not to worry. Even though Ron trusted Dr. Nahum, he was overcome with almost ceaseless anxiety and cold, dark dread; after all, this was *leukemia*. Yes, it was slow-moving and treatable, but it was still a serious disease.

After a long period of time during which Ron felt defeated and overwhelmed, he decided to become part of the solution. He began to conduct research into CLL and into which doctors were the most experienced in terms of treating patients with the disease. When he timidly told Dr. Nahum what he was doing, the doctor smiled and said that Ron was doing the right thing. Then Dr. Nahum gave him the phone number of Dr. Kanti Rai, a recognized expert in the field.

Ron immediately called Long Island Jewish Hospital to schedule an appointment with Dr. Rai, who was known for a number of highly regarded research papers on the staging of CLL. In fact, the Rai System is used throughout the United States to gauge the stages of the disease. The scale that he developed ranges from Stage 0, which means there is a high lymphocyte count and no enlargement of the lymph nodes, spleen, or liver and near normal red blood cell and platelet counts, to a disastrous Stage IV, which indicates lymphocytosis plus thrombocytopenia (too few blood platelets), with or without anemia, enlarged lymph nodes, spleen, or liver.

During his consultation with Ron, Dr. Rai agreed with what Dr. Nahum had diagnosed and with his regime of monitoring blood test results and watchful waiting.

Ron also consulted Dr. Ian Flinn of Johns Hopkins University Hospital in Baltimore, Maryland, who was recognized as an expert in interpreting the composition of CLL B-lymphocyte antigen CD20.

In 2001, Ron and Lucy traveled to MD Anderson Cancer Center at the University of Texas in Houston, the top CLL research hospital in the country. Ron was hoping to be included in a clinical trial involving CLL patients that was being conducted there. After three days of tests, including another bone marrow biopsy, he was told that because of his age[41] he was not eligible for any of the clinical trials. A physician there recommended that he go home and begin the combination treatment of chemotherapy and a monoclonal antibody as soon as possible. The doctor said that the hospital would mail Ron's test results, along with instructions and recommendations, to Dr. Nahum.

At the beginning of 2002, Dr. Nahum initiated Ron's treatment at his clinic. At one point during a short period of remission a lymph node in one of Ron's armpits began to swell, so Dr. Nahum sent him to Jersey Shore Medical Center in Neptune, New Jersey for a biopsy. A few days later, Ron was assured that the swollen lymph node was not a serious matter and that, in time, it would return to its normal size.

Over the course of the next decade, Ron received six treatments, each one involving six hours of IV infusions, most of them a combination of Rituxan, which is a monoclonal antibody, and a variety of chemotherapy agents. He was also treated with Campath. Two other treatments, involving a combination of Treanda and Rituxan, were the most effective in terms of producing a long-lasting remission.

The treatments generally did not cause serious side effects, although Ron did suffer from chronic fatigue, which prevented him from engaging in athletic activities, such as playing tennis. However, on three occasions he developed shingles; those painful outbreaks may have been

---

[41] He was 61.

instigated by the chemotherapy treatments, which weakened Ron's immune system. The first shingles episode, which occurred in 2001, caused him great discomfort, but was short-lived and quite manageable, as was the most recent one in 2012. However, the second outbreak, which occurred in 2002, persisted for six agonizing months, during which time Ron suffered continuous, excruciating pain, as if blisteringly hot steel blades were slicing through his midsection from the inside. During that extended period of hell, Ron ate very little, slept fitfully, if at all, and was able to stand for only short lengths of time. As if the pain were not enough, that flare-up hit him just as he and Lucy left for a visit to Kim, who was married with children and living in Rochester, New York. When they arrived in the area, Ron was in such agony that he stopped at a nearby motel and checked in, insisting that Lucy go on to their daughter, son-in-law, and grandchildren without him. He said that he would visit them in a day or two. After Lucy reluctantly left him, promising that she would be back soon, Ron trudged in slow circles in the parking lot of the motel, whimpering with each of the burning, stabbing starbursts of pain.

In mid-January 2010, Ron and Lucy fled the biting cold, snow, and gray skies of south-central New Jersey[42] for the bright sun and comforting warmth of Florida for a month. They rented a house in Boynton Beach, where Lucy planned a 70th birthday party for Ron. Since Ron had been in the middle of CLL treatments, Dr. Nahum made arrangements with a hematologist/oncologist in that part of Florida to administer the last two weeks of therapy.

Ron's birthday party was a roaring success and served as a much-needed, invigorating tonic for him. He was happy and Lucy was pleased. The only disappointment was that their son Ken, who had planned on flying to Florida from Washington, DC, where he had been on a business trip, had been unable to make it because a snow and ice storm

---

[42] At the end of 2005, the Isaacsons had moved from their large home in Marlboro to a ranch-style house in an active adult community in nearby Jackson.

had cancelled his flight.

A day after returning to New Jersey, upon drying himself after a shower, Ron was alarmed to see a swollen red rash on the skin of his left armpit where Dr. Nahum had conducted a lymph node biopsy a month before Ron and Lucy had left for Florida. Ron immediately called Dr. Nahum's office. A complete blood count analysis determined that Ron's white blood cell count was far below normal and other readings were also anomalous. At the same time, Ron had a body temperature of 101^0 F. The physician, suspecting that the site of the biopsy had become infected, instructed Ron to go to Jersey Shore Medical Center, where he was immediately admitted.

Ron was assigned to an isolation unit; all nurses and physicians treating Ron, as well as all visitors to his room, had to wear surgical masks. Despite the fact that Ron was hooked up to an intravenous drip containing a powerful antibiotic, his fever did not go down; in fact, it increased to 102^0 F. His white blood cell count was close to zero and his other blood readings were far below normal. He was classified as neutropenic, meaning his immune system was severely, dangerously compromised. After 10 days at the hospital, when his fever broke and blood counts finally returned to normal, Ron was allowed to go home.

During the winter of 2012, Ron and Lucy rented a house in Delray Beach, Florida. They spent quite a bit of time talking about his state of depression. They had done this for years, but at this point Ron was more willing than before to verbalize the dark thoughts that ran through his brain. He told Lucy that each time he heard about a friend or relative becoming seriously ill or when he learned of the death of someone who was close to him, he feared that she or others he loved would become ill. He explained that he often felt vulnerable. Lucy said that she understood, and asked him to promise to seek professional guidance. He said that he would do what he had to do to deal with his years-long depression.

When they returned to New Jersey at the end of March, Ron

made an appointment with Dr. Jason Cohen, a psychiatrist. At the conclusion of the initial consultation, Dr. Cohen prescribed a potent anti-anxiety medication for Ron. The doctor also advised him to make an appointment with a psychologist/therapist. A few days later, Ron went to the office of Bernice Garfield, a licensed professional counselor. He consulted her every other week for nine months. On occasion, Lucy accompanied Ron to his sessions. As a result of his talks with Bernice, Ron eventually understood that he had the ability to exert a degree of control over his moods and over his chronic depression. During this period of time, Ron also began to experience a strong need—in fact, a powerful drive—to share the story of what his parents and what he and Eva had endured in Europe during those dark, brutal years so long ago.

Little by little, Ron pulled himself out of and rose above the worst of his chronic depression. At the same time, he remained in remission and felt stronger and more vigorous than he had in years. When he completed his last treatment for CLL—involving the use of Treanda—at the end of November 2013, he sighed with relief. Unfortunately, just a few weeks later, he developed a severe, very painful sinus infection which made breathing difficult. He and Lucy had already committed to renting the same house in Delray, Beach, Florida as the winter before, so, at the beginning of January 2014 they packed their belongings, put Cosette, their black cockapoo, in the car, and drove south.

In Florida, an infectious disease specialist determined that Ron was suffering from an infection caused by a tenacious, extremely difficult to treat pathogen, Methicillin-resistant *Staphylococcus aureus*, commonly referred to as MRSA. He was treated with a 30-day regimen involving a powerful antibiotic infusion drip.

When Lucy and Ron returned to New Jersey at the beginning of April he was still not feeling back to normal.

In May of 2014, Dr. Nahum arranged for Ron to receive an immune globulin infusion treatment at Monmouth Medical Center in Long

Branch, New Jersey. The eight-hour procedure did the trick. Within a matter of days Ron felt much better. Later that month, grateful that he was feeling back to his old self, Ron and Lucy left their worries behind and embarked on a Caribbean cruise.

Ron spent some time during that vacation thinking more deeply than usual about his life and how he could go about telling his story. He had reached an age and was at a place in which he savored each and every good day and was grateful for the health and happiness of those who were dear to him. This more thoughtful philosophy and approach to everyday existence was partially due to his health issues. In addition, for reasons he was unable to explain, powerful floods of decades-old memories of his parents and of Eva and of their time in Belgium and Bolivia and their first days in America washed over him more often than they had in the past. He spent a great deal of time reflecting on the uneven path—with its perilous, cold, dark, low places and its exhilaratingly luminous summits—that he had traveled during his 74 years on Earth, and he could not help but wonder where he was headed.

TWENTY-EIGHT

Commemorations, Ceremonies, and Stumbling Stones

Ron participated in two noteworthy events in 2013. The first was enlightening and led to much soul searching; the second was enormously gratifying. And then, during the year that followed, he developed an unexpected connection to Germany which opened up a bittersweet path to the future.

The first was a *Yom HaShoah* (Day of Remembrance of the Holocaust) event at Brookdale Community College in nearby Lincroft, New Jersey. Each of the several Holocaust survivors in attendance, including Ron, was escorted to his or her seat by a United States Navy petty officer and later asked to light a candle in honor of the six million Jews who were victims of Nazi genocide.

One of the guest speakers that night, Dr. Suzanne Vromen, Professor Emeritus in Sociology at Bard College, spoke movingly of her experiences during the Holocaust: in 1941, during the time of the Nazi occupation of Belgium, she and her immediate family escaped to the safety of the Belgian Congo, where she was able to attend the Institut Marie-José at Elisabethville, a school run by the Sisters of Charity of Gand (Ghent). She also talked about the interviews that she conducted in Belgium decades after the war and the book that she had written as a result of her research: *Hidden Children of the Holocaust: Belgian Nuns and Their Daring Rescue of Young Jews From the Nazis.*

Toward the end of the evening, Ron and Lucy had a chance to speak with Dr. Vromen, and Ron purchased a copy of her book. Days later, as he thumbed through it, he stared in disbelief at a group photograph of female students at Miséricorde. Among those children was his late sister Eva. It was a copy of the same photograph that he had found among his mother's belongings, one of the two he had thought of when he and Lucy had visited Miséricorde in 1985.

Although Ron had studied his copy of the photograph hundreds of times, as he stared at it now in this important book, it touched him deeply; at the same time, it disturbed him. The fact that the photo was out there, for the world to see, added another, sadder layer of reality to his understanding of what he and Eva had experienced. Seeing the image of his sister, dead now for almost 42 years, grieved him because he thought he saw on her face the anguished longing for her parents and the fear that she must have experienced. He thought he could almost feel her pain. He clearly felt his childhood sense of abandonment.

The second important event that year was "Homecoming 2013," a 50th year reunion of the 1963 graduating class of the United States Merchant Marine Academy. The joyous four-day celebration, which commenced on September 26 and involved many events, was highlighted by an elegant banquet ceremony at which alumni from several different years of graduation received commemorative plaques and were honored by the president of the USMMA Alumni Association Foundation, Captain James F. Tobin.

Ron's Special Achievement Award reads as follows:

RONALD R. ISAACSON '63 was born in Antwerp, Belgium in 1940 after his family had escaped from Germany a year earlier. In 1941, the Nazis and Gestapo began to round up all the Jews they could find in now occupied Belgium. Due to the compassionate citizens of Belgium and a local Catholic convent he and his entire family were able to survive the holocaust. In 1953, he came to America and six years later was nominated to Kings Point. He served on active duty, worked at Grumman as a test engineer and established and ran his own successful business, Petro-Marine. From holocaust survivor to Kings Point graduate and a successful business owner, he has truly lived an "acta non verba" life.

The next evening, the members of the class of 1963 enjoyed a dinner celebration at the Claremont Hotel in Roslyn, Long Island. At one point that night, James Gallagher, the class reunion committee chairman, announced the names of the award winners and read the description on each of the commemorative plaques. Later, many of Ron's classmates congratulated him; several said that they had been surprised to learn that he was a Holocaust survivor.

It gratified Ron to reconnect with those men and receive their kind words of admiration. He derived great satisfaction and felt a profound sense of pride when he thought about how he was a member of a special cadre of men, graduates of the United States Merchant Marine Academy.

Nine months later, in June of 2014, Ron's sister Susan, after hesitating for a moment, did what she normally did not do: she opened an email from a complete stranger, Thomas Schroer, who lived in Germany. In his email, Mr. Schroer explained that he had recently been contacted by an organization based in his town, Dinslaken, asking whether he had any information about Jewish people who had been born in or had lived in that town and had fled or been taken away by the Nazis. Mr. Schroer, who was intrigued by the question, began conducting research, eventually coming across the name Walter Isaacson, who had been born in Dinslaken and later married Else Margot Landau. At some point, he had heard about or had skimmed through a copy of Margot's short memoir *Story of My Life*. When Mr. Schroer's research led to the name Susan Isaacson Jaffe, who was living in Seattle, Washington, he wondered whether she was Walter and Margot's daughter, so he contacted her.

In reply to his email, Susan wrote, "I am indeed the daughter of Walter and Margot Isaacson. How did you find out about her memoir and how did you find me?" She also told him about her brother Ron. Mr. Schroer answered her questions, and then he asked whether she and her brother would be willing to allow a woman named Anne Prior to contact them about the *stolperstein* project on which she was working.

The German word "stolperstein" means "stumbling stone." The *stolperstein* project, developed by German artist Gunter Demnig, who was born in 1947 in Berlin, is dedicated to remembering and honoring the victims of the Holocaust, both Jews and non-Jews. Each *stolperstein* is a concrete block which is covered with a sheet of shiny brass. Demnig engraves on the brass covering all of the pertinent information about a particular victim of the Holocaust, such as his or her name, date of birth, and when he or she fled or was transported to a concentration camp or had been killed. Demnig then installs the block, or *stolperstein*—if possible, with family members of the victim present—in the sidewalk in front of a building in the city or town (in Germany or another country) in which the person had lived.

An example of an inscription on a stumbling stone reads as follows (translated from the German):

HERE LIVED CHAIM SHATTNER
BORN 1867
DEPORTED 22.9.1942
THERESIENTSTADT
MURDERED 20.12.1943

Each *stolperstein* serves as a metaphorical stumbling block—as if it were an actual impediment. By catching the attention of pedestrians, it causes them to stop and look down and read what is written. It informs them of the heinous crime committed against that individual by the Third Reich. More than 48,000 *stolpersteine* (the plural of *stolperstein*) have been installed in the sidewalks of cities in Germany, Austria, Switzerland, Luxembourg, the Netherlands, Belgium, France, Italy, Norway, Hungary, Croatia, Poland, Russia, Ukraine, Slovakia, and the Czech Republic. Demnig has explained that his inspiration for the project is the Talmudic saying "A person is only forgotten when his or her name is forgotten."

The person who Thomas Schroer had said would be contacting Susan and Ron, Anne Prior, was born in Dinslaken in 1956. In addition to her work in reference to the *stolperstein* project, she is currently writing a book about what happened to the many Jews who had lived in Dinslaken during the dark era of the Nazi regime. Many of those people had, like Walter and Margot, fled to Belgium. She has discovered that, beginning in 1942, more than 25,000 of the German Jews who had fled to Belgium were transported to the Mechelen (Malines) transit camp (as had been Margot's parents), and from there to concentration camps. Only 1,200 of those people survived the war.

When she contacted Ron and Susan, she reported that her own research had led her to believe that the Walter Isaacson who Thomas Schroer had discovered was, despite the seeming connection to someone named Else Margot Landau, not their father. The man who Schroer had come across during his research had been a livestock dealer who had been born on July 18, 1909; Ron and Susan's father had been born on November 15, 1907. However, after more intensive digging, she unearthed photographs of Oskar and Jenny Landau, Ron and Susan's (and Eva's) maternal grandparents, which had been taken at Mechelen shortly before they were transported to Auschwitz.

On October 13, 2014, Ron received a package from Anne Prior. It contained a photograph of a grave whose headstone read "Emma Isaksohn," with June 1941 as the date of death; despite the alternate spelling of her last name, Ms. Prior said she was sure it is a photo of the grave of Ron and Susan's (and Eva's) paternal grandmother—who died in a hospital in Cologne, Germany in the aftermath of a surgical procedure.

Ms. Prior went on to explain that the artist Gunter Deming wanted to create and install a *stolperstein* for each of the members of the Isaacson and Landau families.[43] She invited Susan and Ron and their

---

[43] In February 2015, he installed *stolpersteine* for Sally Isaacson, Oskar Landau, and Jenny Landau in Dinslaken.

families to attend ceremonies and the unveiling of the *stolpersteine* honoring their family members in Dinslaken sometime in 2016.

Ron has said that he and Lucy are planning on traveling to Germany to participate in one of the ceremonies.

He is profoundly touched and cannot help but experience a sense of deep appreciation in reference to the fact that a noteworthy number of German citizens, along with several non-governmental organizations in that country, have attempted over the years, in small but meaningful ways, to recognize and honor the victims of Nazi persecution. He says that he feels especially grateful to Anne Prior, Thomas Schroer, and Gunter Deming for their efforts in reference to the *stolperstein* project. At times, he thinks about how painful it must be for Germans, both those who were alive during the era of the Third Reich and those who were born after the war, to acknowledge the depth of the unspeakably evil deeds committed by that government and by their fellow countrymen. He says that he cannot help but experience a small measure of relief and a degree of consolation when he reflects on the fact that some Germans are paying homage to his parents, grandparents, his extended family, and others who suffered grievously at the hands of the Nazis.

For several decades, Ron's parents had received reparations payments from the government of West Germany because they were victims of the Holocaust, but he, as a child of Holocaust survivors, had never been compensated. Then, in 2014, he learned from a neighbor and friend, Harry Wiko, who had been born in Shanghai, China in 1942, about a new reparations program. Harry, whose parents had fled Germany in 1940, making their way to Shanghai, where they joined thousands of other Jews who had sought refuge there, told Ron that the new program was based on a 2014 agreement between the German government and the Conference on Jewish Material Claims Against Germany. Germany has agreed to make quarterly payments for life to each individual (totaling around 75,000 people worldwide) who were born between January 1, 1928 and August 1945 and who had been placed in a concentration camp or ghetto, forced into hiding, or had to live under a false identity for at least six months during the era of the Third Reich.

Ron filled out and submitted an application for the program, and at the beginning of 2015 he received his first payment from the government of Germany. He understands that this very modest monetary compensation is the result of tough negotiations between the German government and advocates for victims of the Holocaust, and is not based purely on German attempts to make amends. Indeed, that had been true in reference to all previous German reparations programs. Nevertheless, he feels that it represents official acknowledgment on the part of the German government of how he and his family had suffered, physically and emotionally, at the hands of the Nazi regime.

Remembering the Past and Looking Toward the Future

Ron and Lucy plan to participate in a *stolperstein* ceremony in Germany in honor of the Isaacson and Landau families and pay tribute to the others, Jews and gentiles, who suffered in body and spirit at the hands of the Third Reich. They imagine it will be a demanding, painful journey. Walter and Margot had found their 1986 passage to Duisburg difficult because it brought to the surface a jumbled mix of conflicting emotions: at the same time that tender memories of times and people and places and events gently washed over them like a summer rain shower, leaving them feeling serenely satisfied and languidly refreshed, they fell victim to sharp-edged recollections that left them shivering with cold, dark dread.

Some say that time is a continuum: what has happened and what is occurring and what will take place in the future are inextricably linked. Ron is not sure about that, but there is no doubt in his mind that in order to understand the present and plan for the future one must comprehend the past. And so, he and Lucy will travel to Germany in 2016, where they will be reminded of a ghastly era and pay homage to those who endured much misery during that time and in that place.

Now, when he thinks about his life, more than accomplishments and successes, Ron's mind turns to those who mean the most to him: Lucy, his wife of 52 years; his son Ken, a senior vice president at the New York Federal Reserve Bank, Ken's wife Julie, an accomplished pediatrician, and their children Alex and Zachary; his daughter Kim Jennifer Parks, a managing director of digital operations and commercial print for a large daily newspaper in Rochester, New York, her husband Michael, a manager of photo shoots used in advertising, and their children Ethan and Emerson; his sister Susan Jaffe, a dentist, and her husband Robert, a primary care physician, and their children Benjamin and Miriam; and Eva's children Sidney and Ilana.

He often thinks of Eva, the big sister who took charge and acted like a mother to him during their many months away from their parents. When those thoughts come to mind, he is profoundly grateful to her and to the nuns who risked their lives to shelter them.

And then, there are his grandparents and his mother and father. If his parents had not confronted the many terrifying situations thrown at them and made so many difficult decisions whose outcomes had the potential to be, at best, dangerous and, at worst, calamitous—to run from Germany and then to travel illegally to the Netherlands and then to Belgium—they might not have lived long enough to have conceived him. They and Eva might have been rounded up and killed in what they had thought was their homeland or they might have been transported to one of the many extermination camps that stained the landscape of Europe. In any of those hellholes they would have been exposed to cold, disease, and malnutrition, and, if they survived those punishing ordeals, they would eventually have been murdered in a scientifically efficient and highly professional manner. That had been the fate of the vast majority of the Jews who remained in Germany after *Kristallnacht*. If Ron's parents had not had the determination and strength to repeatedly do whatever they had to do to protect themselves and keep him and Eva safe while they lived in Belgium, they would most certainly all have become victims of the mass murder machine, along with the millions of others throughout Europe.

This story of a family that escaped the darkness and made their way to the light is a testament to the unconditional love of a mother and father who repeatedly faced harsh realities and did what was necessary to safeguard their young son and daughter. Time after time, they disregarded their own needs and swallowed their fears to ensure that their children would not only survive from day to day, but have an opportunity for a bright future in what they hoped would be a better world.

The End

Please post reviews of this book on amazon.com.

Made in the USA
San Bernardino, CA
17 November 2015